STRONG MAN OF CHINA

CHIANG KAI-SHEK, HEAD OF THE NATIONAL GOVERNMENT,
NANKING, 1928

STRONG MAN OF CHINA

THE STORY OF CHIANG KAI-SHEK

BY

ROBERT BERKOV

WITH ILLUSTRATIONS

HOUGHTON MIFFLIN COMPANY · BOSTON

The Riverside Press Cambridge

1938

The Riverside Press
CAMBRIDGE · MASSACHUSETTS
PRINTED IN THE U.S.A.

CONTENTS

ILLUSTRATIONS

THE PEOPLE OF THE STORY

Thumb-nail sketches of the principal Chinese and foreign characters in this book, arranged alphabetically.

BORODIN, MICHAEL — chief of the Russian political advisers at Canton from 1925 to 1927, the period of the Chinese-Russian alliance. A resident of the United States until his adult days, he was a master politician, a shrewd adviser, and a skillful propagandist. He is credited with much of the political success of the Kuomintang revolution. Today he holds the comparatively unimportant post of editor of the *Moscow Daily News*.

CHANG CHING-KIANG — retired millionaire, veteran revolutionist, close friend and financial benefactor of Chiang Kai-shek.

CHANG HSUEH-LIANG — the 'Young Marshal.' Former war-lord of Manchuria, which he inherited from his father, 'Old Marshal' Chang Tso-lin, and lost to the Japanese in 1931–32, he is best known as the kidnapper of Chiang Kai-shek in December, 1936. He was formerly a drug addict but has been cured.

CHANG TSO-LIN — the 'Old Marshal,' uncrowned king of Manchuria, leader of the northern alliance against Chiang Kai-shek and the Nationalists in 1925–27. In 1928 he was killed when a bomb exploded under his train as he was returning to Manchuria from North China.

CHEN CHIH-MEI — military leader of the Shanghai area at the time of the anti-Manchu revolution, Chiang Kai-shek's patron and friend.

CHEN CHI-TANG — erstwhile war-lord of Canton and boss of Kwangtung Province, the 'King under Southern Skies,' unseated by Chiang Kai-shek in 1936.

CHEN KUO-FU — one of the famous and mysterious Chen brothers. Receiving little publicity in China and entirely unknown abroad, he is one of Chiang Kai-shek's closest associates. With his brother, Chen Li-fu, he has directed the powerful 'C.C. Corps,' generally regarded as Chiang

Kai-shek's OGPU. He is a nephew of the late Chen Chih-mei, through whom Chiang originally met him.

CHEN LI-FU — the second of the Chen brothers, and like Chen Kuo-fu a potent influence in the Chinese government and trusted henchman of Chiang Kai-shek. Chen Li-fu holds a degree of Master of Science from the University of Pittsburgh, is known as a philosopher, organizer, and administrator. He is believed responsible for the ethical concepts of Chiang's New Life Movement.

CHIANG CHING-KUO — only natural son of Chiang Kai-shek. Sent to Moscow in 1925 during the period of the Kuomintang-Communist alliance, he remained there after his father split with the Communists, and did not return to China until 1937, after Nanking's *rapprochement* with the Chinese Reds.

CHIANG HSI-HOU — older brother of Chiang Kai-shek. He held a minor government post in his native province of Chekiang until his death in 1936.

CHIANG KAI-SHEK — China's Number 1 man, the Strong Man of the East. Official titles include: President of the Executive Yuan (equivalent to Premier), Chairman of the Military Affairs Commission (the highest military post in China), and Vice-Chairman of the Standing Committee of the Kuomintang Party's Central Executive Committee (the highest executive post in China's ruling party, the chairman of this committee having died).

CHIANG MEI-LING — Madame Chiang Kai-shek, the Generalissimo's American-educated wife, whom he married in 1927. A graduate of Wellesley College, she is her husband's confidante, adviser, secretary, and foreign liaison agent. In addition she holds the post of Secretary-General of the National Aeronautical Commission and as such is in complete charge of China's air force.

CHIANG SHU-AN — father of Chiang Kai-shek, merchant of Chekiang Province. He died in 1896, when Chiang Kai-shek was nine years old.

CHIANG WEI-KUO — adopted son of Chiang Kai-shek. Half-Japanese, he is the real son of a high Chinese official, who is a close friend of Chiang, and a Japanese waitress. Chiang Wei-kuo's Japanese features have led to the baseless theory that Chiang Kai-shek himself is of Japanese descent.

FENG YU-HSIANG — the 'Christian General,' former commander of the 'People's Army.' Tall, stout, and doughty, he wears peasant clothes and affects the greatest frugality and simplicity, a living protest against luxury-loving officials. After having flirted with many causes including Christianity and communism, fought on opposite sides in the same military campaigns, and revolted three times against Chiang Kai-shek, he has finally made his peace with the Generalissimo and lives peacefully at Nanking. Officially, he is the Number 2 military man to Chiang.

GALENS, GENERAL — chief Russian military adviser to Chiang Kai-shek and the Nationalist army in the Canton days, under the Kuomintang-Communist alliance. Today he is known as Marshal Vassili Bluecher and commands the Soviet Russian army in eastern Siberia.

HU HAN-MIN — the third of the southern revolutionary leaders with Chiang Kai-shek and Wang Ching-wei. Always conservative and anti-Communist, Hu remained a consistent advocate of democracy in China and bitterly opposed what he regarded as Chiang Kai-shek's ambition for dictatorship. He died in 1936.

JOFFE, ADOLF ABRAM — former Soviet Minister to China, who negotiated with Doctor Sun Yat-sen the Kuomintang-Communist alliance.

KUNG, H. H. — successor to T. V. Soong as Minister of Finance. He also is a brother-in-law of Chiang Kai-shek, having married Ai-ling, the eldest of the Soong sisters.

LI TSUNG-JEN — co-leader of the Kwangsi clique, military master of remote Kwangsi Province. He has revolted twice against Chiang Kai-shek, but in the Chinese-Japanese conflict of 1937 forgot his private grievances against the Generalissimo and joined the common front against Japan.

PAI CHUNG-HSI — the other leader of the Kwangsi clique and Chiang Kai-shek's most implacable enemy until 1937, when he too went to Nanking and pledged allegiance to China's strong man in the campaign against the foreign invader. Pai is considered China's ablest military strategist and is a civil administrator of extraordinary ability. The régime of Li Tsung-jen and himself in Kwangsi Province in recent years has deserved the adjective 'model.'

SOONG, T. V. — brother-in-law of Chiang Kai-shek and member of the so-called 'Soong dynasty.' A Harvard graduate, he is a financial expert and has served twice as Minister of Finance. He is considered the nation's outstanding financial brain and regarded by many as the ablest leader in the country next to Chiang Kai-shek himself.

SUN FO — son of Doctor Sun Yat-sen by the latter's first marriage. He has been closely associated with Chinese politics since his father first established an independent government at Canton. Today he serves Nanking as president of the legislative yuan. He is considered a leftist in politics and has been one of the chief advocates of closer relations between China and the Soviet Union.

SUN YAT-SEN — the father of the Chinese Republic and saint of the revolution. Almost single-handed he organized the overthrow of the Manchus, but later found himself constantly in opposition to republican opportunists and organized several independent régimes at Canton. He died at Peking March 12, 1925, and straightway became the martyr of Kuomintang nationalism. His place as president of the Kuomintang has never been filled, although Chiang Kai-shek has frequently been urged for the post.

SUNG CHEH-YUAN — Number 1 political-military figure of North China until the 1937 Sino-Japanese conflict. Removed as governor of Chahar Province in 1935 for supposed anti-Japanism, he subsequently made himself *persona grata* to the Japanese military and achieved the much more important post of chairman of the Hopei-Chahar Political Council. The overlord of the Peiping-Tientsin area as well as his former domain of Chahar, he headed a quasi-independent régime outwardly subordinate to Nanking but actually under the thumb of the Japanese military.

WANG, C. T. — former Minister of Foreign Affairs, now Chinese Ambassador at Washington. A Yale graduate, he is able, clever, and eloquent.

WANG CHING-WEI — one of the three leaders of the Kuomintang revolution following Sun Yat-sen's death, the other two being Chiang Kai-shek and Hu Han-min. Considered a leftist in the early Canton days, he has grown progressively more conservative and in late years has been outspokenly anti-Communist. He was shot and seriously wounded at Nanking in November, 1935, presumably at the direction of those who considered him too conciliatory to Japan.

WU PEI-FU — old-time war-lord of Central and North China, who once dreamed of unifying all China by force. Arch-enemy of Old Marshal Chang Tso-lin, he lost his crucial battle with the Manchurian war-lord through the defection of Christian General Feng Yu-hsiang, his supposed ally. Today he lives in retirement in a North China monastery.

YANG HU-CHENG — military leader of Shensi Province, who with 'Young Marshal' Chang Hsueh-liang kidnapped Chiang Kai-shek in 1936. He, rather than the Young Marshal, is believed to have been the ringleader of the plot. He went to America and Europe in 1937 to 'study military science.'

YEN HSI-SHAN — the 'model governor' of Shansi Province, a late convert to the Kuomintang Nationalist cause and later a rebel against Nanking. Too powerful a person in North China to be liquidated, he has in recent years been on seemingly friendly terms with Chiang Kai-shek, but continues as sole boss of his Shansi domain.

YUAN SHIH-KAI — Manchu dynasty politician who became the first president of the Chinese Republic and tried unsuccessfully to make himself Emperor, thus stirring up Sun Yat-sen's second revolution.

CHAPTER I

CHINA'S CHIANG

THE story of China — a story more than four thousand years old — has become the tale of a single man. What that man says is his country's policy. What he does becomes his people's history.

His name is Chiang Kai-shek. He is the best known and the least known of all living Chinese. The world press headlines his name with regular frequency. He crushes a rebellion here, he averts a rebellion there. He hurls his troops against the Communists, he makes peace with the Communists. He is kidnapped, he escapes. He attempts to stave off war with Japan, he finds himself at war with Japan. And casual readers of newspapers in London and New York and Prague become vaguely aware that a Strong Man rules China, that his name is Chiang.

As one commentator has remarked, all the confusing old three-syllable names that used to index Chinese politics can now be forgotten — the names and their bearers have ceased to be of the slightest importance. In their place stands one man — a small, frail, volatile but tremendously energetic man — who oddly enough has become the *alter ego* of that powerful, sprawling, sleepy giant that is China.

Yet he remains, to his own countrymen no less than to the western world, a virtually unknown character. His life and career are the subjects, simultaneously, of reverent myths and too-familiar tea-house gossip. He is alternately acclaimed a saint and hero and denounced as brute and assassin. Between the uncritical accolades of professional patriots and apologists and the unreasoning philippics of disgruntled politicians and proletarian pamphleteers, the man himself remains strange, mysterious. He is a recluse in the most populous nation on earth; he is the most shadowy of the world's great men.

But his power and his importance are neither uncertain nor mysterious. Of his hold on the 450,000,000 Chinese there can be no doubt. On the part which he appears destined to play in the grim struggle of the Far East there is almost no difference of opinion. Because that struggle, from every indication, will inevitably affect the play of world forces with which it is inseparably connected, the essential nature and character of the principal Asiatic protagonist must, it would seem, be understood and evaluated by the world audience.

For here is no obscure Oriental war-lord, no chief of a comic-opera principality. Here is a chief of state and a ruler, one who stands with the Hitlers and Mussolinis and Stalins of the western world — however much he may dislike the comparison — one who, as much as they, may soon see his name written large on the pages of history.

CHAPTER II

CHIKOW CHILDHOOD

IN THE village of Chikow, tucked away among the mountains of Chekiang Province, the villagers prepared for the Great Cold. Housewives took last-minute stitches in padded winter garments, small boys gathered firewood from the surrounding hills, the last crops were stored away.

Soon tradesmen from Ningpo, some thirty miles to the northeast on the coast, would bring orders for cross-stitch embroidery and the women would settle down to spend the winter months with flying needles.

The day for most of Chikow's population was inauspicious, but in wine merchant Chiang's house there was excitement — a second son was born. The gods were kind to the Chiangs, had sent them double assurance that the ancestral tombs would be swept and joss paper always burned at the family shrine.

It was the fifteenth day of the ninth moon of the Year of the Pig. The foreign calendar hanging in the mission compound said October 31, 1887.

Wrapped in swaddling bands lay China's future leader. Bright red eggs were sent to friends and relatives to announce his birth.

On a lucky day thirty days later the baby's head, save for a topknot, was shaved, his small arms were forced into a gorgeous red silk robe, and a charm was hung around his neck.

So arrayed, he was carried before the ancestral tablets

and presented with thanksgiving to the household gods. Then Chiang Shu-an, the proud father, gave his second-born a 'milk name,' Jui-tai, to serve his childhood.

Guests bearing presents gathered for a feast. Warm Chekiang wine flowed freely, food was copiously served. Chiang prestige was upheld.

Who were these Chiangs? The name is a common one, though not the most common in China. The Wangs and the Changs are the Smiths and Joneses of old Cathay. The Chiangs correspond to the Robinsons.

The forbears of the Chikow Chiangs originated in North China, migrating to Chekiang Province some time after the downfall of the Ming Dynasty in 1644. Most of the ancestors had been farmers, but by the time young Jui-tai's grandfather came to manhood, a trend toward small business had set in. The men traded principally in salt and tea.

In Chekiang, after somewhat of a struggle to earn a livelihood for his family, Grandpa Chiang finally obtained control of the local salt monopoly. The family fortunes improved, but Grandpa never achieved riches.

He was a kind-hearted old soul, constantly helping distressed friends and relatives. He dabbled in Chinese-style medicine. With a flair for social welfare work, he provided free medical aid for poor villagers. That was his pleasure. Solace he found in Buddhism.

When the Taiping Rebellion swept the province, trade came to a halt, and the salt business was ruined. Chiang Shu-an, the father of baby Jui-tai, assumed control of the salt office and the wineshop, and succeeded in reviving the family fortunes. Grandpa retired by degrees and became a respected village elder, while his son developed into a typical merchant of the lower middle class, neither envied nor despised but respected by all.

He constantly urged his two sons to study, hoped they

would pass the imperial examinations and enter the realm of statesmanship. Regretting that circumstances had forced him to cut short his own education and enter business, he had the usual Chinese reverence for a scholar. In those days the men of learning ranked at the top of the social scale, and enjoyed a monopoly of political posts. At the bottom, respected by none, were the soldiers.

Papa Chiang Shu-an died at the age of fifty-three. Jui-tai was nine years old. Once again the Chiang family fortunes took a turn for the worse. Grandfather was too old to scrape for a living. The children, Jui-tai, his older brother Chiang Hsi-hou, and his sister, Jui-lien, were all too young to shoulder responsibility.

The mother perforce became the head of the family. Business was bad and funds were scarce. But Mrs. Chiang, the daughter of a merchant from the district of Fenghua, was a resourceful woman. She busied herself with needle-work to supplement the family income.

She was determined that her sons should succeed. Shortly after her husband died, she put young Jui-tai in school for the first time. Had he lived in America, he would have had to answer to the truant officer years earlier; in China he was lucky to go to school at all.

His mother speedily made him realize, young as he was, that the family circumstances were poor, that the matter of earning a living was a real and earnest thing. Under her tutelage he learned at first hand the realities of economic struggle, came to appreciate the nobility of manual labor.

'A fatherless child like you must be carefully brought up before he can expect success in the world,' she told him. 'Our house and name must be carried on by an heir who can keep untarnished the good reputation of our family.'

He went to the village school. Each day, when he returned home, his mother questioned him on what he had learned. He was seemingly an indifferent student in those first years, and showed little aptitude for any learning, but she saw to it that he absorbed each lesson.

His mother paid particular attention to his behavior, and not without reason. He was inclined to be a mischievous lad, and was always getting into scrapes with near-by shopkeepers unless constantly watched. Mother Chiang made him report in detail how he had spent every minute of his time outside of school. Thereby she formed in him the habit of accounting strictly for all his time, a habit which has stayed with him to the present day.

Later he went to the Feng Lu higher primary school in Fenghua. Here he apparently showed for the first time an interest in his studies, and he was described as a brilliant student, although most of his classmates were his seniors by many years.

He was sent to Fenghua not only to attend school but to learn a trade. Relatives of his family had a shop there and he was apprenticed to them.

Life with his relatives was far from pleasant. They had scant use for the youngster, who was more than ordinarily mischievous. They worked him hard, day and night, and cuffed and kicked him when he annoyed them with his pranks. His relatives regarded themselves as his benefactors and looked on young Chiang as an ingrate. At school also he had trouble — he found it difficult to get along with his fellows, and he was badly used by the older boys.

Tiring of the treatment and feeling abused, he ran away to join the provincial army. Nothing could have been more humiliating to his family. A soldier in the family was almost as bad as a leper. Most of his relatives became convinced that he would come to no good end.

At about this time he discarded his 'milk name' and chose for himself a dignified man's name. He called himself

Chieh-shih. The name, freely translated, means 'clean as a stone.' It was not until later years, when he became associated with the southern Chinese who pronounced the same characters differently, that he came to be known as Chiang Kai-shek.[1]

---

[1] The family name comes first. If Franklin D. Roosevelt lived in China, he would write his name Roosevelt Franklin-delano.

CHAPTER III

SOLDIER, HUSBAND

THE year Chiang Kai-shek was born, a youth named Sun Yat-sen left Canton for Hongkong to study medicine. The trip marked the start of a revolutionary career which led to the overthrow of the Manchu Dynasty, the establishment of a republic, the martyrdom of Sun Yat-sen, and ultimately to the supremacy of the Chikow-born Chiang in a new and revitalized government.

While the youngster was growing up, a series of catastrophes fell upon the Middle Kingdom. China, which had regarded itself as the greatest, wisest, richest, most civilized nation on earth, was subjected to repeated pressure by foreign nations who used warships and cannon balls when the Manchu rulers showed the slightest hesitation in granting their demands for territory, concessions, and the sacred right to sell opium to the Chinese people.

The process came to a painful climax when China went to war with Japan in 1894 and took a sound beating from the 'dwarfs of the eastern sea.'

Probably the result made not a vast amount of difference to the bulk of the Chinese population, but it had a profound effect on world history. The Chinese were eventually pushed out of Korea by the Japanese, who then proceeded to lead a frenzied international race to grab loose parts of the once-great empire.

Britain had started the process with the Opium War, culminating in the first of the 'unequal treaties' which established foreign rights in China, but it remained for Japan to set the style in territorial conquest.

From 1895 to 1899 China's diplomats yielded to alternate bribery and force, and a series of intrigues in the Imperial Household at Peking merely paved the way for the collapse to follow.

Some of the political leaders in China saw the trend of the times. They took steps to forestall disaster. Among the measures was the creation of a new military school at Paotingfu, the first of its kind in China. It was designed to be a Chinese West Point or Aldershot, and one of its features was the recruiting of likely looking students from all parts of the Empire. Examinations were held each year to select the student body.

Young Chiang, eighteen years old at the time, took the examination conducted for the purpose by the Chekiang provincial government. To the surprise of his Fenghua relatives, who had concluded that the youth would never be more than a tramp soldier, he took first place in the tests, and was chosen for the next class at Paotingfu.

In 1906, with about forty other Chekiang youths who had been successful in the examinations, he went north to learn how to be a soldier in the foreign fashion.

His mother took the occasion of his departure to give him some homely advice. 'Since the death of your father,' she reminded him, 'I have made every sacrifice to enable you to study. It is not because I want you to snatch a high government office or to amass a fortune, but because I want you to be of service to the country, and to maintain the good reputation of your forefathers.'

The latter consideration undoubtedly carried the greater weight with young Chiang. Service to country was far from a well-developed virtue in those days, and patriotism was an unknown phenomenon. A man owed respect and allegiance to his family, and there his obligations ended.

Meanwhile, Mrs. Chiang had commissioned a go-between, or marriage broker, to find a suitable bride for her son. Soon after reaching puberty, every man in China must marry, not for his own welfare but for the benefit of his family. He must see that the family name is continued. He must provide male descendants to continue the ancestral worship, and he must provide a daughter-in-law to wait upon his mother.

Chiang Kai-shek, they say, was only fifteen or perhaps a year older when the fortune-tellers matched his horoscope with that of young Miss Mao of Fenghua and found them suited to each other. The exact date of the wedding is uncertain; there are no official records and no marriage register.

Until the day the young bridegroom sent a grand red-lacquer sedan-chair for his bride, he had neither seen nor spoken to her. She came to him, gorgeously arrayed in heavily embroidered red silk becoming to the daughter of a comfortably situated bourgeois family about equal in rank to the Chiangs.

His family funds were low. To acquire plenty of 'face' among his friends and relatives, new and old, Chiang borrowed heavily to finance his wedding.

Three days after the ceremony, the young couple, in accordance with old custom, paid their first call on the bride's parents. In his youthful desire to please his father-in-law, so the story goes, Chiang brought along a number of professional and amateur actors. Theatrical people were in the lowest strata of society in those days, and frowned upon by the respectable. In a conservative rural community like Fenghua, feeling on the subject was even stronger than in the sophisticated larger cities.

Unaware of the social misstep he was making, Chiang

presented a show. Father-in-law was shocked and disgusted. There was a family row. Chiang was told to leave.

Deeply hurt, Chiang never forgave his father-in-law. Although no romance had entered into his union with Miss Mao, their later estrangement and separation is generally believed to have been motivated by this first quarrel with her family.

Chiang's selection for the military academy at Paotingfu meant separation from his wife, of course. But meanwhile a son, Ching-kuo, had been born.

The young husband went off to study, and he acquitted himself well, according to the records. He won high marks in infantry tactics, and acquired a knowledge of basic military science which was to be the foundation of his martial success in later years.

CHAPTER IV

RISING SUN — AND DOCTOR SUN

ONE year at Paoting and Chiang had absorbed all the military knowledge that the China of his day could give him. He was not an officer, not even a finished soldier, but his country could teach him no more. If he wanted to be anything more than an obscure minor officer in some provincial army, he had to go abroad for advanced study.

Most of the young Chinese students, civil as well as military, were being sent to Japan. The year was 1907, Japan was basking in the glory of her victory over Russia, and the world had suddenly begun to sit up and take notice of the little brown men.

China, prey to foreign aggression and filled with fear of the white man's next move, was looking to Japan with new respect and admiration. The old contempt of the Chinese for the 'monkey men' still prevailed, but an increasing number of Chinese stood ready to admit that the 'monkey men' had their points. The thought of a new, strong Japan leading the Orient in resistance against the encroachment of the Occident was, if not fully crystallized, certainly beginning to take form.

But even the small journey across the Yellow Sea to Japan required money, and Chiang was dependent on the Paotingfu scholarship for his living. With no rich relative to stake the youth to a few years of study in Tokyo, it was clearly up to his immediate family to provide funds.

While Chiang's mother was ready to scrape together the

cash needed to send her son to the Japanese capital to learn the ways of the latter-day samurai, all the relatives, near and distant, howled their protest. It was bad enough to have the young man go off to study soldiering, leaving his wife and boy. To spend more money on learning militarism among the dwarf men was madness.

Old Mrs. Chiang tried to borrow, but nobody would lend. Those who had money were ready and willing to help her support the family, they said, but to throw money after that scamp of a son was to plant rice seed in the eastern ocean.

She was forced to fall back on her own resources. She plied her needle with new vigor, scrimped and saved, and finally accumulated the few dollars to buy his ticket to Japan. His tuition at the Military Staff College in Tokyo was taken care of by the Paotingfu authorities. His mother had to supply his living expenses. That she did so regularly and without complaint testified to her belief that he was not entirely wasting his time by studying the despised art of soldiery.

He remained in Japan four years. He saw the country become more and more westernized. He watched the beginnings of the process which transformed the peaceful land of the rising sun into Dai Nippon, the world power. The impression on Chiang was profound. He cannot have escaped the lesson that in a world of power diplomacy, successful diplomacy requires real power. If he, like hundreds of others, became convinced that what China needed was a shot of Japan-virus, the reason was easily understandable.

Meanwhile, he studied military science with the thoroughness of the Japanese themselves. And he learned Japanese. To study at the Staff College he had to understand it perfectly, speak it fluently.

In those days Japan was the center of liberal and even radical movements, with the domestic and international situation receiving equal attention from the young Japanese intellectuals. China, the nearest neighbor, was naturally an object of friendly attention, and the Japanese cities were filled with Chinese students, businessmen and revolutionists, living, talking, some of them plotting, with comradely Japanese.

Sun Yat-sen had become a real force, though at times it seemed that he was destined to be an ever-defeated visionary. He had traveled to Europe and America and had visited the Chinese communities in the South Pacific. Observers with sufficient acumen could see that the Chinese monarchy was being subjected to progressively increasing strain, that it was bound to break before long.

After the menace of the Boxers to the Imperial Court had been diverted to foreigners in general and had resulted in the *débâcle* of the Legation siege with another humiliating treaty for China, the imperial government proceeded to carry out, in a clumsy sort of way, a complete reform of the nation's political organization. In 1905 those who ruled at Peking decided on a gradual movement toward a constitutional monarchy.

But when the Empire attempted to strengthen the authority of the central government, as a first step toward introducing democracy on the western model, the people of the provinces, who through the years had become accustomed to the *laissez-faire* government and its concomitant peaceful anarchy, objected. A crack-up was inevitable.

Sun Yat-sen and his group were doing all they could to hasten the crack-up. Their base of operations at the time was Japan. The Tung Meng Hui, 'common alliance association,' had been formed by Sun in 1891. By 1907, when Chiang came to Japan, it was a flourishing and powerful organization, with branches in every part of the world and a strong hold on the sympathies of the younger Chinese.

Chiang had not been in Japan long before he joined the Tung Meng Hui as a matter of course. Chinese revolutionary leaders were always passing through Japan. Many of them were living there. Becoming a member of the Tung Meng Hui was like joining a Chinese Residents' Society.

As a member, Chiang met many of the outstanding leaders of the movement, men who were to rise to high posts in the Chinese Republic and who in turn were to become Chiang's subordinates. But he was without fervor. He was a student trying to get an education that would enable him to make a living. He subscribed to revolution in theory; in practice he remained aloof.

Then he attended a meeting at which Sun Yat-sen presided. He listened to the tremendously energetic doctor as he addressed the group. Sun was an orator, and had in his favor a passionate delivery as well as a respectable intellectual case. He captivated his hearers, and he made a convert of Chiang.

The date was 1910, and it marks Chiang's abandonment of the passive life in favor of a revolutionary career. He plunged into the anti-Manchu movement, attended meetings, spread the gospel of revolution by speech and writing. Those who were with him during those days in Japan say that before his conversion he had many friends, few intimates. After his enlistment in Sun's fight for the overthrow of the monarchy in China, he had more friends, no intimates — the cause became his mistress.

CHAPTER V

UPSETTING THE DRAGON THRONE

WHEN the revolution came, it was not the grand campaign that readers of history imagine. It was a series of local revolts, and the monarchy went to pieces more as a result of its own decrepitude than because of the force opposing it.

The virtue of the revolution was that it had an organization ready to take control. Young men and older ones, nurtured on the doctrines of Sun Yat-sen, were prepared to administer the government and to transform it in a few years into an epitome of American democracy, British peacefulness, German efficiency, and Utopian harmony.

As a military campaign, the revolution was disorganized and disjointed. The revolutionary armies were small, weak, and scattered. Their finances were meager and the sources of their supplies precarious. Handfuls of 'dare to die' corps which seized village authority and conducted marches from one village to another provided most of the heroics.

Here and there the revolution met complete suppression and collapse, and some of its leaders were lucky to escape abroad. The Manchus, able to keep in fairly close touch with them, had them followed and often persecuted. Overseas Chinese, particularly those in Japan, were indignant.

Chiang had just finished his schooling after four years in Japan. Shortly after the first revolutionary outbreak, he returned to China, landing in Shanghai. Through his connections he met Chen Chih-mei, dissolute but kindly war-lord of the Shanghai area, an imperial officer but in complete sympathy with the revolution. He stayed at Chen's house awaiting the signal for the next revolutionary outbreak in the district. It was at this time that he became acquainted with Chen's two nephews, Chen Kuo-fu and Chen Li-fu, later to become his own right-hand men.

When the insurrectionary movement reached Shanghai, Chiang was named commander of the Eighty-third Brigade, a military group composed partly of imperial deserters and partly of raw troops hurriedly recruited for revolutionary purposes. This force participated in the capture of several towns near Shanghai from the Manchu forces, and Chiang's handling of the unit drew praise from his superiors. Despite his youth, he demonstrated that he had mastered his military science, and Chen Chih-mei in particular was impressed. He took a decided liking to the youth.

Chiang was then given command of a regiment, and led three thousand men to Hangchow, Wenchow, and Taichow, all in his native province of Chekiang. His exploits sounded impressive, but the truth was that he encountered practically no opposition. As soon as a force was led against a town, imperial authority collapsed. Officials resigned or fled, and revolutionary leaders, mostly military, assumed authority. The progress was gratifying but hardly exciting.

Chiang was twenty-two and eager to make history. But history appeared to be rather difficult to make. He accepted the circumstances philosophically and settled down to workaday affairs. He decided to make his regiment a model of discipline, and succeeded in converting the unruly, loot-hungry soldiers into a respectably behaved unit.

The passion for system and orderliness which is characteristic of the man today began to be evident then. He wanted his troops in superb condition and perfectly trained. By the end of the Chekiang campaign he was well embarked on the program, and by the time the active phase of the revolution in Central China had ended, his troops were a model regiment.

Chiang brought his men to Shanghai, where they became part of the garrison force. While the revolution was still running its course in the outlying areas, Chiang again met Chen Chih-mei, who was still outwardly loyal to the Empire. He pointed out to Chen the importance of Shanghai as a supply base for the revolution, urged that it be utilized to support the campaign. With Chen he formed an organization called the Tung Chi She to send ammunition into the interior. At the same time he maintained a Shanghai unit of well-seasoned troops for use in emergency.

Hankow, the 'Chicago of China,' seven hundred miles up the Yangtse River, which had been seized by the revolutionists, finally fell to the imperial forces. Chiang and his associates retorted by taking over Shanghai. They then moved up the Yangtse and captured Nanking. Doctor Sun had his heart set on Nanking as the capital of the new régime, and the capture of the city permitted the formation of a provisional government there.

But it soon became apparent that the revolution was far from revolutionary. Its leaders met at Nanking, drew up a provisional constitution, and elected Sun Yat-sen president. The task of transforming a nation was hardly as easy. The Manchus abdicated, but they gave Yuan Shih-kai, veteran politician and former associate of the Empress Dowager, a mandate to establish a republic. Yuan and his group held the real power. Besides, they were experienced administrators. It was clear to Sun and his followers that they must either fight a long civil war, with dubious chances of success, or compromise with those in power and hope to introduce reforms gradually.

It resulted in compromise, of course. The young Nanking

idealists had drafted an enlightened constitution, but wielded no power to carry out its precepts. Sun realized the situation. He agreed to resign, but he made a deal. In return for his resignation in favor of Yuan Shih-kai, the Peking officials would accept the Nanking constitution. Yuan and his associates agreed, and Sun and his associates retired. There was nothing else to do.

The capital remained at Peking, and the country went on as usual, despite its slightly loftier resolutions. Several new administrators settled down to their tasks in various parts of the country, but the essential machinery of government remained as it had been under the monarchy.

Chiang, meanwhile, had made much progress of a personal nature. He had demonstrated his military ability, and was well regarded by his superiors. He rose in rank and importance and his material situation improved accordingly. At the age of twenty-five, he was considered more than fairly well-off.

His mother's sacrifices for him in his student days were not forgotten. As soon as he had lifted himself above the poverty line, he began sending small sums of money home to Chikow. As his circumstances improved, he made fair-sized remittances for the improvement of the family home.

Chiang prestige was on the up-grade once more. His mother was able to say 'I told you so' to the once-critical relatives, and the scoffers were forced to admit that the army man was doing pretty well for himself. As Chiang's income continued to rise, he became even more generous, and constantly remitted funds to his wife and son as well as to his mother.

CHAPTER VI

COUNTER-REVOLUTIONIST

THE end of the revolution against the Manchus and the establishment of the republic demonstrated two things only too clearly — that there was no republic and that there was no room for revolutionists.

The Emperor had abdicated in February, 1911, but life went on in China much as it had done for several centuries before. The hopes of Sun Yat-sen and his fellow-idealists were thoroughly dashed. The evils against which they had inveighed were tolerated — the Emperor himself lived in the Forbidden City and held a mock court which a disconcertingly large number of people regarded as the real thing. The country was a 'republic with an emperor in reserve,' and the democracy of which Sun and his colleagues dreamed was as remote as the working democracies of the western world.

The government, as was to be expected, fell into the hands of the professional politicians. Chiang, of course, was not among them. As the Sun revolutionists retired to private life, Chiang joined them, planning for the day when a real revolution would come to China.

The fault, it might be mentioned, did not entirely lie with Yuan and his satellites. The revolutionary movement itself was unripe. It had not had sufficient time to develop new leaders and to give them the experience they needed to govern. Yuan and his group were older, wiser, craftier, well versed in the ways of ruling a docile people. The Manchus had been driven out, not by a spontaneous uprising of China's millions, but by the small band of revolutionists in league with a group of enlightened officials. The masses took no part in the movement, and the nation was no more ready for a republic than it was for communism.

Sun Yat-sen, after resigning the presidency, grasped the reality of the situation and realized the weakness of the revolution. He knew that the masses must be educated for political change and he saw that in a country as disorganized as China, the education must be effected by a powerful revolutionary body, sure of its ideology and cohesive in its personnel.

The Tung Meng Hui, which Sun had organized in Japan and which Chiang had joined, became the Kuomintang, the national revolutionary party, literally, the 'association of the people of the country.' Sun himself was responsible for enlarging the scope of the group and was carried away by the thought that numbers would bring strength.

Chiang Kai-shek's first indication of political acumen was his opposition to the broadening of the organization. He argued that homogeneity was preferable to size, that a revolutionary party had to be sure of its personnel, and that to admit workers indiscriminately would ultimately prove dangerous. The leaders disagreed and cried him down as a conservative. Chiang, having acquired self-assurance as a result of his military advancement, showed himself a stubborn proponent of what he believed to be right. His tongue was nimble and his temper quick. Many of his associates called him headstrong. He quarreled with some of them and abandoned party activity for some time.

The aftermath of the anti-Manchu revolution proved the correctness of his viewpoint. Kuomintang members, Doctor Sun speedily learned, were of too many minds and motives.

More important than honest differences of opinion among the members was the fact that opportunists had filtered into the organization without any genuine revolutionary fervor. They saw a chance to acquire power quickly and paid lip service to the cause of revolution in order to advance their fortunes under a new order. When the Yuan group took over the government and the Sun crowd retired to private life, the opportunists lost interest.

Sun was not discouraged. He never was. He started reorganizing the party. There is no evidence that he noted the vindication of Chiang's earlier contention. Chiang was an obscure party worker, and the revolutionary doctor hardly knew of his existence. With a few close associates Doctor Sun retired to Canton and began the new revolution, the people's revolution. Chiang Kai-shek remained in Shanghai.

The government at Peking fared poorly. Removal of the imperial authority resulted in considerable chaos and confusion which foreign intrigue and constant pressure only aggravated.

The foreign powers meddled freely in the affairs of a helpless China, and resorted freely to bribery and blackmail where force proved inconvenient. By every conceivable trickery the powers, or their business representatives, rapidly obtained a financial strangle-hold on the country. The fact that they were able to enlist the willing aid of corrupt Chinese officials only lessened the chance of bringing order out of chaos.

In 1913, only a year after Sun resigned the presidency, the so-called Reorganization Loans to the Yuan Shih-kai government indicated the corruption which had reached the highest places. As Yuan himself became more accustomed to sole power, and as he saw the condition of the country at large growing worse and worse, he easily persuaded himself that what China needed was monarchy. With his own experience and ability and the authority of the monarchical tradition, Yuan told himself, and eventually others, it should not be hard to revivify China.

The movement toward monarchy proceeded slowly. But the 'second revolution' was already under way. Chiang Kai-shek was active in it. He worked with Chen Chih-mei, under whom he had first been introduced to revolution. Chen was still the Number 1 military man of the Shanghai area. He could not afford to take an openly revolutionary stand. He remained ostensibly loyal but actually worked closely with the anti-Yuan factions.

Chen finally plotted an open outbreak against Yuan Shih-kai. The plan called first for the seizure of the gunboat *Chao Ho*, lying on the Whangpoo River near Shanghai. A number of the sailors were revolutionists. The plotters also intended to seize the Kiangnan Arsenal with a small military force whose base was in the French Concession of Shanghai.

Chiang was a member of the overland party. It made a brief attempt to approach the arsenal, but was overpowered not far from its goal.

The naval part was at first more successful. A party of men captured the vessel, but then found themselves unable to proceed further. The other gunboats refused to join the revolt, and the *Chao Ho* was left riding peacefully at anchor. The single vessel couldn't make war on the rest of the Chinese navy, feeble as the navy was. On receiving word of the failure of the land force to capture the arsenal, the revolutionists quietly abandoned the boat.

Chen Chih-mei was dismissed from his post as overlord of Shanghai. Chiang Kai-shek lost his army job as a result, but became more active than ever in the underground movement. He traveled to all parts of the nation raising funds for the coming revolution and stirring up anti-Yuan sentiment. Finally the revolutionists were ready to strike, and Chiang went to Canton.

Sun Yat-sen and his associates, having established a stronghold in the Canton area, revolted. They started what they called a 'punitive expedition' against the north. Chiang Kai-shek was a part of it, but he was still in the most minor of positions and hardly known to the southern leaders.

What the northern expedition hoped to accomplish at this time is difficult to see. It had neither military strength nor resources. Nor could it command any popular support when nine tenths of the people of the nation were in complete ignorance of its existence.

The revolution was crushed in something like two weeks, as the northern government moved effective military forces against it. Chiang Kai-shek, with Sun Yat-sen and others, fled to Japan. It was the first time that he had actually been thrown into close contact with the father of the Chinese Republic.

His funds had disappeared and he was poor again. He wrote to his mother for money. To each appeal she always replied with a small amount of cash. The relatives, again positive that Chiang was a hopeless ne'er-do-well, urged her as usual to have nothing to do with him.

In those days, there was nothing romantic about revolutionary work, and literature had not glorified the lives of idealists who plotted against despotism. But Mother Chiang remained loyal to the son, whose headstrong ideas she could not understand, and sent him the few dollars she managed to scrape together. He had enjoyed prosperity once, and she felt sure that he would recoup his losses.

By 1915 Yuan was proceeding with his plan to seat himself on the Dragon Throne. He issued orders for elections to be held throughout the nation with a view to establishing a monarchy. The elections, of course, were a farce. The masses knew no more about voting than did they about metaphysics, and only those people voted who had been paid and instructed, but Yuan announced that a 'large majority' of the electors had favored a monarchy.

The Council of State, which Yuan controlled, thereupon formally invited Yuan to ascend the throne. He declined three times, with becoming modesty. He finally accepted and announced that the enthronement would take place January 1, 1916.

He never became Emperor, as the world knows today. A rebellion broke out in Yunnan, remote southwestern province of China. It was Christmas Day, and the date is observed as a purely political holiday in China today. Chiang Kai-shek, who again had been traveling about the nation organizing anti-Yuan activities, was largely responsible for hiring the Yunnan mercenaries who staged the initial revolt.

The uprisings spread rapidly to other provinces. Yuan became panicky. Even the Japanese government warned him to abandon his plan to make himself Emperor, and his courage completely left him. He first postponed the enthronement date, and then renounced his claim to the title of Emperor.

The old man's heart was apparently broken, and he didn't last long. On June 6, 1916, he died.

But before he passed on, Chen Chih-mei, Chiang's patron and protector, was murdered, at the instigation of the military governor of the province, and Chiang lost a powerful friend.

The Empire had collapsed, but the revolution was still far from accomplished. The anti-Yuan outbreaks had been no more than a series of sporadic uprisings by paid troops.

After Yuan's death the same old professional politicians, all seemingly ardent republicans, continued to rule the roost at Peking.

Chiang remained a revolutionist.

CHAPTER VII

BROKER

CHIANG returned to Shanghai, without funds or influence. No longer was he the gay young army officer with plenty of money and little work. Nor was he the earnest underground revolutionary. He was an impecunious young man in search of a job.

This period of his life is obscure. At times he seems to have fared well, at other times he was decidedly down on his luck. Early in 1916, he counted himself lucky to get a job as a junior clerk in one of the then small Chinese commodity exchanges. A war was raging in Europe, markets were booming, and the Chinese, who rank with the world's most reckless speculators, were plunging heavily.

Fortunes were being made and lost, but Chiang drew a wage, that, even by Chinese standards, was most modest. He lived in a dingy little room by himself. Each morning he went to a near-by hot-water shop, paid his copper, received a potful of water, and shuffled back to his room to make his toilet.

He had no decent shoes. And he ate none too well. Like hundreds of clerks in the Chinese shops, he was unable to afford even the humble meals of the cheapest restaurants, and bought his food from the itinerant street vendors. Some of the old food vendors near the Gold Bar Exchange on Kiukiang Road today say they remember him; a few insist he still owes them money.

It was a dismal time for the future Strong Man. But he

had his friends. The most important was Chang Ching-kiang.

Before the 1911 revolution, Chang made his fortune as a curio dealer in Europe, and was one of the major share-holders in a large bean-curd establishment in Paris, the profits of which went to finance Sun's revolutionary activities. At one time he gave Sun a check for $250,000, and later contributed $1,000,000 to the cause. He also advanced the money to Chen Chih-mei to start the revolt against Yuan Shih-kai in 1913.

While Chiang Kai-shek was clerking at the exchange, Sun established a 'constitution-upholding' government at Canton. This government controlled four southern provinces and parts of two others in Central China.

In the Canton régime were Sun Fo, son of Sun Yat-sen and known as the 'crown prince,' T. V. Soong, a brother-in-law, later to become China's leading political financier, and other progressives. But the Doctor had his own troubles. He had appointed a number of his relatives to office besides Sun Fo and T. V. Soong. Unlike these two, most of the relatives were incompetent, and some were avaricious. Furthermore, the Kuomintang government had failed to bring all the reforms that its enthusiastic adherents had promised. Gambling and opium, for example, were not abolished as some had expected, but were taxed for revenue.

The Canton merchants, disgusted with the abuses of the government and afraid of the radicalism of some of its followers, organized a militia unit to hold it in check.

Up in Shanghai, the revolution-financier, Chang Ching-kiang, still kept in close touch with Sun Yat-sen and his government, and was in entire sympathy with its aims. In the youthful Chiang Kai-shek the businessman-revolutionist saw real ability waiting for an outlet.

He backed Chiang Kai-shek as an exchange broker. The

World War was in full tilt, markets were bullish, and Chiang emerged with a comfortable fortune in a relatively short time. Some say that he was rich in less than a year.

In 1920, with the war over, the crash came. Chiang was caught. When settlement day came around, he was short approximately $30,000, with no prospects of raising the sum anywhere.

Chang Ching-kiang learned of his protégé's deficit, and paid his debts. Then he sent him down to South China with a letter of recommendation to Doctor Sun Yat-sen.

Chiang had seen and worked with Sun before, but he was far from an intimate of the veteran revolutionist. Enthusiastic apologists for Chiang say glibly that he worked with Doctor Sun for forty years, indicating that Chiang started his revolutionary career at the age of nine. Others have pointed to his bankruptcy in Shanghai and said that he had a dark record in the files of the old mixed court at Shanghai. Evidence fails to support the allegation.

During Chiang's stay in Shanghai, he undoubtedly came into contact with the leaders of the secret societies which even today dominate Chinese urban life to an unbelievable extent. Some of the societies, notably the Green and Red societies, had their inception in the early days of the Manchu reign, and began as strictly anti-Manchu revolutionary organizations. Others started as social and mutual-protection groups. Most have financed themselves by running the opium traffic, gambling, protection rackets, and kidnapping business; others specialize in gun-running, and some deal in murder for pay. But plenty of respectable people belong to them, and if Chiang's association with the organization leaders doesn't exactly qualify him for sainthood, neither does it make him a gunman or assassin.

That the association formed in those obscure war-time days has proved valuable to him, no one can doubt. It enabled him to subjugate Shanghai some seven years later without sacrificing much-needed soldiers. The allegation that he is in league with the gangs has never been proved, and hence must, as the British news agencies say, be treated with the greatest reserve.

S. C. Chuck

WITH SUN YAT-SEN, 1924

CHAPTER VIII

HIDE–AND–SEEK AT CANTON

CHIANG went south to Canton to find Sun Yat-sen dreaming of and planning for a 'northern expedition,' while his own power in the south rested on only the shakiest foundation.

Sun eschewed the idea of regional revolution. He scorned the belief of many of his followers that it was wiser to transform one portion of the country into a model governmental area and trust the idea to permeate the rest of the nation. A Chinese revolution, he argued, must be carried into the strongholds of the northern militarists, and national power must be administered by a single agency. Otherwise, he insisted, there was no China, and the overthrow of the Manchus had been in vain.

But Chiang saw what Sun failed to realize, that the southern civil government existed only on the sufferance of southern military chieftains who were no better than those who held sway in the north. Chiang realized, long before Sun came to the same way of thinking, that a revolutionary force must have a revolutionary army. A militarist's army lent to the revolutionary cause would always be unreliable. A mercenary force, such as Sun had depended upon to stage earlier uprisings, was worse than useless for a protracted campaign.

The wisdom of Chiang's stand was amply demonstrated in January, 1922. Sun had completed what he thought were adequate preparations for a conquering northern expedition.

The expedition ended almost as quickly as it started. A war-lord named Chen Chiung-ming, nominally Sun's subordinate but actually the military power of the southern government, failed to see the wisdom of sending his troops to fight a crazy crusade against the north. He refused to supply the necessary supplies for the troops who were leading the northward march and who were loyal to Sun Yat-sen. Without supplies there could be no expedition, and Sun was forced to bring his forces back to Canton. The so-called first northern expedition was over.

Sun stripped the war-lord of his offices in the civil government, but nothing he could do could remove the man as a military power.

Sun was not discouraged, changed the course of the proposed expedition, and entrusted the drive to two generals whose loyalty was assured. But among the loyalist generals was a friend of the obstructionist war-lord. Sun failed to dismiss him, apparently because of lack of evidence against him. Chiang Kai-shek decided that the man was dangerous and urged Sun to get rid of him. The Doctor, who was inclined to trust everyone, demurred. Chiang and Sun got into an argument over the matter, and Chiang, whose temper was hot, found it difficult to keep his peace.

Events soon proved Chiang right and Sun wrong. The general turned out to be the traitor Chiang suspected. On June 16, 1922, a division of troops composed largely of doughty Hunanese, the 'fightingest men in China,' instigated by the traitorous general, headed for the presidential quarters. At the same time troops of the hostile war-lord began to bombard the section where Sun resided, with the intention of killing him.

Chiang learned of the plan at the eleventh hour and rushed to warn Sun. Both, with Madame Sun, escaped in disguise. They made for the naval headquarters, where a meeting was held, attended by leaders loyal to Sun. There were disconcertingly few of them.

Had it not been for Chiang's timely warning, there is no doubt that the first president of the Chinese Republic would have died then and there, and the era of Sino-Russian co-operation which gave the western world the 'jitters' for several years would never have come to pass.

The strength of the Sun-Chiang group seemed to be in the navy, as the army was apparently not to be relied on. Sun, Chiang, and their followers embarked on gunboats, went to near-by Whampoa, and planned a counter-attack.

It was summer and beastly hot. Life aboard the ships, lying under the blazing South China sun, was trying. Chiang became virtually a servant to Sun, caring for the Doctor's personal wants and making him as comfortable as circumstances would permit. He lived like a common sailor, and worked with the ship's crew as they maneuvered the vessel.

It soon became apparent that a counter-attack was out of the question. They had virtually no ammunition. The situation evolved into a game of hide-and-seek, in which the gunboats bearing Sun and his followers disposed themselves strategically among the foreign men-of-war in the stream off Canton, and the insurgents, who had seized power, were afraid to shell them for fear of creating an international incident.

Finally Sun Yat-sen, his wife, and Chiang Kai-shek managed to spirit themselves out of the south and returned to Shanghai. It was probably the lowest point of Sun's career. Most of his former followers deserted him; many attacked him. He was without funds and as a revolutionary he seemed a has-been. The chance that he would ever return to power seemed slim indeed.

Sun's chief associates in those days were Hu Han-min

and Wang Ching-wei, later to become Chiang Kai-shek's chief political rivals. Hu was a conservative of democratic principles. Wang was of the social-democrat school and in those days was considered wildly radical. Hu and Wang were always bickering over matters of policy.

While Sun Yat-sen was living quietly in the French Concession of Shanghai and Hu and Wang were arguing loudly, a military upset occurred in the south. The war-lord who had ejected Sun Yat-sen was defeated in one of the innumerable Chinese civil wars. His successor, who was amiably disposed toward Sun Yat-sen, and regarded him as a harmless orator who might give his régime some needed prestige, invited the Doctor back to Canton. Sun accepted the bid as a recognition of his greatness, and was back in his old stamping ground with remarkable speed. Before the new war-lord knew what had happened, Sun had given himself the title of generalissimo and began issuing orders in the manner of former days. The military man was considerably taken aback, and sent representatives with polite suggestions that the Doctor leave town again.

But this time Sun had profited by Chiang Kai-shek's advice. He had taken the trouble to gather a respectable military machine around him, and had insured the loyalty of the generals in direct command at Canton. He said no to the war-lord's invitation to leave, and said it with assurance.

The war-lord staged a mild sort of military demonstration, but failed to scare the Doctor. Two generals fought for Sun, and the war-lord, seeing that the task was hopeless, gave up.

Harassed by intrigue and increasingly tired of the wrangling of the doctrinaires Hu Han-min and Wang Ching-wei, Sun Yat-sen came to place more and more faith in the quiet businesslike Chiang Kai-shek. Chiang appeared to have

a knack of seeing through situations and offering practical
advice. He was no political theorist but a practical worker.
And, of considerable importance in the revolutionary trend
which Sun foresaw, Chiang was a trained soldier.

CHAPTER IX

RUSSIAN ENTENTE

THE most important event in the history of the Chinese revolution, and one which had a profound influence on the career of Chiang Kai-shek, occurred while Sun was in Shanghai. Adolf Abram Joffe, an experienced Bolshevik diplomat, was sent by Moscow to Peking in the summer of 1922. His task was to broach the project of Sino-Russian co-operation. He made no headway with the Peking government, but did plenty of spade-work among the nation's intelligentsia.

In January, 1923, he went to Shanghai and conferred with Sun Yat-sen, who had been driven out of Canton the previous year. Sun was eager for aid of any sort that would restore his revolutionary movement to life. He had hoped that America would help him, often said that the United States should give the Chinese revolution its Lafayette. He also had hopes of Germany, which had lost its extra-territorial rights in China as a result of the war and was the first great power to deal with China on an equal basis. But America, disgusted with post-war European diplomacy, was wary of entanglements elsewhere. Germany was too busy with her own struggle for recovery.

The upshot of the Sun-Joffe meeting was a joint statement which launched the Chinese revolution on its most vigorous phase and gave it the force of a crusade.

The statement said flatly that Sun did not believe that communism or the Soviet political system could be successfully introduced into China, because the conditions for a successful establishment of those institutions did not exist in China. Joffe concurred in that declaration.

Both men agreed that the first task of the revolution was to establish national independence. Joffe then stated the Soviet government's entire willingness to renounce all special privileges exacted by the Czarist régime. Nothing was said about Russian advisers, nothing about funds, arms or ammunition. Nothing was said about the part Communist Party members would play in the Kuomintang. All that was left for later arrangement.

But it was agreed that between the two régimes, Chinese Nationalist and Russian Communist, there would be 'most friendly and cordial relations.' That concordat in five years brought the Kuomintang armies in triumph to Peking.

Sun went back to Canton in 1923, and Chiang Kai-shek followed a short time later. After Sun had survived his first military test, in the threat from the new war-lord of Canton, he sent Chiang Kai-shek to Moscow to study Soviet military methods and political institutions.

Chiang went and observed. He stayed a year. Some said that he signed an agreement which brought the Russian advisers to Canton. There is no evidence that he did. He was as yet a person of no consequence at Canton, and he was in Moscow merely as a student and observer.

Sun's power at Canton, meanwhile, rested on paid troops from outlying provinces. His authority did not extend beyond the city. The old war-lord who had banished him the year before was still in power in the remainder of the province outside of Canton, and Sun had difficulty raising money to pay the mercenaries who were keeping him at bay. Taxes were necessarily heavy, and their burden even strained the loyalty of those Cantonese who were counted among his supporters.

Then came Borodin and his fellow-Russians, and all that was changed. The Russians first of all brought funds. But, more important, they brought a plan, a plan for the organization of a government and a real revolution.

They called him Michael Borodin. His real name was Gruesenberg. He was a Russian Jew who had been taken to the United States when a small boy. Educated in America, he operated a business college in Chicago under the name of Berg. Rapidly turning radical, he abandoned teaching, took the name of Borodin, and returned to Russia. His alertness and intelligence soon brought him to positions of trust in the Communist régime, and he was sent as an agitator to Mexico, then to Turkey as chief representative of the Third International.

Under Borodin's influence, the Kuomintang Party was quickly reconstructed on the Soviet model. The province was divided into districts, and the districts into local units, and in each one a Kuomintang organization was established.

The personnel of the local units was carefully selected. The party registers were purged of those who objected to the alliance with Russia. The work proceeded, and it generated enthusiasm. On the last day of 1923, Doctor Sun, in a speech at Canton, happily announced, 'We no longer look to the West, we now look to Russia.' By that time one hundred Russians were in Canton, as advisers and military instructors.

In the north, civil war broke out, seemingly for the thousandth time. Wu Pei-fu, dominant North China military figure, decided it was time to prosecute his long-cherished desire to conquer all China. With ample forces and equipment he moved north once more against the Manchurian armies of Chang Tso-lin, the 'old marshal.'

But his chief subordinate, Feng Yu-hsiang, who delighted

to call himself the 'Christian General,' turned back as soon as Wu and his forces were well out of Peking, and seized the capital city. Wu was left to meet the 'old marshal' alone, and was badly beaten. Thereupon the 'Christian General' and the 'old marshal' joined forces for a time, removed the President of China, and installed their own man as 'provisional chief executive.'

It was a bald piece of treachery on Feng's part, but the Christian General had goodChristian excuses: The President had been corrupt; he was generally believed to have elected himself by bribery. Getting rid of him was put forward as a good piece of business.

With Wu Pei-fu out of the picture, the northerners invited Sun Yat-sen to come to Peking and discuss the formation of a truly national government. Sun, ever willing to avert hostilities if possible, accepted the invitation and went up to the north. But he was a sick man when he arrived at Peking, and held most of his conferences in the Peking Union Medical College Hospital. In the midst of the conferences, which were to stave off Sun's new 'northern expedition' for which preparations were already under way, Sun died of cancer of the liver, March 12, 1925.

Before that, however, Chiang Kai-shek had returned to Canton and begun reorganizing the Whampoa Military Academy, which was to become the nucleus of Nationalist China's military force. He went to Shanghai and recruited some of the soldiers of a defeated army, into whom he instilled new enthusiasm. He placed them under special training, and they became the first students of the new academy.

He also persuaded Chen Kuo-fu, nephew of Chiang's old patron, Chen Chih-mei, to come to Canton and help him at the school. Thus began an association with one of the two Chen brothers, who today are among the most powerful and mysterious figures in the Nanking government.

It was Chiang's desire to make Whampoa a national school, and he took pains to bring students from as many provinces of China as possible. Besides forming the character of the new school, this widespread selection had a distinct propaganda value through the nation.

He made the northern or mandarin language the official tongue of the academy, and outlawed all regional dialects. Cantonese, which most of the students spoke, was taboo in the classrooms and dormitories.

Enrollment was at first limited to three hundred students. More than fifteen hundred applied. Five hundred were accepted, and the school began its work in earnest.

The academy attracted a high type of young Chinese. The old contempt for the soldier was giving way to militant nationalism. Most of those who enrolled were students of middle schools and colleges, who felt that during the military stage of the revolution they could best serve their country by becoming army officers.

The instructors were Russians and Chinese who had studied at Paotingfu and in Japan. Chiang Kai-shek, although not the commander-in-chief of the Nationalist army, was the principal of the academy and in full charge of the military unit which it came to represent.

The students were taught a new concept in Chinese militarism, to obey their superiors implicitly, and were subjected to the strictest discipline. They were told that they would be placed in command of ignorant men, whom they would have to teach and drill. They were admonished to be good soldiers so that they might be good officers.

Chiang trained his students to think in terms of China as a whole, and exhorted them to fight for the honor of their country and the party, in accordance with the will of Sun Yat-sen, and not for the glory of an individual commander.

There were other new ideas. The students were told that robbery of the people by the soldiery was forbidden, and that the revolutionary army was the servant of the people. They were warned that violations would result in execution without trial. Even if they received no pay, Chiang instructed them, they must fight for the people and for China. And, in addition to military tactics, he and his fellow-teachers taught the students political principles and the elements of propaganda.

As each class was graduated, its members were sent out to serve in the various armies in the Canton area. They soon transformed the haphazardly organized provincial forces into a formidable fighting machine. The chief instructor in tactics was a Russian known as General Galens. Today he is Vassili Bluecher, marshal of the Soviet Union and commander of the Far Eastern Autonomous Red Army which holds Siberia for the U.S.S.R.

Borodin was in charge of the political training institute. Speaking not a word of Chinese and always forced to address crowds through an interpreter, the man nevertheless exerted remarkable power on the Nationalists, particularly the younger men, and was as effective a revolutionary leader as China had ever seen.

His work was to develop agitators and propagandists to go into the provinces and prepare the way for the Kuomintang armies on their projected march to the north. Galens supervised the military instruction. T. V. Soong, Harvard graduate, took over the finance portfolio of the southern government, checked fraud and corruption.

The first test of the régime came before the Whampoa Academy was a year old. The Canton Volunteers, whom the conservative merchants had recruited and paid, were instigated by the still-active provincial war-lord to revolt against the Sun Yat-sen government.

It was a serious threat, coming from within Canton itself. Chiang was ordered to suppress it. With only a few hundred cadets, poorly equipped but superbly trained, Chiang moved quickly against the rebels.

He maneuvered his forces with a speed and a dash that were new to China. He crushed the Volunteers inside the city and beat back the would-be attackers from without. There was much slaughter, and a large part of Canton was destroyed in the struggle. But his action left Sun master of the city, and free from both the danger of further attack and the necessity of relying on inefficient mercenaries.

Sun was impressed. He looked upon Chiang with new interest and with real respect. Soon Chiang became actual leader of the Kuomintang armies and was recognized by the Central Executive Committee of the party as commander-in-chief.

Later, when civil war broke out in the outlying portions of the province, Chiang assumed control of all agencies of the Kuomintang and the government as a war measure. Although an older officer was still officially commander-in-chief, he was distrusted by the Russians, who put him under surveillance, and gradually the actual management of military affairs passed into the hands of Chiang, with the civilian politician Wang Ching-wei assisting and Borodin giving approval to matters of high policy. The non-Kuomintang units of the southern army moved out of the Canton area.

CHAPTER X

RIGHT WING, LEFT WING

CHIANG'S rise to power and influence at Canton was more than dramatic — it was phenomenal. The 1925 edition of 'Who's Who in China' did not even mention his name. A year later he was leading the southern armies on the long-awaited and eventually successful northern expedition. Two years later he was the outstanding military man in the country. In three years he was the head of a government which not only controlled the south but professed to speak for all China.

Events moved rapidly after the death of Sun Yat-sen. The old Doctor, who had been alternately regarded as a wild visionary, a recurrent nuisance, and a dangerous agitator, straightway became a saint and a martyr. His work and his indisputable accomplishments were bound to achieve greater recognition after his death, when the memory of personal disputes had been forgotten, but the magnitude of the popular emotion which converted him into a legendary hero surprised everyone except those who engineered the conversion — Borodin and the Kuomintang leaders.

Sun Yat-sen's will, generally believed to have been drafted by Wang Ching-wei, immediately became a revolutionary Bible. It is still read each Monday morning by all officials, in regular memorial services, and the recitation is followed by three minutes of silence. Because Wang Ching-wei was so close to Sun in his last days he was regarded as the heir to Sun's philosophic heritage.

But in Canton his chief rival, Hu Han-min, held the post of acting-generalissimo. He was young and failed to command even the respect which Sun enjoyed in his lifetime. Once again the old Canton war-lord who had twice engaged Sun in battle rose in arms. Two other ex-war-lords of the region threatened the Canton régime from the neighboring province of Kwangsi.

Chiang Kai-shek stepped into the situation again and snatched security from danger. Assisted by several revolutionary generals, he struck swiftly and defeated the attackers one after the other.

The first battle was fought even before Sun's death on February 14, 1925. With three hundred cadets from Whampoa, Chiang marched out of Canton and met the enemy troops at Tamshui. He repulsed the war-lord's superior force with heavy losses. Five days later the war-lord counter-attacked and was again driven back. His troops became demoralized under the sudden savage attacks of the handful from Whampoa, and broke into headlong retreat. Chiang followed his advantage and determined to end once and for all the threat of regional war-lords to the Canton régime. He sent his cadets in pursuit of the enemy forces, rounded up small detachments, and cut them off piecemeal.

Chiang then reinforced his cadets and swept through the neighboring districts, defeating the forces of the other two war-lords menacing Canton. He finally broke the main force of the enemy troops and stormed the supposedly impregnable stronghold of Waichow, which for hundreds of years had been one of the best-fortified walled cities in the nation. It had successfully withstood scores of invasions. Once, only, back in the Tang Dynasty in the neighborhood of A.D. 700, had it been taken by an opposing force.

Surrounding the city was a huge moat, which had to be

crossed by any attacking force. Chiang surveyed the situation, decided that he could take the town.

Ignoring the dictum that the general must keep to the rear and direct the fighting, Chiang himself with a handful of men plunged across the moat, half-swimming, half-running in the face of heavy rifle and machine-gun fire. Reaching the opposite bank, they made for a small opening in the city wall. Now out of range of the weapons atop the walls, they overpowered the defending detachment and entered the city.

Then, firing their rifles, yelling, and making as terrific a commotion as possible, they drew the attention of the troops inside the wall and the crews manning the guns mounted on top of it. As the defense weapons were swung about and trained on the handful of men who had penetrated the wall, Chiang's reinforcements, in accordance with orders, crossed the moat in small boats and stormed every section of the wall.

Hundreds were killed and wounded. Bodies lay about the rampart, in the moat, and on the city's streets. But the plan was successful. The enemy troops finally hoisted the white flag and the Nationalist troops assumed command. The war-lord fled aboard a foreign warship and saved himself.

It was a costly victory. Only nine hundred men of the original ten thousand with whom Chiang began the attack escaped death or injury. But the fall of Waichow to the Nationalists enormously increased their prestige and stamped them as a military force to be reckoned with. It suddenly put the hitherto little-known Chiang in the rank of military commanders like Wu Pei-fu, 'Old Marshal' Chang Tso-lin, 'Christian General' Feng Yu-hsiang, and the other veteran war-makers.

Some who tell the story of Waichow say that Sun Yat-sen himself, aboard a gunboat in the East River, closely followed the progress of the battle, and on its successful conclusion exclaimed, 'Ah, here is the second Sun Yat-sen. He will one day take my place.' The tale is pure eyewash. Sun at the time was on his deathbed at Peking, two thousand miles to the north.

With Waichow subdued and the enemy troops in the entire area surrendering or in headlong flight, Chiang struck at another malcontent general and captured the coastal city of Swatow. Meanwhile other enemies lurked. An army of Kwangsi and Yunnan troops camped in the southwest and planned to attack Chiang's flank. The Whampoa units struck at the city of Meihu, where the conspirators were concentrated, and inflicted a disastrous defeat after a twenty-four-hour battle. By the end of 1925, Chiang was master of Kwangtung Province.

He had, only a short time before, been made a member of the Central Executive Committee, the inner council and governing body of the Kuomintang. His political influence speedily increased to keep pace with his military eminence. He quickly emerged as a rival to Wang Ching-wei, whose followers had put him forward as the logical successor to Sun Yat-sen as head of the party.

Chiang himself was becoming conscious of his power, and increasingly distrustful of the Russians. He watched with distaste their communistic, as distinct from nationalistic, activities, and viewed with alarm the influence which Chinese Communists were coming to exert in the Kuomintang. Not all the Russians were as clever and tactful as Borodin. Possibly a few of them indicated their impatience with the Chinese whom they were instructing and advising. Apparently several were arrogant and contemptuous of their Chinese colleagues. But Chiang needed their continued help, their expert advice, their knowledge of political organization and mass propaganda, at which he was still a novice. Above all he needed their military supplies.

Likewise with his potential rivals in the party. Many held important military commands. Chiang needed their support. He stayed out of factional fights as well as he could, kept his own counsel, and obeyed party orders like a good soldier.

Then two incidents broke on a startled nation and sped the course of militant revolution. On May 30, 1925, came the first at Shanghai. A series of labor disputes, centering in Japanese-owned mills, had resulted in a wholesale lock-out and the serious wounding of thirteen workers outside one of the factories.

Shanghai students made common cause with the strikers; after holding a memorial service, several of their number were arrested by the foreign police at the border of the International Settlement. The remainder went to the police station demanding that their fellows be freed or that they themselves be imprisoned.

A British inspector, in command at the station, lost his head. He gave a hardly audible warning in the English language to a crowd of about two thousand, waited ten seconds, and ordered his men to shoot.

Six students were killed on the spot, more than forty others were seriously wounded. But the demonstration went on, and firing continued for a few days. The final count was fifteen killed and twenty wounded. All were Chinese.

The Chinese declared a general strike in the Settlement. Every essential business and service in the city of more than a million people halted. The Chinese presented demands to a foreign investigating commission. The commission found the Shanghai Municipal Council to blame, censured its

American chairman, and recommended the dismissal of the Police Commissioner and the trial and punishment of the inspector who had directed the firing on the students.

The same month the Chinese marine engineers at Hongkong struck, in a dispute over housing. The employers stood firm, and in less than two weeks 200,000 workers left the colony.

On June 23, 1925, occurred the second major 'incident,' the Shameen shootings. A parade made its way along the bund at Canton, passing opposite Shameen, the island which comprises the foreign settlement. Someone fired; accounts differ as to whether the first shot came from Shameen or Canton. But the British and French machine-guns, mounted on Shameen in fear of a mob attack on the foreign area, spat bullets into the ranks of the Chinese across the stream. Fifty-two Chinese were killed and 117 wounded.

South China began its boycott of everything British. Although the French were equal participants in the Shameen shootings, and although the Council at Shanghai comprised Americans and Japanese as well as British, the Chinese anger was directed against the Britons, who were regarded as the chief exponents of foreign imperialism in China.

Meanwhile, up at Peking the provisional president had suspended the constitution adopted in 1923, and even the form of representative government in China collapsed.

On July 1, 1925, Canton announced the promulgation of a new national government which purported to speak for all China. Wang Ching-wei was chairman. A model organization for towns and provinces all over the nation was announced. The idea was ready to be carried to all China, propagandists were already at work in the provinces far from Kwangtung, and it remained only for the military machine to export the revolution.

Chiang Kai-shek, then and for some time afterward regarded as a mild radical, was named commander of the student corps of the army. Hu Han-min was foreign minister. But there were internal disputes to settle before the revolutionary armies could march northward with confidence.

The report circulated that Hu Han-min, the other southern civilian leader, a conservative, wanted to oust Chiang Kai-shek, whom he felt to be growing too powerful, and that he had sought the assistance of other military leaders to that end.

On the night of August 24, by order of Chiang, who was still principal of Whampoa, cadets from the academy searched the offices and homes of all government officials, including Hu Han-min. More than one hundred were arrested. Hu himself was taken under guard on a man-of-war to Whampoa.

Four days later Chiang Kai-shek, now commander-in-chief of the garrisons in Canton, was in full control of the city. The left wing of the Kuomintang was firmly established in power, and Chiang was its acknowledged head.

Hu, in one of the Oriental gestures which westerners find quaint, was forced at the point of businesslike-looking weapons to accept an honorary appointment as 'diplomatic envoy of the Canton government' to Europe to 'inspect general conditions.' Chiang sent him to Russia to see a real revolution in operation.

Chiang had been supported in the coup by the military leader who was officially still in command of the army and hence theoretically Chiang's superior. Soon afterward, Chiang and his associate fell out, and the latter decided to move to a more congenial climate; he fled to Shanghai. The party's Central Executive Committee thereupon gave Chiang Kai-shek complete independence in military affairs.

Communist and anti-Communist factions were forming in Canton. Wang Ching-wei, who with Hu Han-min and Chiang Kai-shek formed the southern triumvirate, succeeded in averting an open clash, preaching the necessity of unifying China first and settling internal policies later.

Chiang, however, saw a growing sentiment among many Chinese against the Russians and the Communists. He was in full sympathy. After conferring with his old Shanghai benefactor, Chang Ching-kiang, he issued a statement shortly after Sun Yat-sen's death, announcing that he had ceased to be a Communist and henceforth would base his philosophy on Doctor Sun's 'Three Principles of the People,' nationalism, democracy, and 'livelihood of the people.' That the third principle, according to Doctor Sun's writings, was indistinguishable from socialism failed to trouble Chiang. He had his own non-socialist concordance for the Sun scriptures.

But Chiang did not at the time declare war on the Communists. When a group of ultra-conservatives of the Kuomintang held a conference in the Western Hills near Peking and demanded the expulsion of the Communists from the party and the dismissal of the Russian advisers, the Kuomintang, with Chiang assenting, rejected the demands and affirmed the entente with Moscow. The party refused to accept Borodin's proffered resignation; on the contrary, it presented him with a silver tripod bearing the inscription 'The Co-operative Struggle.'

Early the next year, 1926, following a resolution by the party congress that 'all encouragement be given Feng Yu-hsiang (the Christian General) in the struggle against the northern imperialists and militarists,' Borodin left Canton for the north. His sudden departure was regarded in some quarters as evidence of a split with Chiang.

In March, Chiang was veering decidedly to the right.

P. & A. photo

RUSSIAN ADVISERS TO THE KUOMINTANG

Michael Borodin at the extreme left, General Galens at Chiang Kai-shek's right

Acme

GENERALS YEN HSI-SHAN, FENG YU-HSIANG, CHIANG KAI-SHEK,
AND LI TSUNG-JEN

Without the permission of the Central Executive Committee he suddenly attacked a portion of the workmen's pickets of the Canton Strikers' Committee, the group which had inaugurated the Hongkong boycott. After surrounding the pickets with his own troops, he searched them, disarmed them, and kept them under surveillance. At the same time he ordered the disarming of an army regiment believed to be Communist.

Chiang utilized the services of the Chief of Police, Wu Teh-chen, to make the arrests. Numerous Russians were arrested and ordered to leave Canton forthwith. But, Chinese fashion, Chiang gave them a banquet on the eve of their departure, told them how sorry he was that they found it necessary to go. Hu Han-min, whom Chiang had previously packed off to Moscow, was recalled.

In May, 1926, Borodin returned to Canton. Hu arrived about the same time. Chiang seemed decidedly cool to the Russian. But they had a talk, and after a while they seemingly came to an understanding.

Thereupon, to the amazement of everybody, Chiang turned on the anti-Communists. Chief of Police Wu, whom he had used to arrest the Communists, was himself put in jail, and later sent off to Shanghai.

The only reasonable explanation for the about-face was that Chiang had acceded to Borodin's terms for the management of the government in return for material assistance on the forthcoming northern military expedition.

But at the first meeting of the C.E.C. after the coup and counter-coup, Chiang with fine indignation denounced the outrages attributed to the Communists in South China. He suggested that henceforth no Communists be allowed to hold leading posts in the party of government. The meeting passed a resolution calling for a revision of relations between the Kuomintang and the Communists.

Chiang went further and suggested that the Communists be expelled from the party, but the committee voted him down. It was decided to restrict the number of Communists filling Kuomintang posts, and the Communists were told not to oppose the Three Principles of Doctor Sun. They were also instructed to deposit a list of their members with the C.E.C.

Borodin sat at the meeting and said not a word. He and Chiang, it was obvious, had worked out the procedure beforehand, and Chiang's vigorous Red-baiting was only for 'face' purposes.

The necessity of unity was obvious, however, and the Chiang-Borodin deal need not be condemned. Each was wise enough to realize that he had to make some concessions to the other. The Kuomintang enemies were not far from Kwangtung Province, and were now being financed by the northern militarists. It was time for a clear-cut understanding at Canton.

Wang Ching-wei, meanwhile, had fled to Europe, finding Canton a bit too hot for comfort. Hu Han-min had gone to Shanghai. The disruption of the party seemed imminent when Chiang took charge, supported by party veterans, and called a special C.E.C. meeting to reconcile outstanding differences.

As a result, Chiang became chairman of the standing committee of the C.E.C., the highest effective organ of the party and government. Borodin remained as high adviser. Kuomintang-Communist co-operation was to continue. With most of the veteran party leaders in exile, control came to rest squarely between the military commanders and the organizers of the workers' and peasants' groups under Communist domination — in short, between Chiang Kai-shek and Borodin.

CHAPTER XI

NORTHWARD MARCH

FOR ten years Sun Yat-sen had talked of an anti-northern expedition. His troops never crossed the borders of Kwangtung Province. A little more than a year after Sun's death the troops of Chiang Kai-shek were on the march, pouring into Hunan Province en route to Hankow, the Chicago of China.

Chiang assumed command of the Nationalist army at Canton, June 11, 1926. At a subsequent meeting of the C.E.C. he was given dictatorial powers for the duration of the expedition. He immediately started moving his regiments northward. In August the Nationalist armies entered Hunan, and by August 9 they had reached the city of Hengchow.

Look at a map of China. You will see that the distance from Canton to Peiping as the crow flies is more than thirteen hundred miles; by rail or road it is nearly two thousand. Even from Canton to Hankow is a respectable distance. For the southerners to have started a purely military expedition aimed at Peking and to have expected the northern militarists to await their arrival would have been naïve. To march was to give notice of their marching, and to warn the northerners to take defense measures.

Hence three steps were necessary. One — to have an understanding with the man controlling Hunan Province, lying between southern territory and Hankow. Such an understanding would enable the southerners to make a quick dash through Hunan and be knocking at the gates of Hankow before the northerners could prepare to defend them. Two — to propagandize so thoroughly the areas through which the Nationalist armies were to pass that resistance would melt away and the southerners would be hailed as deliverers of an oppressed people. Three — to push the propaganda behind the enemy lines, so that strikes and demonstrations would harass the enemy's rear and bring demoralization.

All three steps had been taken some time before. All that remained was to test their effectiveness. First of all, a minor Hunan war-lord who had grown dissatisfied with the régime of Wu Pei-fu was seen and 'fixed.' It was arranged that he would 'welcome' the Nationalist armies and join the revolution. To bring about such proper and noble sentiments on his part, silver was lavishly dispensed, ample arms and ammunition were assured him, and he was given to understand that in the new order he would become an eminent and respectable figure.

When the Nationalists reached Hengchow, they waited for the gentleman to act. He did not fail them. He moved on Changsha, capital of the province, and occupied it. The Nationalists joined forces with his troops and shortly after July 13 took charge of the city.

Chiang moved up to Changsha and was hailed as a Messiah. By the end of July the combined forces were on the outskirts of Yochow.

Here the effectiveness of the Nationalist propaganda machine began to manifest itself. Kuomintang agitators had gone among the military units of the province and preached the gospel of the anti-imperialist revolution. As the revolutionary forces advanced, unit after unit which had previously professed allegiance to Wu Pei-fu went over to the southern cause and shouted the Kuomintang slogans.

While the main army of the expedition moved through Hunan, a second started for Nanking by way of Kiangsi Province, and a third plunged through Fukien en route to Chiang Kai-shek's native province of Chekiang.

Wu, of course, heard what was happening, but he was engaged at the moment in a private grudge-war with the 'Christian General,' who had betrayed him. He had bottled up Feng at Nankow, and paid too little attention to the northward-marching Cantonese. His commanders sent him warnings and appeals, but Wu took the threat lightly and thereby made the most serious blunder of his career.

If he had moved promptly and decisively against the Nationalists, his superior equipment and forces, 110,000 men to the Nationalists' 100,000, would have made a real war of it. He might not have won, but he might have given Chiang Kai-shek and the Nationalist movement a severe enough setback to have caused dissension in the southerners' own ranks.

As it was, however, he ignored the warnings and appeals and relied on nondescript troops for the defense of the Hankow area. When he eventually proceeded south, he failed to take his best units with him, and his importance as a Chinese military figure was fast becoming merely historical.

Yochow fell to the Nationalists August 22. Alarmed, Wu hastened from North China. Before he arrived at Hankow, however, the Nationalists had penetrated the province and were advancing on Wuchang, sister-city of Hankow.

The southerners pushed forward quickly, and reached the outskirts of the city early in September. Finding a garrison ready to resist, the Nationalists crossed the Yangtse River west of Hanyang, third sister-city in the Hankow area. There they resorted to negotiation and the judicious use of silver bullets.

As a result, the northern general in charge of the place became suddenly converted to nationalism and the blue and white banners of the Kuomintang flew over Hanyang September 6. The convert general was rewarded with the command of a Nationalist army unit and subsequently pushed forward with the most ardent of the revolutionary warriors.

Hankow was occupied by the southerners September 8 without much difficulty. Of the three cities only Wuchang remained loyal to the north. There the sturdy Honanese garrison was ready to battle for the city to the death, and resisted a series of attacks until October 11. Then, just as an agreement was being reached for the surrender of the city, the Nationalists entered through a ruse, and took the place by surprise.

By this time the war-lord in control of the middle Yangtse area began to be restive. Previously he had turned down the appeal of the Old Marshal Chang Tso-lin, for a coalition of northern generals to beat back the southerners. Now, with Wu Pei-fu in retreat, he saw himself bearing the brunt of the Nationalists' attack. He suddenly perceived the wisdom of the coalition and joined it.

The Peking government had collapsed after a student demonstration which had culminated in a small massacre of the demonstrators. The 'old marshal' set up a military dictatorship.

But in two months three central China provinces fell to branches of the Nationalist armies, and two others were threatened by the approaching Nationalist hordes.

In addition to genuine military reverses, the northern allies were always suspicious of each other. When the Nationalist 'plain-clothes men,' behind-the-line propagandists and saboteurs, appeared, each of the northern generals thought it was an act of treachery on the part of the others, and whole armies fled without the show of a fight.

Meanwhile the Nationalist middle army in Kiangsi captured the strategically important city of Nanchang on September 19, but because of lack of flank protection had to withdraw for a while, and it was not until months later that the Nationalists took the city again and held it.

For a time the war-lord of the middle Yangtse considered suing for peace to save what he could of his régime, and negotiations were actually started, but in the midst of the conversations one of his subordinate generals revolted, declared his independence, and attempted to occupy Lunghua Arsenal near Shanghai. The war-lord, enraged, broke off dealings with the Nationalists and decided on bitter resistance against the southerners.

But plain-clothes agents of the Kuomintang were already active in the stronghold of Shanghai, and labor organizations were full of Kuomintang adherents. Strikes were breaking out daily, and industrial anarchy in the enemy's rear made his position untenable.

Kiukiang, important Yangtse port, was occupied by the Nationalists, again as the result of treachery by a subordinate general. The southerners were now in control of nearly the entire province of Kiangsi and half of Anhwei; they had completely overrun Fukien and were threatening Chekiang.

Chiang Kai-shek himself moved toward Nanchang. The city had been captured by the Nationalists, as noted previously, but had been abandoned when the position appeared dangerous. Chiang besieged the city. In the course of the attack he was reported killed, the first of the rumors which later circulated at frequent intervals.

The northerners caught three Nationalist spies, whom they court-martialed. Under torture the spies gave the password for entrance to Chiang's headquarters. The northerners sent five hundred volunteers in Nationalist uniforms to Chiang's camp. They were discovered by Chiang's own bodyguards, who virtually wiped out the invaders. Only thirty of the five hundred survived. One of them, who had never come within hailing distance of Chiang, reported that the Nationalist generalissimo had died of his wounds. The story spread, but Chiang continued to enjoy the best of health.

For two months the northerners held on to Nanchang. Chiang, through his spies, spread the word that the Nationalist army had been transferred. The northerners, who by that time were being called 'the allies,' sent troops to attack the Nationalists, supposedly on the move, at two points. Chiang trailed them and suddenly attacked one of the northern concentrations, inflicting heavy losses. When the second northern army came to the rescue, the two Nationalist forces united to crush it. Nanchang finally fell for the second time November 8, with the Nationalists taking 100,000 prisoners.

Such tactics were something new to the old-style Chinese militarists. These novel practices, the product of Chiang's own strategy, based on Russian precept, spread terror among the northern soldiery.

Following a hasty conference of the allied generals at Tientsin, summoned by Chang Tso-lin after the fall of Kiukiang November 5, it was decided to send expeditions down two railways, the Peking–Hankow and the Tientsin–Pukow lines, to strike before the two bodies of the Nationalist armies, one in Hupeh and one in Kiangsi Province, could unite.

The Tientsin–Pukow railway expedition sallied down into the Yangtse Valley as scheduled. It actually occupied Pukow, across the river from Nanking. The other expedition, however, never started. Wu Pei-fu was still distrustful of his allies and failed to move the requisite troops.

In January, 1927, a mob of workmen, roused by patriotic anti-imperialist orations, rushed the British Concession at Hankow. British marines were under orders not to fire. Britain had been badly scared by the tide of anti-imperialist nationalism, had decided it was time to stop listening to the die-hard Britishers in China and to formulate a new conciliatory policy. The British high command wanted no more 'incidents' like those at Shanghai and Shameen; the lesson of boycotted, half-deserted Hongkong was still painfully obvious.

Hence the British marines did not shoot. They protected, as best they could, all foreigners in danger, and withdrew to their ships. The mob overran the British Concession, and in a short time it was a British concession in name only and Chinese territory in fact. Not long afterward, Britain formally ratified the rendition of her concessions at Hankow and Kiukiang in the famous Chen-O'Malley agreement. After nearly a century of losing territory to the foreign powers, China had finally increased her dominion. The Nationalists were jubilant and all China exulted.

Spurred by this political success, the Nationalist armies pressed on with their campaign and extended their territorial gains.

On February 16, 1927, Chiang met the northern forces in open battle before Hangchow, and inflicted a smashing defeat. The middle-Yangtse war-lord fled north.

In the hope of saving the situation, the northern troops which had come down from Tientsin and occupied Pukow crossed the river and occupied Nanking. But it was too late to prevent the Nationalists from dominating the entire Yangtse Valley.

On March 22 the Nationalists occupied the Chinese-administered areas of Shanghai. The International Settle-

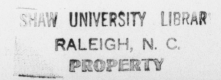

ment and the French Concession, the other parts of the Shanghai municipality, were in panic. The warships and troops of a half-dozen nations had been rushed to the scene and stood ready to halt a possible attack on the foreign areas, which many regarded as imminent.

Another army of Nationalists, meanwhile, had been attacking Nanking for nine days, and on March 24, 1927, two days after the occupation of Shanghai, the Nationalist armies drove the northerners out and entered the seat of Sun Yat-sen's first government.

There then occurred the Nanking 'outrage' or 'incident,' depending on one's point of view. Victorious Nationalist troops, entering the city as the northerners withdrew, began looting and pillaging. Foreign consulates and houses were attacked, including missionary institutions. Five foreigners were killed, and a British bluejacket was fatally wounded. Five others were wounded and several foreign women were reported to have been outraged.

A party from the American consulate made its way to Socony Hill, in sight of the river, and signaled for assistance from foreign warships anchored there. The British and American vessels staged a bombardment which halted the molestation of the foreigners by the troops, and the residents were evacuated the next day.

Chiang Kai-shek reached Nanking shortly afterward. He was plainly upset by the turn of events. He immediately apologized to the Japanese Consul-General at Wuhu, and asked him to communicate with the British and American authorities, assuring them that the southerners had no enmity against either nation and that he, Chiang, would personally settle the incident.

The Nationalist government, meanwhile, had moved from Canton to Hankow and was embarking on a radically left-wing program which Chiang found more and more

distasteful. The fear of reprisals for the Nanking incident
caused the Hankow government to issue a statement blaming the disorders on remnants of the defeated northerners.
The latter were accused of instigating the attack on foreign
consulates in order to involve the Nationalist forces with
the major powers.

The argument failed to convince. American and British
missionaries among the refugees spoke and understood
Chinese; most of them had been friendly to the Nationalist
cause, but they insisted that the soldiers who staged the
attacks were without a doubt southerners, that their speech
labeled them plainly.

Eugene Chen, the Hankow foreign minister who had
negotiated the rendition of the British concessions, said
that more than one hundred Chinese had been killed and
wounded for every foreign casualty. Chiang Kai-shek
himself investigated, and reported that seven Chinese had
been killed and fifteen wounded.

Events in Nanking then assumed a new aspect. Chiang
was preparing to split with Hankow and to set up a new
anti-Communist government at Nanking. He accused the
Communists of being really responsible for the Nanking
attacks. This was believed by those who wished to believe
it, principally by the frightened foreigners. Investigation
showed that the Communists had indeed been busy in the
native areas of Shanghai and up at Hankow, but that the
Nanking marauders were soldiers of good standing in the
regular Kuomintang Nationalist army.

In later years, eulogists of Chiang shifted the whole
blame to Chen Chien, the leader of the forces in Nanking
that day. Chen was said to have been a strong rival to
Chiang Kai-shek, and jealous of his growing power. He
sought, the story went, to embarrass Chiang by attacking
the foreigners. But if Chen was out of favor with Chiang

Kai-shek at the time, there is little to prove it. He retained his command, received a promotion shortly afterward, and in 1937 was chief of staff of the Chinese National Army.

But at any rate Chiang quickly disavowed the Nanking incident, assumed complete charge of affairs, and announced that the Nationalist government intended to deal 'fairly and sincerely' with the powers. He warned the powers, however, not to interfere with the Nationalist movement.

The remainder of Central China soon afterward capitulated to the Nationalist armies, and the first stage of the northern expedition was at an end.

CHAPTER XII

THE TURN TO THE RIGHT

CHIANG had already decided to split with the Communists. The question was, could he carry it through and garner the support necessary to keep him in power, to prevent his being eliminated by Hankow just as he had eliminated the northerners?

It was while he was still at Nanchang that he realized that whoever held Shanghai would hold the purse of China and ultimate power. Up at Hankow and the surrounding provinces the revolution had ceased to be a purely political movement and had already become a proletarian uprising aimed at the creation of a new social and economic order.

The prospect was alarming to Chiang. It was also alarming to the Chinese bourgeoisie, especially those of Shanghai. If they were alarmed enough, Chiang reasoned, they would back him in a new government, and with Shanghai and its customs revenues in his control, he could make himself the real power in China, completely liquidating the Hankow régime.

What had happened was that the peasants whom the Kuomintang had organized had taken the Kuomintang promises literally. Having helped the Kuomintang shake off the old militarists, they now turned and made demands on the Kuomintang. They called for drastic reductions of rent and interest rates. They wanted the abolition of extortionate 'extra' taxes, and in some places sought the, dispossession of the landed gentry.

Furthermore, the peasants had banded into armies to enforce their demands. Wholesale confiscations of land were reported from many areas. The reports terrified the propertied classes in every section of the country. In many districts the peasant organizations actually took over the government, dividing land among the peasants, placing embargoes on salt and rice to bring prices down, and prohibiting the planting of opium.

No one was more frightened by the trend than the orthodox Kuomintang political leaders. They had endorsed the peasant slogans as the armies marched northward from Canton, but were astonished when the peasants attempted to translate the slogans into action.

The actual break between Chiang and Hankow was preceded by considerable bickering, accusations, and counter-accusations. The left-wing group opposed to Chiang was strong enough to call a meeting of the C.E.C. for Hankow in March, 1927. Chiang and several others who thought as he did refused to attend. The radicals elected a new standing committee.

Chiang was deprived of the chairmanship of the important standing committee, although he was allowed to retain his membership in the Central Executive Committee itself. Wang Ching-wei, then considered a radical, was named chairman to replace him.

Chiang went to Shanghai and entered into negotiations with interested groups for the establishment of a new government at Nanking. The needed financial support was quickly provided by the powerful Chinese bankers of Shanghai, who agreed to raise $30,000,000 Chinese currency on the understanding that the Nanking government would be definitely anti-Communist. K. P. Chen, a leading banker who had never before associated himself with politics, was appointed chairman of a group to raise the money. Merchants, bankers, and conservative politicians gladly contributed to the cause.

The military support for the government appeared in the troops from southwest China, led by three important and able generals who immediately declared their allegiance to Chiang. It should be noted that Chiang had no personal army at that time, and hence was somewhat of a phenomenon in Chinese politics. His Whampoa cadets were scattered among a hundred army units. There was hardly a single regiment which was completely under Chiang's direct control. But he controlled the generals who controlled the army, which was just as effective and, under certain circumstances, probably more satisfactory.

To herald the new movement a 'white massacre' was decided upon, to eliminate the Communists from control of the Shanghai area. Chiang interviewed the heads of the powerful secret societies, virtual gang leaders with whom he had become acquainted in his previous Shanghai residence.

The gangs were charged with the eradication of the Communist military units, the radical union members, and the Red plain-clothes men who had made possible the seizure of Shanghai by the Nationalists but who still took their orders from Communist leaders at Hankow. The regular troops, it was agreed, were more urgently needed for fighting in the field, and the eradication of the urban Reds could safely be left to the hired thugs.

The job was done with bloody thoroughness. Thousands of workers were shot. The victims also included hundreds of intellectuals. Approximately fifteen hundred were wounded. It was reported that five hundred coffins were stored in a single office and filled in two weeks. Nearly five thousand additional workers and students were arrested. It was a far more spectacular drive than Balbo's raids in Italy, and it claimed several times as many victims as Hitler's blood purges in Berlin and Munich.

The campaign in Shanghai was duplicated on a smaller scale at Nanking and Canton. Labor unions were forcibly closed, armed labor and peasant units disarmed and disbanded. Hundreds and thousands of Communists perished in Shanghai, Nanking, Wusih, Soochow, Changchow, Hangchow, Canton. Firing squads were continuously active in the suburbs of Shanghai. Still more victims perished when 'special committees to clean up communists and reactionaries' started to function. Oddly enough, the purge was organized on principles similar to the early institutions of the Soviet Union.

During the purge, with the co-operation of the secret societies, victims were beheaded as well as shot. Men were kidnapped and forced to make heavy contributions to the military funds. Others were seized because they had corresponded with friends in Hankow. They were granted no hearings. Men with millions of dollars to their names were held as Communists. The *North-China Daily News*, most capitalistic of news organs, was refused the use of the posts for allegedly disseminating a communistic piece of news. Men were dragged out of the International Settlement and forced to admit their affiliations in Chinese territory.

Meanwhile, Chiang sent an ultimatum to Hankow. Communist propaganda must cease. Hankow's orders would not be accepted until relations between the Communists and Nationalists were adjusted. The Nationalist armies must be under the exclusive control of the regular officers, and the so-called political agents with each army must not interfere. The labor organizations must be subject to the orders of the military organizations, he insisted.

Hankow, which was committed to the theory of civil

supremacy over the military, rejected the demands, and deprived Chiang Kai-shek of his military command. April 16 he was proscribed as a counter-revolutionary and dismissed from all posts. Hankow even voted him out of the Kuomintang Party.

The formal establishment of the Nanking government followed. The foreign powers realized that Hankow's power was fast waning and stopped dealing with the upper-Yangtse régime, but they were not yet ready to recognize Nanking.

Hankow and Nanking then proceeded to bombard each other with manifestoes and denunciations. A deadlock quickly ensued. Northern military forces were still dangerously close to Chiang Kai-shek, practically at Pukow, across the Yangtse River from his capital. The situation made Feng Yu-hsiang of the greatest importance.

The 'Christian General' had established headquarters in Honan Province, and both sides proceeded to woo him. He proved coquettish. He agreed fully with the Hankow representatives who came to see him, and said the party should not be disrupted. He agreed fully with Chiang Kai-shek, who also interviewed him, that Communism was to be opposed at all costs. Neither side knew where he stood, and he played his advantage to the utmost.

Meanwhile, affairs at Hankow moved toward a crisis. On June 1, 1927, an Indian Communist, Roy, told Sun Fo, son of Sun Yat-sen, that Borodin had received new orders from Moscow, to replace the Kuomintang with a Communist army, and to confiscate land for the peasants — in short, to establish a one hundred per cent Communist régime.

The news was a bombshell. Borodin had told the Chinese Kuomintang leaders nothing of such a program, which was far beyond what they were ready to support. Borodin was confronted, replied unsatisfactorily. Hankow itself swung away from the new Communist program, and Chinese suspicion of the Russians increased to such an extent as to make further co-operation impossible.

A group of Chinese leaders decided to outlaw Communism; they agreed that Borodin must return to Russia, that a new C.E.C. meeting must be called, and that radicals would be forbidden to hold membership in the committee.

No purge took place. There were no arrests. It was acknowledged that the period of Kuomintang-Communist co-operation had come to an end, and Borodin, Galens, and the remaining Russians went overland to Moscow. A number of Chinese left-wing adherents, including the widow of Sun Yat-sen, followed them soon afterward.

With the Kuomintang leaders at Hankow themselves turning against the Communists, the way was being cleared for a reconciliation between Hankow and Nanking. But Hankow was the legitimist government, the heir to Canton, and the upper-Yangtse leaders could never forgive Chiang Kai-shek, who had brought about the split. They had got rid of Borodin. They insisted that Nanking get rid of Chiang.

The military council at Nanking discussed the problem of reconciliation with Hankow. Most of the members agreed that it was the only possible way to save the Nationalist cause from complete failure.

The meeting was simple, its procedure blunt, its tone dramatic. Someone suggested that Chiang take a subordinate position in the army. Chiang immediately resigned as commander-in-chief. For some minutes no one said a word. Then an unimportant member of the Council arose and discussed the importance of union with Hankow and the necessity of all Kuomintang members being good friends again. Chiang Kai-shek rose, left the room, and went to Shanghai by special train.

One of the southern generals was appointed to take his place as acting commander-in-chief of the Nationalist armies. A number of other leaders resigned, including the bitterly anti-Communist Hu Han-min, and the way was open for a rapprochement.

In Shanghai, Chiang conferred with his wealthy old friend, Chang Ching-kiang, and then went to his birthplace near Fenghua. Almost the entire Nanking government arrived in Shanghai the following day, ostensibly to ask him to return to office. This, however, was merely to save 'face,' as the leaders could have informed him two nights before if they had wanted him to stay.

But as far as the public knew, Chiang was ready and eager to step out. 'I am willing to sacrifice my position in order to assist the unification of the party and to make possible the accomplishment of the chief objective of the Kuomintang,' he announced.

Shortly afterward he left for Japan.

Conferences opened with representatives from Nanking and Hankow in attendance, and in September an arrangement was concluded to consolidate the two governments. The office of commander-in-chief which Chiang Kai-shek held was invested in a commission.

But the leaders lacked a strong man, and quarreled. Wang Ching-wei went to Canton and found a strong pro-Chiang group against him. He returned to Shanghai, became disgusted with the factional strife, and left for Europe after announcing that Chiang Kai-shek was the only man able to save China.

The southern militarists pledged their allegiance to Chiang Kai-shek, urged him to return and resume office. The northern troops were constantly on the point of capturing Nanking itself, and the march of the Nationalists toward Peking had been halted since summer.

By August 30, in fact, the former war-lord of the middle Yangtse, taking heart from the disorganization of the Nationalists, had stolen across the Yangtse and had placed seventy thousand men on the Nanking side of the river, outnumbering the Nationalists. The latter, however, succeeded with naval support in dispersing the northern troops, and the war-lord fled once again, evacuating Pukow and removing the menace to the Nationalist capital.

The next day the Communists at Canton rose and seized the government. Three days later they were suppressed by anti-Red forces, mostly from Kwangsi Province, which massacred two thousand persons. At the proposal of Chiang, who then assumed command of the Nanking troops, the Nationalist government severed diplomatic relations with the Soviet Union.

On January 4, 1928, Chiang resumed his posts, but promised to resign on the conclusion of the northern campaign. Five days later he returned to Nanking, and on February 1 the Central Executive Committee elected him chairman of the National Military Council. The ruling, adopted at Hankow the previous year, that the commander-in-chief could not be chairman of the military affairs or other standing committees was abolished. He was back in power and stronger than ever. He had observed the old maxim, 'Never resign until you are indispensable,' and had found it a wise precept.

CHAPTER XIII

MEI-LING

WHEN Chiang sailed for Japan, he was ostensibly en route to the United States on the usual 'tour of inspection' taken by Chinese big-wigs not wanted at home. Actually he went to do a little reconnoitering of the China scene from the shores of the near-by islands and to propose marriage to Miss Soong Mei-ling.

The reconnoitering was soon done. Chiang decided that it would not be long before China would need him again, and he decided to stay within easy calling distance.

He took the opportunity to interview a number of Japanese leaders. One of them was Mitsuru Toyama, the leader of the notorious Black Dragon Society, a strange mixture of gang leader, reactionary politician, patriot, and messiah. Toyama was an advocate of Pan-Asianism, the doctrine of a common front among the Asiatic nations against the western powers. It was a doctrine to which Sun Yat-sen at one time subscribed. Today the Japanese are its only advocates; the Chinese will have none of it.

What Toyama said to Chiang or Chiang to Toyama has not been recorded. But the Japanese leader was more than friendly and he arranged quarters for Chiang at the home of a wealthy neighbor.

Chiang also visited Viscount Eiichi Shibusawa, a leading industrialist and an earnest student of the Chinese classics. In a small pavilion on Shibusawa's estate, Chiang met a number of Japanese political and economic leaders. Among them was Kenji Kodama, then manager of the Shanghai branch of the Yokohama Specie Bank. Kodama urged Chiang to abandon his idea of going to the United States.

'You must go back to China and complete the revolution,' he counseled Chiang, with obvious concern for China's welfare. Chiang returned soon afterward, but that Kodama's advice had anything to do with his decision, as the Japanese say, seems doubtful. All the evidence indicates that Chiang had made up his mind some time before, after a series of earnest conversations with moderate Chinese leaders who trekked to Japan to tell him how much he was needed at home.

Chiang's enemies are fond of saying that at that time he reached an understanding with the Japanese which has continued to this day. The idea is fantastic. Chiang at the time represented the best prospect of a strong and unified China, and a strong and unified China was the last thing the Japanese wanted.

Japanese policy for years had been based on the allegation that China was a weak and disorganized state, needing the overlordship of a strong, protective Japan. To strengthen the allegation, Japanese agents continually schemed with disgruntled politicos, ambitious regional war-lords. The more civil strife existed in China, the stronger was Japan's case. Chiang's rise to power and the northward march of the Nationalist armies foreshadowed the end of such civil strife. His absence from China, with the northern militarists still active in the Yangtse Valley, appeared to encourage it.

A few Japanese interested in economic activities, like Kodama, might have desired a stable China for the promotion of Japanese trade, but they had no voice in Japanese policy and even less influence on Chiang Kai-shek.

He had friends in Japan, of course, and he was not anti-

Japanese. Speaking at Miyanoshita during his visit, he said that any disputes between China and Japan had arisen as the result of mutual misunderstanding. Both nations had been equally responsible.

'A dispute among brothers requires less cause than among others,' he remarked piously. He was obviously far from the anti-Japanese firebrand that the Nipponese represented him to be in later years. On the other hand, he has never spent much time preaching about the beauty of Sino-Japanese friendship. From the time of the Tsinan incident, when his own forces first clashed with the Imperial Japanese army, he has insisted the evidence of real friendship must come from Japan.

His other mission to Japan was of the heart. Five years before, at Shanghai, he had met Miss Soong Mei-ling, sister of Madame Sun Yat-sen. He was struck by her beauty and intelligence, but the subject of marriage was not broached at the time. For one thing, Miss Soong was an ardent Christian and the daughter of a stern Christian family. Chiang's religious life seemed to have been confined to bowing before his ancestors' tombs.

Then there was the un-Christian matter of concubines. He was said to have had two of them. One of them was generally known as Madame Chiang in the Canton days, and many foreigners thought she was his wife. Incidentally there was an actual wife, the Fenghua bride, although not many persons knew if she were living or dead.

But Chiang by this time was eager to marry the charming Miss Soong, and set about proving that he was not encumbered with too many liabilities. Before setting out for Japan he packed the best-known concubine off to the United States. Her departure was in the nature of a public ceremony, and the old Dowager Empress herself could have wished for no more pomp.

The Shanghai newspapers carried numerous photographs of the event, and the stories left no doubt that the lady in question was General Chiang's lady. Incidentally, when she arrived in San Francisco, a group of Chinese students held a reception for her. To reciprocate the kindness she entertained the students by singing a low-class Soochow folk song. The students were insulted. She has not been heard from in recent years.

After getting rid of this lady, Chiang went to Japan and confronted Miss Soong and her mother with proof that he had been legally divorced from his Fenghua wife a number of years before. Old Mrs. Soong, a woman of remarkable character, had been opposed to Chiang as a prospective son-in-law for some time, and the rest of the family, except Mei-ling, was far from cordial. Mrs. Soong asked Chiang if he was ready to become a Christian.

It was a temptation to say yes. But Chiang told Mrs. Soong that he couldn't become a Christian to win Mei-ling. It wasn't like joining a club or a secret society. Christianity, as he saw it, had to be understood before being embraced. He would be glad to study it, he said. Meanwhile, he was sincerely desirous of marrying Mei-ling and of being a good husband to her.

Mrs. Soong was impressed by what he said and his manner of saying it. She gave him a Bible and told him to study it. He promised to do so. Meanwhile, he outlined to Mei-ling his plan to make China a great nation, to reform old practices and to make of Sun Yat-sen's three principles a living force among the people of China. He asked her to join him and to help him. Some time during his visit in Japan she indicated her willingness, and the Soong family, against her obviously made-up mind, withdrew its objections to the marriage.

Chiang returned to Shanghai and announced that he was

WITH MISS SOONG AT THE HOME OF DOCTOR H. H. KUNG

MARRIAGE TO MEI-LING
SHANGHAI, 1927

S. C. Chuck

GENERAL AND MADAME CHIANG
AT A HANGCHOW RESORT

going to marry Mei-ling. Speculation immediately arose as to his other domestic ties. George Sokolsky, well-known American newspaperman, who had known members of the Soong family for years, called on him and put the question bluntly: what about the wife in Fenghua?

Chiang had a ready answer, 'In the tenth moon, in the tenth year of the Republic [October, 1921], I was divorced, in accordance with Chinese custom, from my first wife, who is now living at Fenghua.' He showed Sokolsky a document of divorce which he said had been registered with the proper judicial authorities at Fenghua. It indicated that Chiang and the former Miss Mao had been divorced on grounds of incompatibility.

Asked about the 'lady who is traveling in America,' Chiang replied tolerantly, 'Foreigners perhaps do not understand all the intricacies of the Chinese family system. That lady has been divorced in accordance with Chinese custom.' The custom, of course, was quite familiar to Sokolsky and other foreigners. The second concubine did not figure in the conversation. That there was such a person was known to many who were close to Chiang Kai-shek. Today she is understood to be living comfortably at Soochow.

But concerning his status at the moment, Chiang was not the least doubtful. 'I am at present married to no one, and am free to marry in accordance with the most monogamist practices. Miss Soong would not consent to marriage under any other circumstances and I should not dare to ask a lady of her character to marry me in any other circumstances.'

Chiang ridiculed the idea that he was about to make a political marriage. He said he had courted Mei-ling for years, but remarked frankly that the Soong family had always objected to his aspirations.

Shortly after his return, they were married, and China

obtained thereby a First Lady whose activity in national affairs is not duplicated by the wife of any chief of state in the world today.

Most Americans know that she is a graduate of Wellesley, and take some pride in the fact. Less well known is the fact that her entire family has an American background.

She was born in Shanghai in 1892, the daughter of Mr. and Mrs. Charles J. Soong. Her father was a native of Kwangtung Province, in South China, while her mother came from Kiangsu, the province in which Shanghai is located.

Charles Soong, as a young man, was brought to the United States by an uncle who was in the silk and tea business in Boston. A number of the Boston Chinese students used to frequent his shop, and Charles worshiped them. He wanted to go to school in America, but his uncle was against the idea, said it was better to learn a business and make money. Charles pleaded, uncle was obdurate. The youth was so keen on getting an education that he eventually ran away to get a job and earn enough money to give himself the schooling he desired.

He next showed up as a cabin boy on a steamer plying between Boston and Savannah. Thus he was introduced to the State of Georgia, to which he later brought his family. Mei-ling was a child when her family moved to America. They first lived at Summit, New Jersey, where she attended a private school. Then they moved to Macon, Georgia. The two older sisters, Soong Ai-ling and Soong Ching-ling, entered Georgia Wesleyan College. Mei-ling was too young for college; she studied under private tutors at Macon and lived at the college dormitory with her sisters, under a special dispensation.

The rest of the family meanwhile returned to China. Father Soong was engaged in the Christian literature business for a while, marketing the Chinese edition of the Bible, and eventually branched into other business, becoming fairly wealthy.

Mei-ling entered Wellesley, as soon as she was old enough, and was graduated with honors. At college she was known as Miss Mayling Soong. She was as popular as she was brilliant, and received the Wellesley and Durant scholarships, the first Oriental student to be so honored.

On her return to China she devoted herself to social service and a thorough study of the Chinese classics. She was appointed a member of a Child Labor Commission to investigate labor conditions in the industries of the foreign settlements of Shanghai. She was the first Chinese woman named to such a group.

She was married to Chiang Kai-shek in Shanghai December 1, 1927. An ardent Christian like her father and mother, she insisted on a Christian marriage ceremony. The couple applied to the Reverend Z. T. Kaung, a Chinese Southern Methodist minister, at that time pastor of the Allen Memorial Church. He inquired into Chiang's previous marriage, and apparently was not satisfied that the General was free to marry again. He declined to perform the ceremony.

Other arrangements had to be made. On the appointed day a religious ceremony was performed privately at the home of the bride's mother on Seymour Road, Shanghai. Doctor David Yui, now dead, who was then general secretary of the Y.M.C.A. of China, but not a minister, officiated.

The couple then went to the ballroom of the Majestic Hotel on Bubbling Well Road, where a politico-religious rite equivalent to a civil ceremony took place. The ballroom was decorated to resemble a foreign-style church. From the lounge on the left of the bandstand, a path of scarlet cloth bordered with white standards led to an alcove

on the opposite side of the room. Clusters of white chrys-
anthemums and ferns lined the path. In the alcove an
arbor had been erected. At its rear stood a portrait of
Doctor Sun Yat-sen draped with the national and party
flags.

One thousand guests, including a number of foreigners,
were massed in the ballroom along the scarlet pathway. As
the bride appeared on the arm of her brother, T. V. Soong,
the audience broke into loud applause.

The bride and her brother walked toward the alcove,
where they were met by the groom, in approved church
style. They then faced the venerable Tsai Yuan-pei,
eminent scholar and veteran revolutionary politician, who
delivered a speech.

The speech over, and the couple presumably thoroughly
united, the wedding party retired for the inevitable photographs. Tables were set and feasting began on a grand
scale, in accordance with age-old Chinese custom. The
bride and groom soon disappeared and left on a honeymoon
trip to Hangchow and Mokanshan, scenic resorts in
Chiang's native Chekiang Province.

Some democrats muttered at the splendor of the wedding
celebration. It was alleged that Chiang had spent more
than a million dollars Mex. on gifts and entertainment,
but the real figure, although undoubtedly sizeable, was
probably considerably smaller.

Not long after the marriage, Madame Chiang began
taking an active part in national affairs. At first her activity
was in the realm of social welfare. She inaugurated the
movement for the establishment of the Officers' Moral
Endeavor Association, a sort of Chinese military Y.M.C.A.
She established schools in Nanking for the children of
revolutionary heroes. One is for the Sons of the Revolution, another for the Daughters. Five hundred boys and

three hundred girls, descendants of Kuomintang veterans, are taught to be self-supporting and impressed with the spirit of service.

She encouraged the formation of clubs for Chinese women in widespread sections of the country. She began to write articles in Chinese and English on the new spirit of China, and her essays were published in the United States and Europe as well as in China.

Then she turned to political affairs. Today she serves as a member of the legislative yuan or department. She assists in the execution of the National Economic Reconstruction Movement. She is secretary-general of the National Aviation Commission; it is one of her most important posts, in which she has been charged with the complete reorganization of the aviation arm of the Chinese military forces. When the New Life Movement was inaugurated, she became the director of its women's division.

When the Communists were driven from Kiangsi Province, and it became apparent that a social and economic reconstruction program must follow the military campaign, she helped organize the Kiangsi Christian Rural Service Union, in co-operation with foreign missionaries, and became its first president.

But of greater importance, she became her husband's chief adviser, confidante, and secretary. It is fair to say that any national question is subject to her consideration as much as his. She is no 'yes man' — she often disagrees with her husband on matters of policy, and he respects her judgment. With her fluent knowledge of English, spoken and written, she has become his foreign liaison agent. When foreign visitors interview him, she translates and explains. When he issues statements or manifestoes, she translates them into English.

She is also an interpreter of the western world to him.

Each day she prepares a digest of world news from the English language press, and keeps him abreast of developments abroad. She has introduced him to western literature, and given him an appreciation of western music.

Chiang's marriage to Mei-ling was one of the important events of his life. If he has avoided becoming just another Chinese war-lord, it is largely due to his wife. Since that December day in 1927 on which he married her, he has become a far greater figure in Chinese life. It would be ridiculous to say that he is what he is because of her; the man was a character of no mean force before he met her. But the changes in his personality, the development of his national vision, and the modifications of some of his policies are without a doubt directly due to her influence and hers alone.

CHAPTER XIV

ON TO PEKING

NINE days after his marriage the government asked him to resume office as generalissimo. Wang Ching-wei, his chief political opponent, who had found himself balked by his own lack of military power and the continued dissension among government leaders, agreed to retire in the interests of the party and the nation.

Chiang faced a sad prospect. The flush of success had faded from the Nationalist cause. Wang Ching-wei was off to Europe. So was Hu Han-min, the third of the old Canton triumvirate. So was Sun Fo, son of Doctor Sun Yat-sen.

Civil war was rife. Fighting in Canton was particularly fierce. As a result of the Communist coup and its bloody suppression, Canton was a wreck. Its bund in many places was a mere heap of cinders. The remnant Communists, having formed a military unit, retreated toward Swatow, where they still constituted a menace to the Nationalist régime in the south.

The Nanking government, in fact, had begun to break up. Regional chiefs were ready to seize power for themselves and revert to the days of the war-lords. The northern militarists, emboldened by inaction and dissension at Nanking, were threatening the citadels of Nationalist power.

The party leaders decided to stake everything on the successful continuance of the northern expedition. The

Nationalist armies must march north again, bringing the hope of a unified China and the end of the military dictatorship at Peking.

But the expedition could not start until the government had been rehabilitated. There was only one man to hold the government and at the same time direct the military campaign. He was Chiang. So they turned to him once again and offered him the supreme command of the Nationalist forces.

Chiang accepted, but with a reservation. He announced that at the conclusion of the military operations he would resign. He promised to join peacefully in the movement to usher in the era of political tutelage, the transitionary period which Sun Yat-sen had said must intervene between the military campaigns and the introduction of representative democracy on the western model.

As Chiang returned to the helm, he received an outright pledge of support from Christian General Feng Yu-hsiang and Yen Hsi-shan, the so-called 'model governor' of Shansi Province. Although Yen had come to power under the old style militarists and was actually named a member of the northern coalition against Chiang's armies, he had been persuaded to throw in his lot with the Nationalists.

Chiang had learned not to expect real help from prospective allies unless it was to the interest of the allies to provide it. Events indicated that it was to the interest of both Feng and Yen to aid the Nationalists. Feng wanted to be a military power in his own right, an ambition which would never be satisfied as long as Wu Pei-fu and Old Marshal Chang Tso-lin held the north. Yen coveted a clear title to Shansi Province and was not averse to taking over Peking. Both saw steady revenues in a Nationalist victory, oblivion in continued rule by the northern militarists.

But before resuming the northern expedition, Chiang

turned his attention to the civil government. His first move was to convene the Central Executive Committee for the first time since it had met at Hankow. The Committee proceeded to rescind formally the agreement with the Communists. Chiang Kai-shek himself was named chairman of the Central Political Council, the highest effective governmental organ. T. V. Soong, now Chiang's brother-in-law, became minister of finance.

Another step of the greatest importance was the election of Chiang to the chairmanship of the National Military Council, which was now raised to equal rank with the Central Political Council. Until then the political council, the civil arm of the government, was acknowledged supreme. Hereafter, it would share eminence with the military arm, and presumably yield to it in case of national emergency.

But, to allay the suspicions of the civilian democrats, a deadline for military dictatorship was established — August 1, 1928. For that date a Kuomintang party congress was summoned, to plot the course of the government during the coming period of political tutelage. The move was to serve as assurance that a party, and not a personal dictatorship, was the aim.

The new government was organized January 7, 1928. Three days later Chiang in a manifesto announced his intention of suppressing all Communist uprisings. He also reiterated that he would resign when the northern expedition was completed, 'in order to make amends for my evasion of duty last year.'

In March he began preparing for the resumption of the military campaign. An American observer, Doctor Arthur N. Holcombe, records that despite the bustle of preparations he was calm and deliberate 'as if at a tea party.' He was happy with his bride, and frequently strolled with her to places of scenic beauty near Nanking. Care-free and chatting gaily, he traveled about without the semblance of a bodyguard.

The offensive began April 9. The northerners resisted as they had done in the past. Sharp encounters took place. The peaceful countryside became a no-man's land of dead and dying. Three armies converged on Peking. One was Chiang's own force advancing up the Tientsin–Pukow railway. The second, under Feng Yu-hsiang, started from Honan and marched to the tune of 'Onward, Christian Soldiers,' to the delight of the foreign missionaries. The third was Yen Hsi-shan's army, moving over from Shansi.

Northern resistance was brief. The armies of the Old Marshal and his associates began a retreat, which finally turned into rout.

Chiang Kai-shek's troops reached Tsinan, capital of Shantung Province, on May 2, 1928. The people of Shantung, relieved of the devastations of the provincial warlord, welcomed the southerners. But the Japanese government viewed the southern advance with alarm. Since capturing Tsingtao from the Germans, Japan had regarded Shantung Province as her special sphere of influence. The fact that Japan had been forced to return Shantung to China in no wise lessened Japanese interest in the area.

The Japanese Premier announced that since the Chinese Nationalist armies were advancing toward Peking, Japanese troops would be landed at Tsingtao to protect Japanese interests in the province. Detachments moved up the railway from Tsingtao to Tsinan, supposedly to protect the Japanese army of two thousand at the latter city.

The Chinese sought to pass along the Tientsin–Pukow line through the so-called commercial area outside the city in which the Japanese troops were stationed. The Japanese refused them the right-of-way and sat astride the railroad.

On May 3 the inevitable happened. The troops clashed. Reports conflicted as to what happened, as to who actually fired the first shots. But there was nothing doubtful about the aftermath.

A high Chinese official was killed and many street lecturers, who were expounding the Kuomintang doctrine and might have interlarded some anti-Japanese sentiments, were arrested. At midnight, Japanese soldiers broke into the house of the foreign affairs commissioner of the province, ransacked the house and shot the commissioner. Later they killed a number of persons who had witnessed the shooting of the official.

Chiang suppressed this news for fear of stirring up his own troops and starting a Sino-Japanese war for which he was ill prepared. He instructed all his subordinates to 'avoid conflict at all costs,' and ordered all the Chinese soldiers to return to their original stations, well away from the area in which the Japanese were encamped.

Chiang sent a representative to negotiate with Japanese General Fukuda. While negotiations were progressing, Japanese soldiers set fire to and destroyed a Chinese radio station. Other destruction followed. May 6, Fukuda handed Chiang an ultimatum. It called for the punishment of the Chinese officers under whom soldiers had allegedly molested the Japanese. Fukuda insisted on the withdrawal of the Nationalist armies for a distance of seven miles and an end to anti-Japanese propaganda.

Chiang replied that he would punish all guilty Chinese, but said the guilty Japanese should likewise be punished. He informed Fukuda that measures had already been taken to suppress anti-Japanese propaganda. He agreed to withdraw his troops the seven stipulated miles, but insisted that the Tientsin–Pukow railway line be kept open so that the Nationalists' troop and supply transportation would not be obstructed en route to Peking.

This reply failed to satisfy Fukuda, who rejected it. He also detained one of Chiang's envoys. He prepared to take the entire city of Tsinan and to hold the railroad junction.

May 8, the Japanese received reinforcements from Tsingtao and drove the Chinese seven miles southward. One small body of Chinese troops fled into the walled city of Tsinan, but the Japanese shelled the city and drove them out. The Japanese then occupied the north-south railroad as far north as the Yellow River and blocked all traffic.

The northward advance of Chiang Kai-shek and his troops was thereby halted. The Japanese held the city of Tsinan for a full year.

The news of the original incident leaked out, of course. A wave of indignation spread through China, and a nation-wide boycott of Japanese goods was soon under way.

On May 18 the Japanese advised both the Nanking and Peking authorities that if further disturbances resulted in the neighborhood of Peking and Tientsin, Japan might have to 'take steps' to maintain order in Manchuria. Peking was some distance from Tsinan, where the trouble was going on, and Manchuria was still farther away, but the Japanese professed to be alarmed. They told Old Marshal Chang Tso-lin that he had better withdraw to Manchuria at once. They went further and told him that unless he moved back quickly, his return would be barred by Japanese troops.

The Old Marshal had had enough of civil war in China, anyway, and was apparently quite willing to move back north of the Great Wall, where as long as he played ball with the Japanese, he was more or less boss. The National-ist forces of Chiang Kai-shek, under subordinate generals, were capturing town after town south and west of Peking.

The Old Marshal's troops were in a precarious position. He suddenly announced that he was withdrawing.

On the nights of June 2 and 3 he sent his troops northward along the Peking–Mukden railway into Manchuria. On the third, the Old Marshal himself left for Mukden. But as his special train passed a suburban railroad station, almost within sight of the old walled city of Mukden, it was destroyed by a bomb placed on the roadbed by unknown persons. The Old Marshal and his chief henchman were instantly killed. Several of his other associates were seriously wounded.

The day the Old Marshal was killed, Chiang Kai-shek had returned to Nanking. When the news reached Peking, the Old Marshal's son, 'Young Marshal' Chang Hsueh-liang, ordered a general withdrawal of the Manchurian troops. Peking, the old capital, was open to the Nationalist advance. Chiang's own armies, however, could not move up and take over the city as long as the Japanese blocked the north-south railroad. Chiang appointed Yen Hsi-shan to take over both Peking and Tientsin.

So Yen's troops, not true Kuomintang Nationalists, but converts and deputies, marched into Peking. But as long as Chiang and Yen saw eye to eye, the effect was the same, and the northern expedition was at an end.

Romantic historians wrote feelingly of the conclusion of the 'long trek from Canton,' but the actual Cantonese veterans who first marched north with Chiang were mostly far to the south in Hunan Province. And a regrettable percentage of them, marching under red banners, had precious little use for the Generalissimo.

True to his promise, Chiang resigned his command. His resignation was not accepted. On June 19, the standing committee of the C.E.C. ordered him to report to the spirit of Sun Yat-sen.

On July 3, Chiang Kai-shek, without his army, traveled
to Peking. Three days later he went to the Western Hills
where the body of Sun Yat-sen had been consigned to a
temporary resting-place, awaiting permanent burial. Accompanied by 'Christian General' Feng and 'Model Governor' Yen, Chiang bowed before the remains of his old
leader, and reported that in his name they had conquered.

Meanwhile, the Young Marshal, it developed, held none
of his father's contempt for the Kuomintang idealists. He
too had definite ideas about China's unity and was willing,
even eager, to reach an understanding with Chiang. To
show his friendliness he himself showed up at Peking and
greeted the Nationalist leaders on the sixth of July.

A session of the Kuomintang Executive Committee had
been summoned, before the campaign, to meet August 1,
1928, but it failed to convene until a week later because of
the difficulty of obtaining a quorum. Chiang proved himself a master negotiator. Shrewdly judging which support
the party and government needed at the moment, Chiang
decided to court the conservatives. But the right-wing
elements were unwilling to attend the meeting if the radicals were likely to dispute control.

Chiang, with the most artful persuasiveness, induced
the radicals to stay away from the meeting. This he did
by promising them full freedom of press and speech, in
short, all the facilities of a 'loyal opposition' except participation in that particular meeting. The radicals accepted,
and proceeded to use their weapons with an unexpected
vigor which later caused Chiang to doubt his own wisdom
in the deal. But in the meantime the committee meeting
went off smoothly. The members gave Chiang a fresh
vote of confidence and named him chairman of the important standing committee.

At the time there existed so-called branch political councils, regional miniatures of the Central Political Council at Nanking. One functioned at Canton, another at Hankow. The common-sense procedure, of course, would have been to abolish the branches and center control at Nanking. But common-sense ran into formidable obstacles. Those in control of the branches feared a Chiang Kai-shek dictatorship, and insisted on retaining the regional groups, ostensibly to retain a decent measure of local autonomy. Radicals held sway at Canton, conservatives at Hankow. Both were opposed to dissolution, and their combined opposition carried the day.

But the internal situation seemed hopeful enough at the time. The Young Marshal was ready to swear allegiance to Nanking. On October 10, the birthday of the Chinese Republic, when the Nanking government marked the anniversary by inaugurating a new constitution, Chang Hsueh-liang was appointed one of the sixteen members of the State Council.

The Young Marshal's switch to the Kuomintang found little sympathy with the Japanese. A week after he had been named to the Nanking Council, a high Japanese consular official in China cautioned him against too close relations with Chiang Kai-shek. But the Young Marshal had his own ideas and ignored the Japanese advice. On December 29 the Kuomintang flag — white sun on blue sky — was hoisted all over Manchuria, and the provinces north of the Great Wall were, nominally at least, an integral part of China.

The diplomatic triumph of Chiang Kai-shek in the matter of Manchuria was matched by success in foreign fields. December 20 the British minister to China presented his credentials to the Nanking authorities, and the envoys of the other principal nations speedily followed suit. The name of Peking, northern capital, was changed to Peiping, meaning 'northern peace,' and Nanking appeared to rule a united China.

A short time before, the relationship between the Kuomintang Party and the National government had been formally defined, under Chiang Kai-shek's direction. The C.E.C. adopted a set of principles for the Period of Political Tutelage which, with commendable optimism, was fixed for six years — 1930 to 1935. All that remained for Chiang Kai-shek and his government to do, it seemed, was to settle down to the arts of peace and the task of reconstruction.

CHAPTER XV

SOLDIERS AND SPOILS

CHIANG soon discovered that disposing of the northern militarists did not dispose of militarism. The problem, as a matter of fact, became more acute than ever. When the Nationalist generals, most of whom still thought in terms of regional war-lordism, were fighting for a unified China, they were also fighting for a place in that unified China. When the northern expedition ended, it was useless to tell the generals and their soldiers to put down their arms and go home to their peace-time jobs. They had no homes and no jobs. For their stations and maintenance they looked to the government which they had helped to establish.

The business of peace-time regulation started off hopefully enough. Not long after the capture of Peking in June, 1928, T. V. Soong called an economic conference at which the disbandment of troops was discussed. It was decided to organize a national commission to reduce the number of soldiers from 2,100,000 to a maximum of 715,000. The plan sounded convincing. Employment was to be found for the discharged armies, and the cost was to be defrayed by a domestic loan. Carrying out the program was another matter.

One month after the economic parley, the first official disbandment conference opened, in July, 1928. Chiang Kai-shek, as President of the State Council, proposed drastic reductions in the regional forces. The other generals failed to see the force of the argument, suspected that Chiang was making a clever play for personal power. The plan dragged along; nothing was done.

By the end of the year 1928, business leaders had become seriously concerned about the enormous military burden which the country was bearing. Sixteen Chinese business organizations, headed by the powerful General Chamber of Commerce of Shanghai, sent a memorial to the government pleading for the disbandment of superfluous troops and the framing of a national budget.

The memorial, although polite, was pointed. The petitioners reminded Chiang that he and his subordinate generals had endorsed the idea of retrenchment at the economic conference six months before, and pointed out that the results had been nil.

'No actual disbandment has taken place, various national and provincial revenues continue to be detained, and no national budget has been promulgated,' the organizations asserted. 'Our debts have mounted higher and higher, taxes have become heavier and heavier, and still the Treasury remains empty.' The allegations could not be denied.

Early the next year another disbandment plan was drawn up, after a series of secret conferences among the leading military chieftains. It detailed plans, which all had approved, for the abolition of all independent commands of regional forces, which were to be placed under the control of a central disbandment commission responsible to Nanking. It was planned to reduce the army to sixty-five divisions, which it was estimated would cost $192,000,000 Chinese currency per year. Arsenals were to be placed under central government control and the manufacture of arms and munitions by unauthorized parties halted immediately.

The commanders had agreed to the plan in principle, but

when it came to shaving down the forces, each wailed that Nanking was discriminating against him, trying to shear him of power for the benefit of the others. Chiang insisted that a unified nation demanded one supreme army, and that any conflicting subordinate command was incompatible with the theory of a strong, modern government.

The theory was sound, but Chiang's motives were suspect. His rise to power, without a really formidable army of his own, had been notable. They believed that he was trying to solidify his power by obtaining military support which he did not then possess. What Chiang's real motives were, one can only guess. Certainly he was human enough to realize the stature he was beginning to assume as a national figure, but in the absence of proof it is difficult to accept the declaration that the entire disbandment program was a plot cooked up to remove every threat to Chiang's continued eminence.

The Christian General wanted the Tientsin and Peiping area. Pai Chung-hsi, early associate of Chiang who captured Shanghai and helped to pacify the Yangtse Valley, had joined the second northern expedition only after receiving a large financial subsidy. He and his associates had lodged themselves in the vicinity of Hankow, and now demanded the Lunghai railway, which would have strengthened their position. Other generals made other demands.

Chiang, in disgust, resigned his command and went off to the town of Chinkiang, but the other generals, including his chief rivals, sent him urgent telegrams to return. A compromise was reached, which was strengthened by the meeting of the chieftains before Sun Yat-sen's grave in Peiping.

But, although a compromise was reached on location of troops, it was broken on the question of money. Each commander wanted money for all his own troops, but there was not enough for all. Too, it was contrary to national policy to strengthen regional military powers; to do so was only to weaken the central government's authority.

Chiang, for more than a year after the end of the second northern expedition, had his hands full maintaining peace among the militarists, keeping them from fighting each other or him. The left wing of the Kuomintang under Wang Ching-wei had by this time entirely withdrawn from participation in the government. The southwest faction also withdrew from active support after a Kuomintang conference had decided to curtail the power of the branch political councils in favor of Nanking.

Chiang argued that the maintenance of the branch councils would only help local militarists to become more powerful. The opposition said that China was too vast a country to be managed efficiently by a central government alone; there must be a measure of local autonomy.

The subject split the party. Even Chiang's old friend and patron, Chang Ching-kiang, ranged himself with the opponents, and left the Nanking session. Chiang followed and pleaded with him to return, but the old man was obdurate.

The January, 1929, conference finally adopted a program fixing the National army at sixty-five divisions, 800,000 men, with an annual expenditure of $192,000,000. The program called for pensions for all officials and soldiers above a specified age who wished to retire. All officers above the rank of major and properly qualified who desired to study would be awarded 'scholarships for study abroad or in the country.' The surplus minor officers were to be trained as supervisors or overseers of the government's various construction schemes. It was a noble plan even though it was never carried into effect.

Chiang, having temporarily quieted the row among the militarists, proceeded to inaugurate what he hoped would be an era of reconstruction. He recruited a host of foreign advisers — the Frenchman Georges Padoux on judicial affairs, the American Kemmerer Commission on currency and finance, the American Henry Killam Murphy on architecture for the government buildings at Nanking, and, most important of all, the German General Max Bauer, who was named adviser in military affairs.

Bauer had been an associate of General Erich von Ludendorff. He came to Nanking to reorganize the National army and to industrialize the disbanded troops. He first came to China in the winter of 1927 during the Canton coup, and visited Nanking, but returned to Germany with a Chinese mission.

He returned in November, 1928, as personal adviser to Chiang, and he announced that he had no contract with the national government. The statement was greeted with hostility in many circles, which feared further growth of Chiang's power.

The other military chieftains saw in the German's expert technical advice a force which would eventually lead to their own destruction.

Bauer died suddenly of smallpox at Shanghai only a few months after coming to China. Rumor had it that Chiang's enemies had poisoned him.

CHAPTER XVI

THE BREAK-UP

IF ANYONE thought that the year 1929 would see the beating of swords into plowshares in China, he was to be disappointed. The year marked the first open revolt against Chiang Kai-shek's régime from within the ranks of its supporters.

The Kwangsi clique, one of the strongest units of the Nationalist advance, was the first to rebel. The clique was headed by Li Tsung-jen and Pai Chung-hsi. Li was the nominal leader in his capacity of chairman of the Hankow branch political council, but Pai was the brains of the group.

Pai had been the first southern commander to occupy Shanghai in 1927, when nearly thirty thousand foreign troops had been poured into the non-Chinese areas of the city in the fear of a Chinese outbreak. He was and is one of the most astute military commanders in China, with military skill matched by his effectiveness as an administrator. Even today, in the poor and remote province of Kwangsi, he has made his territory a model of progress and efficiency.

In 1929 he and his associates held full sway in Central China, with Hankow as their headquarters. But the province of Hunan, lying between their headquarters and their home base of Kwangsi, was held by a subordinate general who did not hold the same views as the Kwangsi clique and who looked to Nanking rather than to Hankow for guidance.

The immediate cause of the warfare which followed was the action of the Kwangsi clique in unceremoniously booting out this head man of Hunan. But the dismissal, like most occurrences which cause wars, was purely incidental.

Conflict arose over the principle of the branch political councils. Chiang Kai-shek had definitely decided to eliminate regional authority such as the Kwangsi clique maintained. He insisted that a national government must be truly national, and that the idea of having deputy bosses in various sections of the country was tolerable only if it were clearly understood that they were really deputies. It was the old dispute between regionalism and federalism.

The Kwangsi clique maintained, and many disinterested observers agreed, that conditions in China required local autonomy under sectional chiefs; that only matters like foreign relations, affecting the nation as a whole, should be administered by the central government.

In the United States the two schools argued it out and compromised to set up a three-power system of government with a complicated system of checks and balances. In China no amount of oratory could prevail, and the opponents went to war.

Nanking moved after the Kwangsi clique had dismissed the Hunan governor, appointed a man of its own, and moved its troops toward Changsha. The Kwangsi leaders, however, insisted that Chiang Kai-shek had forced their hand, provoking the actual fighting after working out plans for a military campaign with General Bauer.

Chiang blamed the trouble on a quarrel over money, letting it be known that the old Hunan governor had remitted revenues directly to Nanking, while the Kwangsi leaders had insisted that he must deal with Nanking through them. Kwangsi retorted that the old governor was a Nanking stool-pigeon, and that if they were going to run

Central China properly they had to control Hunan Province as well as the rest of their territory.

Chiang Kai-shek answered. The National Congress on March 27 expelled the three leaders from the party, termed them rebels and counter-revolutionists. The same day the government ordered a punitive expedition under Chiang.

The Generalissimo boarded a battleship, and sailed to the upper Yangtse to direct the fighting. He announced that he would 'pacify' the situation in one week. In hardly more than a week the Kwangsi troops were in retreat from Hankow toward Hunan.

Chiang sent his chief of staff to Peking to organize aeronautical headquarters; in a short time Nationalist planes were flying over the ranks of the Kwangsi armies. The planes were few and decrepit, and the damage they did was small, but their appearance marked the first time that aircraft had been used under a definite campaign plan in a Chinese civil war.

But the war thus far was a matter of maneuvers and movements, and there was little actual fighting. In quick succession a number of commanders subordinate to Pai Chung-hsi announced their support of Chiang Kai-shek and denounced Pai with vigor. It was obvious that 'silver bullets' were again being used in some quantity.

Pai himself was at Peking. As one after another of his former commanders deserted to Nanking, he found himself cut off in the unfamiliar northern country. It would have been suicidal to hurl his small personal force against a Nanking army so vastly superior in numbers and equipment. He was forced to relinquish his command and flee to South China by sea.

When Chiang himself reached Hankow, he abolished a series of exorbitant taxes including business excise levies, thereby assuring himself the gratitude of the Hankow commercial interests, little and big. Again he insisted that he would resign and go abroad as soon as conditions were settled.

He returned to Nanking in May and proclaimed that peaceful unification of the country was his only policy. As a policy it was excellent. The only drawback was that he never got a chance to carry it out.

At first the Kwangsi leaders attempted to establish another government at Canton. But the local political chieftain announced his loyalty to Nanking. The Kwangsi leaders sent their troops into Kwangtung Province, but met stiff resistance and were forced to retreat into their own territory.

Shortly afterward Chiang Kai-shek sent troops from the north to Canton and started an expedition into Kwangsi Province itself. The stronghold of Waichow fell to his troops and the Kwangsi rebellion, if it could be dignified by the name, was at an end.

No sooner was the Kwangsi revolt in collapse than Feng Yu-hsiang, the erstwhile 'Christian General,' went on the warpath. Feng had been disgruntled ever since he failed to get a rich and comfortable province after the Nationalist arms had triumphed. He and a number of military leaders in the northwest began to plot against Nanking. Soon they were conferring with the so-called 'reorganizationists,' political opponents of Chiang, under the leadership of Wang Ching-wei.

When the Kwangsi troops revolted, Feng joined them. There is some evidence that he actually instigated their movement. But he did little to help them in their own cause. When Chiang Kai-shek's forces were pursuing the Kwangsi men in the far southwest, however, Feng moved.

His armies immediately destroyed the Yellow River bridge on the Peiping–Hankow railway and other railway bridges in Shantung Province. Having thus cut himself off from possible large-scale troop movements by rail from Nanking, Feng sat down and waited.

Chiang was more or less prepared. Although dependent on 'Model Governor' Yen Hsi-shan's benevolent neutrality, Chiang quickly got in touch with Feng's two chief subordinates. Soon, to the surprise of some and not of others, the two generals proclaimed their undying devotion to Chiang Kai-shek and their unswerving allegiance to the Nanking government.

Feng retreated to the west, destroying more railroad bridges and tunnels as he went. Only a small portion of his subordinates followed the example of the two deserters. A majority of the troops remained loyal to Feng, in spite of the fact that many of them had not been paid for something like three years.

Nanking opened the campaign by expelling Feng from the party and ordering his arrest. The Model Governor at this point offered to mediate. That meant more than it appeared. Yen, it was to be noted, was a late convert to the Kuomintang cause. His troops, and not Chiang Kai-shek's, had taken over North China for the Nationalists. Nanking needed a loyal Yen to maintain control of the north. Yen's offer to 'mediate' was in fact a covert announcement that he was in alliance with Feng, and that Chiang Kai-shek had better, therefore, treat Feng nicely.

The situation was a grave one. Chiang Kai-shek needed Yen's support and loyalty. But he could not truckle to the Christian General without losing much 'face' for himself and compromising the entire authority of the Nanking government.

It was not a pleasant thing to do, but he did it. June 25, Nanking canceled the mandate for Feng's arrest 'in view of his meritorious services in the past.' Feng agreed to relinquish his military command and to go abroad for the usual 'tour of inspection.'

The wily Feng had got off scot-free and remained in the good graces of the Nanking government, while the Kwangsi group whom he had egged on to revolt were out of power, in exile, and more or less in disgrace.

Meanwhile, Chiang had gone to meet the train bearing the remains of Sun Yat-sen from Peiping to Nanking. He returned to the capital, noted with satisfaction that the envoys of eighteen major foreign nations had turned up, in top hats and morning clothes, for the state funeral. He proceeded to stage the most splendid burial service that China, renowned for elaborate funerals, had ever seen.

June 1, Doctor Sun Yat-sen was buried in a crypt behind a shining mausoleum on near-by Purple Mountain, overlooking the city which he had made the first capital of the Chinese Republic in 1912, and which was now the seat of a new and stronger government, one which the foreign powers did not hesitate to recognize. The only jarring note was offered by Madame Sun Yat-sen, who on her arrival at Harbin from Europe started denouncing the Nanking government and kept on denouncing it until her departure from China the following September.

CHAPTER XVII

FENG AND YEN AGAIN

THE Christian General did not stay loyal long. Chiang Kai-shek continued in his refusal to give him Shantung Province, which the Japanese had recently evacuated, a year after seizing it in the Tsinan 'incident.'

Chiang was determined to extend national territory. He realized it would have to be a gradual process. He knew he could not drive out war-lords from the regions which their armies occupied. But he was insistent that the area held by the war-lords not be extended. He could tolerate Feng in the far northwest of Chahar Province; he refused to let him take over Shantung.

The result was that when the next anniversary of the first revolution rolled around, October 10, 1929, twenty-seven generals of the People's Army in northwestern China, former subordinates of the Christian General, issued a ringing denunciation of Chiang Kai-shek and the Nanking government. This was rebellion; Chiang replied that it must be suppressed.

A few days later he announced the personnel of his high command against the rebels, but the loyalty of some of his generals was in doubt. One was imprisoned at Nanking a short time after his appointment was announced. Another repudiated Chiang Kai-shek's authority and openly joined the rebels.

Chiang planned to send one of his armies down the Yangtse River with the idea of attacking the rebels in the rear, but the move did not materialize. On the other hand, early in November Chiang found himself embarrassed by the reappearance in Hupeh Province of one General Hu, with a force variously estimated at ten thousand to forty thousand men and the slogan, 'Hupeh for the people of Hupeh.' Here was regionalism in the open. Hu marched on the Yangtse River port of Ichang, but was defeated and withdrew into the interior.

November 21, Chiang Kai-shek assumed the offensive, attacking Loyang, in Honan Province, the home base of the People's Army. The rebels retreated, leaving behind large quantities of arms and ammunition.

But early the next month the two generals who had forsaken Christian General Feng the previous May revolted against Nanking. This revolt began with a mutiny at Pukow, where troops had been concentrated preparatory to transportation by steamer to Canton. The mutinous troops looted Pukow, and could have easily taken Nanking, across the river, as the capital was short of troops, all the picked units having been sent to the various war zones in the north.

For some unknown reason the general in charge of the mutineers chose not to attack Nanking, the fall of which might have meant a severe loss of prestige to Chiang Kai-shek. Instead, the 'gray general,' as he was known, moved his troops up the Tientsin–Pukow railway, taking rolling-stock with him as he went.

The revolt was finally settled through the mediation of an outside general, and Chiang saw to it that thereafter troops of unquestioned loyalty were placed in strategic places like Pukow.

Chiang, although making a few inconsequential advances, was registering little real progress against the major foe, the leaders of the People's Army, who were more experienced field commanders and not disposed to be bribed. Chiang made a strong effort to procure the active co-operation of Model Governor Yen. In December he turned over to Yen the command of all Nanking forces north of the Yangtse. If Chiang thought Yen would then use his new command against the People's Army, he was mistaken. Yen singled out one of the rebels whom he never had liked anyway, and attacked him, but remained indifferent to the main campaign.

Chiang Kai-shek then ordered a subordinate general to move his troops up the Tientsin–Pukow and Lunghai railways, but sent his own troops behind to make sure of no treachery ahead.

The Model Governor looked askance at this advance of military force northward. He regarded it as a revolver directed at his own head. On February 10, 1930, he telegraphed Chiang Kai-shek suggesting that they both return to private life. He urged Chiang to 'abandon his ambitions.'

Telegrams then began to fly faster than bullets. While keeping up with the correspondence, Chiang concentrated all his best troops in the neighborhood of Hsuchow on the north-south railway. He brought most of his troops out of the Hankow area for the concentration. His most modern equipment was assembled and he conferred ostentatiously with his German advisers.

Yen thereupon gave up his proposal to resign and see the world, and concluded a definite alliance with old Feng, the Christian General. The latter resumed command of the People's Army, received funds and supplies from Yen, and the war was on.

Chiang realized that a battle against the combined strength of Feng and Yen was likely to be long-drawn-out and bloody. He appealed to Young Marshal Chang Hsueh-liang, up in Manchuria, for aid in crushing the revolt. The Young Marshal, however, remembering for the moment his father's disastrous experience in venturing south of the Great Wall, elected to sit tight in Mukden.

When hostilities began, Chiang Kai-shek appeared to have a vastly superior military force. But the rebels had the advantage of fighting in their own territory, and were able to disrupt Nanking transport lines. They also knew the art of instigating guerilla chieftains to stage disconcerting raids in various parts of Central and South China, thereby preventing Chiang from concentrating his full military strength against the main Feng-Yen forces.

Only one maneuver remained before the opposing forces settled down to war in earnest. Han Fu-chu, erstwhile subordinate of Feng but a man with healthy ambitions of his own, proceeded to send his troops to join Chiang's at Hsuchow. Feng and Yen sent a bandit leader to prevent the junction. He failed, and General Han formally joined Chiang Kai-shek.

For his action this former deputy of Feng Yu-hsiang was later given the overlordship of Shantung Province, for which Feng had originally started hostilities and which he never got.

CHAPTER XVIII

RUSSIAN INTERLUDE

WHILE still busy with the Kwangsi imbroglio and the Feng-Yen threat, Chiang Kai-shek suddenly found himself mixed up in a quarrel which he did not start and which concerned him little. The other party to the quarrel was Soviet Russia, which made it serious.

Toward the end of May, 1929, Chinese police at Harbin, in Young Marshal Chang Hsueh-liang's dominion, raided the Soviet consulate there. Subsequently the police broke into three other consulates. In each, they reported, they had found proof that the Russian officials and employees of the Chinese Eastern Railway had been using their positions to foment a Communist revolution.

The Chinese Eastern Railway, pushing across northern Manchuria to provide a short cut for the Trans-Siberian Railway, had been built by the Russians in Czarist days. When Soviet Russia made a new deal with China, part of the deal was that Russia should share operation of the railway with China. As a result the road was jointly administered by Chinese and Russians, and high offices were divided fairly equally among both nationalities. The Russians, however, actually managed the line, as they had done before.

In June the Soviet Consul-General at Harbin and a number of other officials were arrested, the telephone and telegraph systems of the C.E.R. were seized, and the Russian trading offices in Manchuria were closed. The Russian manager of the railway and a number of his staff were removed and deported, and replaced by Chinese officials.

If the Manchurian Chinese who carried out the coup thought that the Soviet Russians would take the seizure calmly, they soon realized their error.

On July 13 came the expected official Soviet Russian protest, but with it came a stinging ultimatum. The Moscow comrades gave the Manchurian authorities exactly three days to restore the *status quo ante*, failing which the Soviet would start military operations.

Young Marshal Chang Hsueh-liang, who had not long before pledged allegiance to Nanking and hoisted the Kuomintang flag in his territory, blandly referred the matter to Nanking. He was a loyal Chinese, he informed the Russians, and the little fracas involving the Russians would have to be settled by Chiang Kai-shek's capable Foreign Minister, Doctor C. T. Wang, today China's envoy at Washington.

The Russians weren't particular. They sent the same ultimatum to Nanking. C. T. Wang, clever, affable, Yale-educated, and eager for a diplomatic triumph, plunged into the crisis with vim.

Before the three-day deadline had expired, he had dispatched to Moscow a note which would have done credit to the eloquence of Eugene Chen, who had restored the Hankow British Concession to China. Making the Manchurian quarrel Nanking's quarrel, C. T. lodged what amounted to counter-demands for the release of Chinese merchants said to have been arrested by the Soviet government, and for the protection of Chinese merchants lawfully residing in Soviet territories. This was in the best Eugene Chen 'red herring' technique, but the Russians, being quite familiar with herrings, refused to be diverted.

On July 18, back came the second Soviet note, making it

clear that Moscow would stand for no nonsense. China would please return the railway to its former management, the note said, or Moscow would withdraw its diplomatic mission and consuls from China, recall all its citizens from the C.E.R., sever all railway communication with the Chinese Eastern, thus cutting off the principal revenue of the railway, and would demand the immediate departure from Russia of the Chinese diplomats and consuls.

The Chinese reply indicated no alarm, and Soviet Russia acted. Fifty thousand Red troops, well equipped and perfectly disciplined, quickly concentrated east of Irkutsk and moved toward the Manchurian border. The Young Marshal moved heavy detachments, somewhat more slowly, northward. It was estimated that he had dispatched about sixty thousand men, reinforced with airplanes, armored trains, tanks, etc.

Nanking continued to handle the matter diplomatically, but Chiang Kai-shek was growing alarmed. America's Secretary of State, Henry L. Stimson, called the attention of both China and Russia to their obligations under the Kellogg Pact, and received in return a verbal wrist-slapping from Comrade Litvinoff.

Before either Chiang Kai-shek or the Young Marshal knew what was happening, Soviet planes were raining bombs in the vicinity of Suifenho, on the eastern Manchurian border. On the western side, the Soviet land forces advanced. Their leader was none other than General Vassili Bluecher, who under the name of Galens had been Chiang Kai-shek's old military adviser at Canton and during the northern expedition.

It was disconcerting, to say the least, to have one's military teacher as one's potential enemy, but Chiang Kai-shek showed no signs of flinching. The fight was Chang Hsueh-liang's, but the Young Marshal was a Chinese and it was up to Nanking to help him. Chiang offered to move his own troops northward, despite his preoccupation with rebellion at home. Chang Hsueh-liang's associates curtly refused. They hinted that Chiang Kai-shek himself had stirred up all the trouble with the crazy Russians in order to have the opportunity of sending troops into Manchuria, and eventually taking over the territory. Chiang contented himself with sending financial aid, estimated at $2,000,000. This rejection of freely offered military help may have accounted for Chiang's hesitation in making a similar tender when the Japanese ran riot in Manchuria at the end of 1931.

Suddenly, while C. T. Wang was still trying to get the whole matter settled through the League of Nations, the Soviets unleashed a real attack and came thundering across the Manchurian border with infantry, artillery, and aircraft.

On October 13, the Russians captured the town of Lahasusu in a combined land and water attack. They sank two or three Chinese gunboats and sent the Chinese garrison into precipitate retreat.

Airplane raids then began on Chailanor, and along the C.E.R. between there and Hailar. Another Soviet force crossed the western Manchurian border. The invaders did not exceed a division in strength, but their thirty airplanes wrought havoc with the countryside and completely destroyed the morale of the Chinese forces. The Young Marshal had a few airplanes, but nothing seems to have been heard of them.

Manchouli, Chailanor, and Hailar on the western front and Mishan on the east were occupied in succession. At Chailanor the Soviet forces captured the bulk of the Seventeenth Brigade, one of the Young Marshal's crack units, and annihilated the remainder.

The Manchurians were in panic. Their forces were in retreat, and the population of Harbin was in greater fear of the retreating Chinese than the possibility of capture by the Russians.

The Young Marshal decided to take matters into his own hands. He apparently had had little to do with the original dispute, which had been stirred up by his associates and subordinates. But he saw that matters were going from bad to worse. His own armies were being decimated on the field, and he suspected the Japanese of itching to step in and take over his territory on the pretext of maintaining law and order. Nanking, meanwhile, was still exchanging notes with the League of Nations and the western powers and getting nowhere.

The Young Marshal decided that it was better to lose face than to wait for Nanking's pleas to reach the ears of the Kellogg Pact signatories. He put in a hurry-up call for the veteran diplomat, Wellington Koo, sometime ambassador at Washington and London, who at the time was out of favor with Chiang Kai-shek and was passing his days in France.

Koo, with no official diplomatic status, hurried back to China from France, avoided Nanking, and went straight to Manchuria, where he began negotiations for peace without regard to Chiang Kai-shek's government.

On November 26 he announced that Chang Hsueh-liang was ready to accept the terms of the Soviet note of July 13, and to restore the railroad to its pre-hostilities status. Accordingly, a preliminary agreement was signed at Nikolsk-Ussursk on December 3, 1929.

Nanking still insisted on putting its finger into the pie. C. T. Wang proposed that the belligerent parties withdraw their troops to points thirty miles on each side of the frontier. Comrade Litvinoff rejected the proposal, and also refused to entertain any foreign representations or mediation.

Wellington Koo advised Chang Hsueh-liang that it would be wise to accept all the Russian conditions, and the Young Marshal capitulated. On December 22 formal minutes were signed at Khabarovsk between the Soviet and Chinese delegates, bringing the conflict to an end. The agreement called for the return of the railway to its former conditions of management, the reopening of the Soviet consulates in Manchuria, and a conference at Moscow for the settlement of outstanding questions, including the resumption of diplomatic relations.

To save face, Chiang Kai-shek's government had to 'ratify' the agreement, thereby giving it binding force as far as Nanking was concerned. But it was a secret to no one that the Young Marshal had made his own peace; its nature was indicated by the fact that the Soviet consulates were to reopen in Manchuria, although diplomatic relations between Russia and China were still in suspension, and there was not a single Soviet diplomat or consul in all the rest of China.

CHAPTER XIX

WAR IN THE NORTH

MEANWHILE the dispute with Feng and Yen turned into a crisis and soon into a war. Chiang Kai-shek found himself with not only a military enemy in the field, but a thoroughgoing political movement which resulted in the setting up of a new government at Peiping.

It was a serious crisis even aside from the threat of armies and guns. Feng Yu-hsiang and Yen Hsi-shan formed a coalition with Wang Ching-wei. It was a strong combination psychologically as well as tactically. Feng, although his obvious flirting with Moscow had cost him the enthusiastic support of the missionaries and churchmen who had prayed for his success as the Christian General, was still a potent figure in the country. His troops were well disciplined and, despite the defection of some subordinates, entirely loyal to him. Their courage was acknowledged. He himself continued to affect the garb of a Chinese peasant and lived simply, a living protest against official extravagance.

Despite the obvious inconstancy of his own allegiance, he was difficult to discredit. He lived frugally, devoted himself to the building of schools and the encouragement of agriculture, spoke out sharply against the luxurious living of the Nanking officials, and denounced corruption. He was extremely popular among the masses.

Yen's administration of Shansi had already become known as 'model.' He also affected simplicity, scorned political maneuvers in other parts of China, and devoted himself ostensibly to the welfare of the Shansi people. His armies were well fed, well paid, well equipped, and well disciplined.

Wang Ching-wei was acknowledged by most as the ideological heir to Doctor Sun Yat-sen in the Kuomintang. He was generally regarded as the leader of social democratic ideals in China, and he had a loyal following among the intelligentsia.

The chief criticism directed against Chiang Kai-shek was that, as a military man, he had acquired undue political power and was busy converting Kuomintang trusteeship into personal dictatorship. Feng and Yen promptly announced that they were only rude soldiers, with little interest in politics, and would fight for a democratic government, which they would entrust entirely to Wang Ching-wei and his followers. As a propaganda gesture it was excellent.

The movement started in characteristic fashion with an exchange of telegrams. At the end of 1929 revolts had already broken out and had been quelled. By November 30 Honan Province had been cleared of rebellious troops, and Chiang thought he had brought the campaign to a successful conclusion. He returned to Hankow November 22.

But on February 10, 1930, Yen telegraphed Chiang and asked him to retire, 'in view of the impossibility of uniting the country by force of arms.' This was designed to put Chiang in the light of an ordinary war-lord, another Wu Pei-fu. Yen advised Chiang to 'abdicate his seat' and go abroad with him. He reminded him of his frequent promises to retire. It was as nearly insulting as a polite Chinese communication could be.

Chiang replied by calling on Yen to co-operate for the good of the country. Yen answered equivocally; the gist was that his ideas and Chiang's on the good of the country differed. Chiang said that since the government and party were not yet firmly seated, it would be shirking his duty to retire at that time.

Yen retorted that Chiang had been responsible for placing military power above power of the party and the civil government. The allegation was true; whether the action was justified or not depended on one's point of view. Some argued that a reasonable amount of chaos wasn't so bad if the essential democratic rights were maintained. Chiang's view, obviously, was that peace and order came first, and that the Chinese people could wait a bit longer for their precious rights, which they had never enjoyed previously anyway.

While all this palaver was going on, Feng's and Yen's troops were moving southward. Chiang inquired, as if he didn't know, why the troops were moving. Yen said he would never attack Nanking, but accused Chiang of making military preparations.

The talk still continued, however. From Manchuria, the Young Marshal telegraphed urging peace. Yen suddenly resigned all his posts, and said he was going abroad with Feng. But they stayed on the order of their going, and in the meantime the military preparations continued. On March 18 Yen's forces forcibly took over all the government institutions in Peiping, and disarmed the Nanking troops in the vicinity.

April 1, Yen assumed command of what he was pleased to call the National forces at Taiyuan. Feng was deputy commander. On April 5, Chiang replied by ordering the arrest of Feng, but significantly not that of Yen, whom he still hoped to win over.

Fighting broke out first in Shantung and in Honan. Yen then made definite plans with Wang Ching-wei for a new government at Peiping, which presumably would again become Peking, the northern capital.

Hostilities on this occasion were not characterized by the rapidity and decision with which Chiang conducted his previous campaigns. He was obviously in grave doubt as to the attitude of the Shantung provincial armies, and was prepared to evacuate the province entirely rather than take needless risks.

There was little serious fighting until the end of May when the Nanking forces advanced up the Lunghai railroad line and occupied Lanfeng, a few miles from Kaifeng, Feng's old stronghold. Feng's People's Army counterattacked with its best units on the following day, May 23, making a wide turning movement from Chengchow to Hsuchow, culminating in a sweep to the northeast for an attack on the south flank of the Nanking forces.

Another army simultaneously attacked Chiang's north flank, and the People's Army counter-attacked along the Lunghai. The Nanking forces were compelled to beat a hasty retreat, suffering losses which were variously estimated at from four thousand to fifty thousand killed and wounded.

Yen meanwhile had struck a blow at Nanking revenues in the north. On June 16, Yen's men took over the Tientsin customs, and money collected was withheld from Nanking. As the customs revenues were security for a number of foreign loans, the action threatened international complications. B. Lennox Simpson, a British journalist, was therefore made the 'front' man to bandy protests with the foreigners.

While this was going on, the Yen-Feng forces, reinforced by some South China troops who were still on the loose, penetrated Hunan Province and captured the capital, Changsha, threatening Chiang's rear.

Chiang was forced to place sturdy units on the defensive along the Honan and Shantung fronts, and only with difficulty recaptured Changsha on June 17.

A lull in operations followed, lasting until about June 20, when Chiang with about 100,000 troops launched an offensive toward the northwest. Success attended its early phases, but he was soon driven back.

There the situation appeared to reach a stalemate. It became apparent to both sides that Young Marshal Chang Hsueh-liang up in Manchuria held the key to the situation. If he translated his loyalty to Nanking into action and moved south of the Great Wall to menace Feng and Yen in the rear, then the rebellion was doomed. If he maintained neutrality, Feng and Yen might yet carry the day against Chiang. At any rate, a long and bloody conflict was in prospect.

Both sides proceeded to woo the Young Marshal. On June 21 the Nanking government appointed him deputy commander-in-chief of the National forces, and sent envoys to Mukden to seek his assistance. Not to be outdone, Feng and Yen appointed the Young Marshal a member of the State Council of their own prospective government, and set aside several portfolios in their cabinet for his nominees.

A government conference now formally opened in Peiping. Wang Ching-wei was elected to the standing committee. A manifesto was issued in orthodox Kuomintang style, promising to call a people's convention in the shortest possible time, in accordance with Doctor Sun's wishes. It was also announced that the government would not be restricted to Kuomintang members, that it would not be too centralized, and that local and national functions would be clearly differentiated.

Rumors were circulating at Shanghai and elsewhere that

Chiang, apprehensive of the result of the campaign, was depositing huge quantities of money in foreign banks. The reports were given credence in many foreign circles, but many well-informed observers were skeptical. Acknowledging that much Chinese money was being sent abroad, the American-owned *China Weekly Review* said that the bulk of the funds represented government remittances for arms and munitions, and did not mean that Chiang himself was sending his money to safety.

Chiang, meanwhile, without waiting for the Young Marshal's decision regarding intervention, staged a general offensive on all fronts, throwing all his resources and power into one tremendous demonstration, in the hope of cowing his opponents and bringing the conflict to a speedy close.

The Nanking forces advanced in three columns, and by August 13 one of its Cantonese divisions was within eight miles of Tsinan. They recaptured the city on August 15, the Shansi evacuation assuming the proportions of a *débâcle*. It was claimed that thousands of prisoners, 30,000 rifles, 230 field guns, and quantities of military supplies were captured. Chiang did not attempt to cross the Yellow River but withdrew the bulk of his forces almost immediately, transferring the units to the Honan front.

Yen's forces fell back in disorder to the vicinity of Peiping, necessitating Yen's own departure for field headquarters.

Up in Mukden, meanwhile, the Young Marshal had decided to throw in his lot with Chiang Kai-shek. He prepared to move troops south. Yen knew what was coming, and on September 13 telegraphed Wang Ching-wei that he intended to retire.

His foresight was unerring. On the seventeenth the Mukden commanders conferred, and on the eighteenth, one year to the day before the Japanese took his own territory, the Young Marshal issued a stentorian call for a halt to all military operations. All problems, he said, should be settled by the central government. The implication was plain. As soon as the telegram in which he made the announcement was issued, Mukden troops stationed at the Great Wall city of Shanhaikwan began to march on Peiping.

Yen ordered his troops to retreat, and the civilian members of the newborn northern government fled to Tientsin. The Young Marshal's troops moved into the Tientsin-Peiping area September 21, and by September 30 the northeastern army units held both cities on behalf of Chiang Kai-shek. The change-over was entirely peaceful, Yen's troops offering no resistance. Military and civil officials waited at their posts, handed over their duties to the Mukden replacements, and then withdrew.

Chiang's own forces then captured Kaifeng, in Honan, on October 3, and the city of Chengchow three days later, thereby bringing the campaign in Honan to a close.

The campaign against Feng and Yen had lasted more than six months. It was the bloodiest civil war ever fought in China. Chiang said that a half-million men participated on the rebel side. Nanking reported 30,000 of its own men killed and 60,000 wounded, but the Yen-Feng troops were said to have suffered 150,000 killed and wounded.

The long campaign taxed Chiang's physical vitality. Edgar Snow, American newspaper correspondent, interviewed him and found him much aged, thin, worn, and nervous, 'sick at heart with another rebellion,' and at the needless sacrifice of troops against his own countrymen.

While still in the field in Honan, Chiang Kai-shek telegraphed Nanking proposing an amnesty for all political offenders except Communists, Yen Hsi-shan and one of Yen's subordinates. It was noted that he did not include Feng among those to be denied mercy.

He also urged that the Kuomintang convene in plenary session as soon as possible to decide a date for the calling of a national convention and for the promulgation of the national constitution.

Much importance was attached to his statement. He was apparently acceding to the demands of the 'reorganizationists,' after all, assuring the masses of his intention to carry out the process of democratizing China.

On October 10, the birthday of the Republic, Chiang issued a manifesto outlining the future tasks of the national government. Chief among them were the eradication of communism, for which he set a six-months time limit, and the enforcement of a district autonomy system. He was, it was obvious, listening at last to the voice of those who opposed extreme centralization.

Yen, Feng, and Wang, meanwhile, were at the city of Shihchiachwang, and, having nothing better to do, announced their retirement. It was an obvious and routine gesture, but its official announcement gave the cue for a triumphal return to Nanking of Chiang Kai-shek. The Young Marshal accepted Nanking's appointment as deputy commander-in-chief of all armies, and the country was, apparently, once again unified.

November 12, the birthday of Doctor Sun, saw the son of the Old Marshal at Nanking, taking an active part in the session of the Kuomintang. The much-discussed People's Congress was summoned for May 4, 1931.

Yen fled to Dairen. Feng stayed with his own troops in the far northwest. Eventually both generals and Wang Ching-wei forgot their grievances against Chiang, and made their peace with Nanking. But by that time he had other troubles to think about. There was a Communist state in South-Central China, and later a separatist government at Canton. Less than a year later the Japanese struck in Manchuria.

CHAPTER XX

A NEW CHRISTIAN GENERAL

ONCE more Chiang Kai-shek settled back to survey a united country and to prepare for the reconstruction which he realized was sorely necessary if China was to be given any security in the future. But in the meantime he took time out to attend to his own spiritual life.

Off on the Honan front he carried with him at all times a Chinese edition of the Bible given him by his wife's mother. Old Mrs. Soong exerted a profound influence on Chiang. For all his eminence as a military man, he was almost humble in her presence. Three years before, he had married her daughter, but had declined to become a Christian without understanding Christianity.

Chiang read the Bible. He was impressed. It was probably the first major non-Chinese work to which he devoted any attention. The biblical characters were as fascinating as the old Chinese heroes, but it was emotionally that he succumbed to the Testaments.

Huddled in his cold quarters as winter descended upon the northwestern plain, Chiang never missed a day of reading the Bible. There were many days when he must have wondered at the outcome of that war which he was waging against the northern militarists. It was a hard campaign. He could not be sure of the loyalty of many of his high generals, and the national armies were meeting stiffer resistance than at any time since the Kuomintang legions marched north from Canton. There were undoubtedly times when he pondered if it was all worth while, if he was wrong and his enemies were right, if China after all had better go on being the same old China that it had been since Manchu days.

Soon he acquired the habit of saying prayers at his bedside, when he arose in the morning and before he retired. He began to feel that at last he had found the spirit of a true Christian, and that he was ready to join the church.

He communicated his desire to his wife when he returned to Nanking after the conclusion of hostilities against the north. Members of the family got in touch with the Reverend Z. T. Kaung, the same Chinese Southern Methodist minister of Shanghai who had refused to perform Chiang's marriage ceremony because of what he considered irregularity in his divorce.

Pastor Kaung, although glad to see the faith making headway among the eminent, still managed to keep his perspective. He wanted to be sure that this was a *bona-fide* desire for baptism, and not a personal whim or a political maneuver.

He questioned Chiang as to why he wanted to be a Christian. Chiang replied without hesitation. First of all there was the influence of his Christian wife, whom he wanted to join in religion. The pastor knew that Chiang had told Mrs. Soong he would not become a Christian in order to win Mei-ling, but would promise to study Christianity.

Then, too, Chiang informed the pastor, he had studied the Bible, particularly the New Testament, and it had affected him profoundly. Finally, and he offered it for what it was worth, he had learned that the officers and men on whom he could rely implicitly were almost all Christians.

Pastor Kaung was convinced of Chiang's sincerity in desiring to be baptized. The matter was arranged.

Early on the morning of October 23, Chiang and his wife arrived in Shanghai by special train from Nanking. Wearing a simple Chinese long gown, without the formal black silk overjacket, Chiang went to the home of his mother-in-law, Mrs. Soong. There, in the presence of Mrs. Soong, T. V. Soong, Madame H. H. Kung, the eldest of the Soong sisters, and Mei-ling, Pastor Kaung performed the simple ceremony. Prayers were offered, and Kaung again asked Chiang whether it was his sincere desire to become a Christian.

Chiang replied in firm tones that it was. The minister sprinkled a bit of water over his head, and welcomed the chief of the National government into the church. He thus became the third son-in-law of Mrs. Soong to join the Christian church, the others being Doctor Sun Yat-sen and Doctor H. H. Kung.

Chiang found himself with plenty of company in the government. Other Christians holding high government positions at the time included T. V. Soong, Doctor C. T. Wang, the Minister of Foreign Affairs, and Sun Fo, the son of Doctor Sun Yat-sen by his first marriage. Feng Yu-hsiang was also nominally a Christian, but at the time he was not being held up as a model for the youth of the nation.

The event was given no widespread advance publicity. Although Chiang and Mei-ling had been welcomed on their arrival at the Shanghai North Station by a vast concourse of military and civil officials, Kuomintang leaders, merchants, and bankers, none had any idea of the reason for his visit to Shanghai.

Foreign missionaries, jubilant at the prestige conferred by the conversion, let the news out, and the newspapers soon broke the story.

The next day he and Mei-ling went to Chikow, where,

for all his newfound Christianity, Chiang did not neglect to bow before the tombs of his ancestors, as of yore.

The news, unfortunately, did not arouse rejoicing in all quarters. One commentator remarked cynically that Chiang was seeking aid against the Communists, his latest plague, from 'no less a personality than God Almighty Himself.' Another remarked that God would 'henceforth ride with Chiang in the same military saddle.'

Others suspected him of becoming a Christian largely for political reasons and to improve his standing among foreigners. Both allegations were ridiculous. He obviously could never gain the slightest political advantage by becoming a Christian; on the contrary, he stood to lose much influence because of the probable distrust of high non-Christian officials and leaders who after all constituted an overwhelming majority. The belief that he sought to improve his status among foreigners was childish; Chiang has never had the slightest regard for foreign opinion as such. Nor has he the awe of foreign power which has characterized so many of his contemporaries.

There is no reason to doubt his sincerity in joining the church. He is known to be devoted to Madame Chiang, and she is a most active and fervent Christian. He also has the example of his respected leader, Sun Yat-sen, who became a Christian early in life.

Whether or not Chiang's belief as a Christian has been at variance with his policy as a civil leader is something for the theologians and philosophers to weigh, but the sincerity of his personal religion can hardly be doubted.

Chiang has taken his faith seriously. He still says his prayers regularly, and attends church whenever time permits. A few years ago he was in the habit of taking a Chinese Methodist pastor out for Sunday automobile rides with him and Madame Chiang. While bodyguards bristled about the car, the minister, an old friend of Madame Chiang, used to sit between husband and wife and give them an informal sermon. In late years his days have been too full for church attendance or even Christian talks, but he still reads the Bible daily and he insisted that when he was kidnapped at Sian in 1936 he never forgot to say his prayers.

Incidentally, despite her influence in having her husband baptized, Madame Chiang herself never formally joined the church. Her parents were Southern Methodists, and she regards herself as a member of the church by birth, but she has not gone through the ceremony of membership.

CHAPTER XXI

RED ARMIES, BLUE SHIRTS

WHETHER or not Chiang Kai-shek's conversion to Christianity had anything to do with it, the hardly pious Communists seemed to mark the occasion by suddenly becoming a formidable military force.

Of course, there was nothing mysterious about it. While the country was racked by civil war, as Chiang battled alternately against the Kwangsi clique, the Feng-Yen combination, and the assorted minor militarists who harassed him, conditions among the peasants went from bad to worse.

Rampaging armies are never any respecters of homes and farms, and in China they have been worse than the twin scourges of flood and famine. The Communists as a result of the continued chaos found the countryside receptive to their appeal and, often enough, full of enthusiastic converts.

The respectable people called them all bandits. But there was a difference. There were actual bandits, and there were roving bands of Communists too ragged and ill-equipped to give the appearance of an army but ready to fight against Kuomintang capitalism and its concomitants.

The Communists had their beginnings in the peasants' and workers' corps organized during the northern expedition from Canton. When the break came between Chiang Kai-shek and the left wing, to be followed by the break between the left-wing Kuomintang and the Communists, many of these corps merely continued to travel and fight.

They were sometimes joined by farmers driven to banditry, who were willing to listen to Communist denunciations of Chinese bourgeois revolution and to travel with the Red bands.

After some wandering about without any definite plan, setting up settlements here and there and quickly moving when government troops or militia attacked, the Reds coalesced into several large, permanent armies. These speedily became a threat to the nation-wide authority of the Nanking government.

The Reds, with thousands of men, moved in various groups through the Central and South China provinces, and in a number of cases set up semi-sovietized régimes. The news dispatches referred to bandits or Communist-bandits, but many of these groups had elements of stronger governmental institutions than Nanking itself.

In July, 1930, Communists captured Changsha. The fact that they burned and looted much public and private property was emphasized as proof of their utter depravity. But when the military governor whose troops had failed to hold the city recaptured it with the aid of Nanking troops, he was credited, or discredited, with having killed four thousand persons in retaliation, presumably to reduce his 'guilt' in having let the Reds capture the city in the first place.

Finally, the main Communist bands merged and reached the heart of the Yangtse Valley. With Nanking busy fighting Feng and Yen, the Reds' progress was almost unimpeded. They established what was virtually a Communist state within Nanking territory.

When Young Marshal Chang Hsueh-liang moved his troops south of the Great Wall to provide the intervention which won the war for Chiang Kai-shek and ended the threat of the northern coalition, he permitted Chiang Kai-shek thereby to devote his attention to the Communists for the first time.

In October, 1930, while some of Chiang's troops were still chasing stray detachments of Feng's and Yen's forces, he sent three divisions which had been released from the Honan front to deal with the Reds in three Central China provinces, an area within striking distance of Nanking.

In December Chiang himself assumed command of the campaign. He began by announcing an amnesty to all the Communists renouncing their belief in proletarian revolution and laying down their arms. He also announced, significantly, that he had 300,000 troops, twenty gunboats, and thirty airplanes ready to send against them.

If the Reds were impressed they failed to show it. By reason of their long marches over the country, sometimes without food, together with their long practice at guerilla warfare and the support they almost invariably received from the peasantry, they were in a strong position. Much has been made of alleged Red massacres, their harsh treatment of the populace, and their destruction of property, but the aid and encouragement which the people of the countryside gave them and withheld from the Nanking and provincial soldiery showed how much truth was in most of the stories.

The first drive against the Communists, which Chiang ordered at the end of 1930, resulted in a serious reverse for his own armies. Many of his troops, sent against the Communists, joined the Red legions, taking with them valuable army equipment, weapons, and munitions. It became a standing joke among the Reds, and even their enemies, that the Nanking troops were 'ammunition-carriers for the Communists.' The defections did Chiang's prestige little good.

When Chiang took charge of the anti-Communist campaign in mid-China, he announced that the suppression would be completed in three months. When the deadline expired the Reds were still as unsuppressed as ever, and the time limit was extended until the end of April, 1931.

Communist and other left-wing activity, meanwhile, was growing in the ranks of the students, professors, and other intellectuals. The period of civil war might have had something to do with the growth of the movement, by weakening the authority of the central government and lowering its prestige, but there was also plenty of evidence that the intellectuals, recalling the spirit which prevailed in the days of the northern expedition and the successes which attended the Communist-Kuomintang union, hoped for a return to the era of co-operation with the Reds.

Conditions in the cities, where living costs were rising and workers were shamefully exploited, added fuel to the fire, and intellectual China was soon aflame with communism. Terrorism to stamp out terrorism merely created more terrorism, and crimes of violence against high government officials were frequent.

Chiang himself had at least one narrow escape from assassination at this time, when a former member of his bodyguard penetrated almost to his bed, and might have dispatched him with a revolver if an alarm had not been raised outside and frightened the man into flight.

With actual revolutionary activity coursing through the middle schools, colleges, and universities, and frequent demonstrations a matter of embarrassment to the authorities, Chiang Kai-shek himself, in December, 1930, assumed the post of Minister of Education. The man who had been appointed to the position was still in France. Chiang realized that he could not depend on subordinates to curb what was fast becoming a state of insurrection.

His first manifesto as Minister of Education declared

that the students had 'fallen prey to communism and had sometimes gone the length of calling meetings, distributing handbills, and involving themselves in party conflicts.' They had opposed their presidents, and he pointed out that opposing their presidents was tantamount to opposing the government.

The manifesto began by stating that Chiang's 'heart was pained.' It ended with the stern warning that he was not afraid to shoot students who remained recalcitrant.

The academic repression was soon followed by a new press law which established new definitions of treason, and virtually made it a crime to criticize the party or the government.

Meanwhile, however, the Communist armies renewed their activity in Kiangsi Province. A second Nanking drive was unsuccessful, and Chiang Kai-shek's troops constantly met defeat. One of the chief Nanking generals was killed in action. Another was captured by the Communists and executed. The forces of a third were annihilated.

Chiang changed the command of the anti-Communist forces. He sent the Minister of War against the Reds. Still the results were unencouraging.

Chiang finally decided to take the field himself, assuming direct command and conducting operations from his own field headquarters. He went from Nanking to Nanchang, capital of Kiangsi Province, where he established headquarters.

The main body of his troops was concentrated in southern Kiangsi. Chiang ordered a general offensive, and in two days he seemed to have surrounded the Communists. A week later the Communists commenced a general retreat to the mountainous regions of western Kiangsi, with Chiang's forces in hot pursuit.

The feat was announced as a great government victory,

but it is now known that the Communists were hardly more bothered by Chiang's attack than a man by a fly. When he came too close for comfort, they moved off into more remote areas.

The Communist organization was such that it could actually dissolve into villages and towns. One hour there was a Communist army; the next there was nobody in view but ordinary farmers and workers. It was impossible for Chiang's forces to round up the Communists and destroy them. They slipped through his fingers every time he tried.

Hence, toward the end of July, although the Nanking press agents announced that all the Communist strongholds had been captured, and that the Reds were in full retreat toward the south, they told the truth but failed to explain it. The strongholds were indeed in the hands of Chiang and his troops, but they were empty. The Reds were in retreat of their own volition, in good health, while Chiang's troops puffed to keep up with them and were frequently surprised by counter-attacks and ammunition raids.

While Chiang was pursuing the Reds with less and less success, but at least harrying them out of his own territory in Central China and into the semi-independent areas of Fukien Province, more trouble broke out in the south.

Down in Canton another government was in the process of formation, with an odd assortment of right-wing and left-wing leaders whose principal common interest was a hatred of Chiang Kai-shek. In May, 1931, Wang Ching-wei had issued a manifesto announcing the commencement of a general anti-Chiang campaign. He said that previously Chiang had been able to deal with opposition movements separately and to defeat them with ease. Now, he announced, the Kwangtung and Kwangsi provincial leaders were joining forces against Chiang, and Feng and Yen, who had been quiet for some time, had endorsed their views. Among the leaders at Canton was none other than Hu Han-min, who previously had been Wang Ching-wei's bitter political opponent.

Chiang then was still faced with the growth of a serious oppositionist movement in Canton and the Communist threat in Kiangsi. The protracted campaigns were weakening the power of the government, and its finances were in bad condition.

This is generally believed to account for Chiang's institution of an opium monopoly system in 1931. Previously, China had counted on suppression, and appeared to be making excellent progress in stamping out the drug, considering the difficulty of dealing with foreign elements involved in the traffic.

Soon, without any public announcement, it gradually became known that the Nanking government itself was administering the opium traffic, ostensibly with a view to controlling it. Men who had been associated for years with the fight to suppress opium denounced the monopoly system, warned that it was certain to promote corruption and delay the eventual extirpation of the drug from the country.

Chiang's enemies said he had come to an agreement with the chief of the Shanghai secret societies, giving the gangs control of the traffic in the Shanghai area in return for freedom to carry out a complete control program in every other section of the nation.

The undoubted existence of the opium monopoly, the terrorism against all liberals and radicals, the gagging of the press, the elimination from Kuomintang councils of all except those whose allegiance to Chiang and his associates was unquestioned, convinced many thoughtful observers that Chiang was turning Fascist and that his government would soon become a totalitarian state on the western model.

The organization of the Blue Shirts, a secret blood brotherhood of reputed Fascist leanings, lent strength to the belief. Begun by military academy cadets and apparently motivated by a strong anti-Japanese feeling, its existence was long denied by Nanking officialdom, but of its activity there was too much evidence. Finally Nanking gave up the pretense and admitted that such an organization existed. Today the official explanation still classifies the group as a harmless students' club, and vigorously rejects the thesis that it has been responsible for most of the political assassinations in China during the past several years.

Shortly after the Blue Shirts were formed, one began to hear whispers of the 'C.C. Corps.' Named for Chen and Chen, the nephews of Chen Chih-mei (full names Chen Kuo-fu and Chen Li-fu), the corps was ostensibly formed to recruit super-patriots and maintain party discipline.

It quickly became known as Chiang's OGPU. To it were attributed countless acts of terror. Popular opinion has confused it with the Blue Shirts, but the latter is strictly a military group while the C.C. Corps centers its activity in civilian circles. Whether or not the Chen brothers have anything to do with it is impossible to say with certainty, but of its existence and operation there is, in the opinion of unbiased observers, little doubt.

CHAPTER XXII

CANTON DIVORCES NANKING

As the Feng-Yen revolt faded into history and Chinese events moved toward the Manchurian crisis, the nation saw the beginning of an internal political struggle which finally burst the bounds of discussion and confronted Chiang with a new, independent government in South China.

The dispute started with a more or less academic quarrel between Chiang and Hu Han-min over the proposed constitution for China. Under the program which Sun Yat-sen had outlined for the nation, the Kuomintang Party during the period of political tutelage was to prepare the people for full representative democracy. Chiang thought such a democracy required a constitution outlining the powers and functions of the various governmental units.

Hu accused Chiang of trying to make himself dictator through the constitution. He opposed the idea of a provisional constitution during the period of tutelage. Such an instrument, he said, would only enable those who were in power at the moment to perpetuate their power after the period of tutelage ended.

Chiang insisted that Hu was talking nonsense and that his attitude was balking democracy in China. He even accused Hu of flouting the will of Sun Yat-sen and seeking to keep the Chinese masses out of the government. He said Hu was more interested in maintaining the power of the Kuomintang as a party than in introducing the people to democracy.

Each was probably sincere. Hu felt with all his heart that he must save China from personal dictatorship. Chiang regarded Hu as an incurable old fogy. Both men were headstrong; each was used to having his own way, Hu because of his past eminence in the party, Chiang because of his very real power at the moment.

On February 28, 1931, Chiang, Hu Han-min, Sun Fo, and several others were threshing the question out at the Tang-shan Hot Springs, not far from Nanking. The discussion turned into an argument between Chiang and Hu and the argument became heated. Finally Hu threatened to resign from the presidency of the legislative department of the government and leave Nanking unless his views were endorsed.

Chiang refused to budge, Hu resigned, and two days later the standing committee of the C.E.C. accepted his resignation. The committee named Chiang and ten others to draft a constitution. Lin Sen, an amiable old man of no political importance, was appointed to succeed Hu as president of the legislative department.

The same day Chiang addressed a meeting of government officials to state the cause of the dispute. The split between Chiang and Hu seemed to mark the turning point of Kuomintang history, as the two leaders were hopelessly at variance in their interpretation of Doctor Sun Yat-sen's doctrine.

But Hu did not appear to state his case. He was not seen in Nanking, nor did he turn up in Shanghai, as in the past, with a noisy denunciation of those who disagreed with him. It soon became evident that Hu was the prisoner of Chiang Kai-shek.

He was treated respectfully enough and made more than comfortable, but he had 'lost his liberty of movement,' as they say in China.

Hu's Cantonese friends and associates spread the report of what had happened. The press, controlled by Chiang and his group, said not a word, but the story got around. Finally the rumors became so thick that Chiang felt he had to say something.

In one of the most extraordinary speeches ever delivered by a Chinese statesman, Chiang told everything and at the same time told nothing. It was long and rambling, but it boiled down to this:

1. It was rumored that Hu had lost his personal freedom. But the personal freedom of every loyal Kuomintang member must be restricted. Even he, Chiang, suffered all kinds of restrictions. It was not only incumbent on every patriot to sacrifice his personal liberty for the sake of the cause, but it was perfectly within the right of the party or government to restrict the liberty of any party member whenever circumstance demanded.

2. As a matter of fact all these rumors about Hu having lost his freedom were silly. Weren't his writings appearing in the newspapers? Weren't his statements being quoted? The reports were obviously groundless.

3. On the other hand, in order to avoid 'misunderstanding,' Hu was planning to live permanently in Nanking. In the past, political leaders out of sympathy with the government had fled to the foreign settlements and 'incited disorder.' Even when their own intentions were good, their followers made trouble for the government, and the leaders thus lost prestige. The government was particularly anxious to prevent Hu from falling into such error.

Chiang wound up the oration with a statement which, though polite enough, left no doubt as to his intentions. 'We are really loath to see such a long record as Comrade Hu's wrecked in a single day. Therefore, both for the sake of the public and his own interest, we are anxious to devise

measures to preserve him from ruin. Both in the opinion of
the government and of Comrade Hu himself, it is best that
he should not leave Nanking. Therefore, although he has
already resigned from his government post, Comrade Hu
will not leave the capital.'

Although as an example of Oriental humor the speech
did not receive the attention it deserved, it put a period to
political arguments for the time being.

Meanwhile Chiang's political opponents who were still
at large were muttering that he wanted to be President of
China under the new constitution. On March 23 he issued
a statement categorically denying that he had ever entertained such an intention. He did not need to. He held the
power, and if under the new constitution the President was
to be a figurehead, Chiang was not one to pine for the position.

Chiang prepared for the national people's convention
which had been summoned for May 5, 1931, and which was
to consider the constitution for the forthcoming period of
tutelage. By the time it opened, however, Chiang had a new,
a full-fledged rebellion on his hands in the south.

The trouble started when a number of Cantonese leaders
issued the usual circular telegram of denunciation. They
brought what they termed an impeachment against Chiang.

Chiang could have afforded to ignore the telegram dispatched by the politicians. What was more alarming was
another telegram released by the 'King under Southern
Skies,' otherwise known as the war-lord of Canton, who
openly attacked Chiang, cataloguing his faults and accusing
him of dictatorship. Chiang called on the party elders to
investigate his alleged offenses.

But the anti-Chiang movement gathered strength. Sun
Fo, son of the sainted Sun Yat-sen, and Wang Chung-hui,
first Foreign Minister of the Republic and an eminent

Kuomintang veteran attached to no faction, ostentatiously left Nanking. The defection of these two meant a serious loss of face for Chiang.

Then the Kwangsi generals, who had been sulking in their southwestern mountain province and who had never forgiven Chiang for squeezing them out of the Nationalist picture, contributed another circular telegram denouncing Chiang and Nanking. Chen Chi-tang, the Canton war-lord, promptly announced the re-establishment of friendly relations between Kwangtung and Kwangsi Provinces — a southern coalition.

More ominous was a proclamation by the commandant of the Bocca Tigris forts outside of Canton: all warships passing the forts must have a pass from Chen Chi-tang or they would be fired on. It took no soothsayer to report that Canton was preparing for war.

Chiang, after probing the situation, decided that there would be no war, that the southerners would not fight unless attacked, and that in any event the dispute might still be settled by negotiation.

Since negotiations take time, Chiang Kai-shek dispatched envoys to meet the southern spokesmen at Shanghai, and decided to take himself off to Kiangsi to crush the Communists. The Cantonese would wait, he concluded; the Communists would not.

On May 25, the Canton leaders demanded the retirement of Chiang Kai-shek in forty-eight hours. Chiang returned to Nanking but showed no sign of quitting. On the contrary, he announced that he was now forced to treat the southern leaders as rebels and to suppress them.

When the Canton deadline expired, and Chiang was still in his seat at Nanking, the southerners announced that they were establishing their own Central Executive Committee at Canton. Two days later they proclaimed the establishment of a new national government with its seat at Canton.

The orthodox C.E.C. met at Nanking the next day. Chiang, for all his brave words, was unwilling to fight Canton unless forced. There were too many party veterans, too many old associates of Sun Yat-sen in the south to attack with impunity.

The peace talks dragged on, but the Canton war-lord meanwhile called a military conference at Canton, June 13, to discuss an expedition against Nanking. The Canton political chiefs reiterated that there could be no peace unless Chiang quit.

July 21, the new Canton government ordered a 'punitive expedition' against Nanking. It took the expedition some time to begin moving, but on August 5 the vanguard of the Kwangsi armies entered Hunan Province, 'the Balkans of China.'

Chiang saw that it was a question of quit or fight. He elected to fight. He ordered the mobilization of the central government troops and prepared for war. Despite support of the Young Marshal in the north, the situation was anything but hopeful. Chiang could count on not only a fight with the southerners but further trouble from the restive troops of Feng and Yen, still a formidable military force and far from pacified.

Even the fastest of expeditions move slowly in China, and large-scale warfare did not break out at once. There was some question of the loyalty of the Hunan governor himself. If he let the southerners pass through his area, as another Hunan militarist had let Chiang's own armies pass in 1926, the theater of war would shift to the vicinity of Hankow and conflict would be delayed.

Both sides jockeyed for support. Canton even sent envoys to Japan to obtain recognition of the southern régime. Some said that the southerners were ready to make a deal with Nippon, giving the Japanese a free hand in the Young Marshal's Manchurian domain, in return for recognition of Canton dominance in China proper, but the Cantonese indignantly denied the charge.

Then, while everyone was waiting for the outbreak of a bloody civil war, Japan struck in Manchuria.

CHAPTER XXIII

CHIANG STEPS OUT—AND BACK

WHAT happened at Mukden on the night of September 18, 1931, and afterward has been told a hundred times. What happened inside China, as a result, may have been less spectacular, but it was hardly less interesting.

After the first shock had worn off, and the Chinese realized what was taking place north of the Great Wall, war fever surged through the nation, particularly infecting the always nationalistic students.

As it became obvious that Chiang Kai-shek was not going to lead the nation to battle against Japan, and that Nanking was putting its trust in the League of Nations and the Kellogg Pact, the patriots proceeded to prod the government.

In Shanghai, where feeling was highest and organization best, hundreds of students on September 28, ten days after the Mukden 'incident,' seized a train, rode to Nanking, and joined the students of the capital city in a vast demonstration comprising more than five thousand persons.

The mob moved on the government buildings, shouting for war against Japan, and an end to weak-kneed diplomacy. Terrifying and overpowering the capital police, the students stormed the Ministry of Foreign Affairs, poured into the building, cornered Minister C. T. Wang, and pummeled him severely. Doctor Wang, having lost exceedingly much face, immediately resigned.

The scene was repeated at other government offices, and

the students decided to settle down in the capital until something drastic was done about Nanking's government and its foreign policy in the face of the Japanese rape of Manchuria. Forgetting books and classrooms, they decided to accept no promises but to stay and see that action was forthcoming.

Down in Canton, meanwhile, Eugene Chen, obviously enjoying Chiang Kai-shek's embarrassment, delivered a stinging denunciation of the Generalissimo for 'truckling to Japan.' He discreetly omitted mentioning the fact that only a short time before he himself had visited Tokyo in open relations with the Japanese on behalf of Canton.

Public opinion demanded the merging of the Canton and Nanking governments. Nanking made the first overtures. Chiang Kai-shek named peace envoys who urged the southern leaders to cancel their opposition. Nanking indicated its readiness to come to terms with the Cantonese.

Peace negotiations opened once more. Despite the very real menace of the Japanese campaign in Manchuria, however, the parleys made no progress. The Cantonese demanded Chiang Kai-shek's withdrawal as the price of their support.

On October 14 Chiang released Hu Han-min, as evidence of his desire to reach a speedy agreement with Canton. Hu, once able to leave Nanking, showed none of that fondness for the capital city which Chiang had extolled eight months before, and forthwith left for the comparative safety of the foreign settlements at Shanghai.

Once there, however, he telegraphed the Canton leaders to abandon their attempt to overthrow Chiang Kai-shek, to let bygones be bygones. A week later the Canton peace delegates arrived in Shanghai, and progress was immediately noted.

Chiang sent a letter to the conferees, saying, 'As for all

past complications, whatever may have been the right or wrong, the whole blame may, if desired, be placed entirely at my door.'

Soon the complete reorganization of the government was announced. The President of the national government, it was decided, would be the head of the state but would have no executive responsibility. He was to be a figurehead like the King of England or the President of France. The real executive would be the President of the Executive Yuan, with duties similar to those of a prime minister.

The Canton government was to be automatically dissolved after the reorganization of the Nanking government. But most important of all, it was agreed that Chiang Kai-shek would resign on the date the Canton government announced its dissolution.

Chiang accordingly surrendered all his offices, and immediately retired to his old home at Chikow, declining all offers of honorary posts. He was elected one of three members of the C.E.C. standing committee, with Hu Han-min and Wang Ching-wei, but refused to accept.

The students, however, were still encamped in Nanking, and far from satisfied. Again they invaded the Ministry of Foreign Affairs; this time, reinforced by a group of students from Peiping, they destroyed the building completely. They marched to the central Kuomintang headquarters, seized Tsai Yuan-pei, scholar and veteran conservative political leader, and dragged him out of the building. The guard at the party headquarters fired into the air to disperse the crowd, and finally rescued him, but not before Tsai had been dragged some distance by the students and badly mauled.

Another group attacked the *Central Daily News*, official Kuomintang organ, practically destroying its entire printing plant. Police rushed to the scene, and a free-for-all took place in which one student was drowned while trying to escape.

At this point the government decided that it had had enough. The next morning regular troops surrounded the National Central University, where the students were quartered, and forced them to leave the capital under military escort.

With Chiang out of the government, his associates also submitted their resignations. Young Marshal Chang Hsueh-liang's resignation was accepted; he was given an honorary post at Peiping, supposedly to compensate him for lost Manchuria. That of T. V. Soong was rejected. The government needed his banking support.

Sun Fo became President of the Executive Yuan, actually Premier. The eloquent Eugene Chen replaced C. T. Wang at the foreign office, and Lin Sen became the figurehead President of the National government.

Japan moved into the outlying regions of Manchuria and was soon engaged in stamping out every vestige of Chinese authority. Before long a series of incidents involving Japanese at Shanghai was leading to a new conflict within striking distance of the capital at Nanking.

The new government, which its sponsors had announced would 'put an end to the old régime and inaugurate a new era,' was no more successful than the old, but the fault was not of its own making.

None of the 'big three' — Chiang, Hu Han-min, Wang Ching-wei — would assume his duties as a member of the standing committee of the C.E.C. Chiang stayed in Chikow. Hu Han-min was in Hongkong. Wang Ching-wei was in a Shanghai hospital, reportedly quite ill.

Of more importance, when Chiang withdrew from the government his supporters went with him. The Shanghai bankers who provided the foundation of his government withdrew their backing when he left. His own troops and those of his associate generals were off in the near-by provinces, unpaid and growing restive.

The new government, as a result, quickly found itself in a political and financial snarl and unable to function. Its Cantonese supporters cried sabotage. The old Nanking crowd cried incompetence. Perhaps it was a little of both.

On January 19, Wang Ching-wei, despite his illness, went to Hangchow to confer with Chiang, presumably to urge him to co-operate with Nanking. They both decided to assume their duties, provided Hu Han-min did likewise. January 21, they both returned to Nanking.

The party leaders met at Nanking January 23. Chiang and Wang opposed Foreign Minister Eugene Chen. Chen wanted to sever diplomatic relations with Japan immediately, but the others, particularly Chiang Kai-shek, opposed the step.

Eugene Chen left Nanking, went to Shanghai, and announced his resignation January 24. He left no doubt as to the reason and as to the real situation at Nanking.

'The severance of diplomatic relations has been and is opposed by General Chiang. His opposition is so categorical and uncompromising that he has not hesitated publicly to express himself in a manner that, while gravely hampering me in the conduct of China's policy *vis à vis* Japan, is tantamount to an invitation to the Japanese militarists to do as they please, since no resistance will be offered. This attitude of General Chiang is the logical outcome of his passive policy, and it has much to do with the present Japanese menace to Shanghai.

'As Chiang, in whom all real power resides, is opposed to my foreign policy, I have tendered my resignation.'

The next day Sun Fo came to Shanghai, supposedly to

GENERALISSIMO IN FULL DRESS

persuade Chen to reconsider, but wound up by himself resigning the presidency of the Executive Yuan.

The result was another shakeup in the government and the triumphal return of Chiang. Wang Ching-wei, who now seemed to be in complete rapport with Chiang, replaced Sun Fo as President of the Executive Yuan. Lo Wen-ken, a scholarly Buddhist, became Foreign Minister. T. V. Soong, the financial power of the government and Chiang's brother-in-law, returned to the Ministry of Finance and was also named Vice-President of the Executive Yuan.

Chiang himself was named chairman of the National Military Council, the highest military organ in the government. Co-members were Christian General Feng, Model Governor Yen, and Young Marshal Chang Hsueh-liang.

The government, menaced by Japanese gunboats in the Yangtse River off Nanking, was quickly moved to Loyang, far inland in Honan Province. And exactly one month and seven days after he had resigned all his posts in the Nanking government, Chiang Kai-shek resumed control.

He had acceded to the popular demand, he had withdrawn from the government, he had given way to his critics. He stood aside while his opponents took power, he watched while they made a mess of things. He returned to power under the best of all possible circumstances. The nation needed him; his opponents called him. He was stronger than ever.

CHAPTER XXIV

SHANGHAI—HEROES AND VILLAINS

WAR, real but undeclared, broke out at Shanghai on January 28, 1932. Two days later the National government which Chiang Kai-shek had established five years before at Nanking was moved to Loyang, far from the menace of Japanese men-of-war on the Yangtse.

Chiang, having returned to active duty as a member of the C.E.C. standing committee, went to the new capital. With him went Wang Ching-wei, who had decided, in view of the emergency confronting the government, to ignore his previous illness, which had been partly real and partly political.

The fighting at Shanghai involved marines of the Imperial Japanese Navy and soldiers of the Chinese Nineteenth Route Army. The Nineteenth Army was a Cantonese unit which had been stationed along the Nanking–Shanghai railroad when Chiang Kai-shek resigned and the Cantonese leaders took over the government at Nanking. It was placed there in case the Cantonese found the climate of Nanking not to their liking and desired to leave in a hurry. None of them cared to emulate Hu Han-min's 'voluntary' residence at the capital.

Under such circumstances, it was understandable if Chiang Kai-shek failed to work up the proper amount of enthusiasm for the heroes' rôle which the Nineteenth Route Army proposed to play. Its soldiers were not his soldiers; they came from the south to protect his political adversaries. He was opposed to open warfare with Japan, anyway, believing that the nation was ill equipped to stand a long siege by the Japanese. China, he felt, could not at the time successfully challenge the formidable Nippon war machine. He did not know, any more than did the skilled foreign military observers at Shanghai, how pitifully inefficient that war machine was to appear at Shanghai.

But it was also true that when the fighting broke out at Shanghai, Chiang was in no position to order the Nanking military forces to support the Nineteenth Route Army. This point was generally lost sight of, particularly in foreign countries where the Chinese communities, being almost wholly Cantonese, loudly denounced Chiang for sacrificing the brave Cantonese to the enemy while keeping his own crack regiments far from the battle line.

The fact was that at the time Chiang was merely a member of the standing committee of the C.E.C. He had resigned all his other posts. He was no longer President of the Republic. He was no longer commander-in-chief of its armed forces. Later he was restored to military power, but just then he was without rank in the Chinese army.

In reality, the Nineteenth Route Army was not left to defend Shanghai alone. The Eighty-seventh and Eighty-eighth Divisions, crack troops trained by Chiang, took part in some of the heaviest fighting, and sustained heavy casualties. One-third of their number met death in the battle of Kiangwan, Miaohong, and vicinity. He had ordered them to give the strongest support to the Nineteenth Army.

'No sacrifice is too great to make,' he told them. 'The glory of the Nineteenth Route Army is the glory of China.'

But Chiang kept in touch with Tsai Ting-kai and Chiang Kwang-nai, the commanders of the Nineteenth Route Army. He advised them not to attack prematurely because it would be physically impossible to move reinforcements in time. Japanese warships were stationed on the Yangtse near Nanking, and it was extremely difficult to transport Chinese troops speedily across the river in large numbers. It was necessary to spirit small numbers across, and the process was slow.

Chiang telegraphed the two commanders to station troops at Liuho on the Yangtse River, commanding the Chinese flank, and prevent the Japanese from landing there. In a joint telegram of reply, the two generals agreed to abide by his advice, but they did not, and when the Japanese finally got around to moving there, they were able to land without opposition.

During the critical period of the Shanghai conflict, hundreds of condemnatory telegrams and letters poured in on Chiang asking him why he did not send reinforcements.

Those close to him implored him to tell the truth of the situation. Chiang insisted that the explanation would have to come from the commanders of the Nineteenth Route Army. Finally, irked by the abuse heaped on him, he sent a representative to the other two generals, asking them to make public what had taken place. They promised, but remained silent.

Shanghai newspapers, however, quoted both generals as saying that they had no fault to find with Chiang and that the government had supported them fully with necessary supplies. But since the newspapers printed what they were told to print, this endorsement was unconvincing. Tsai Ting-kai undoubtedly voiced his true sentiments later when he toured Europe and America and denounced Chiang as a traitor. Regardless of Tsai's sincerity in the matter, there is support for the contention that at the time Chiang was not in a position to act otherwise than he did. Tsai's case has been well publicized, particularly in the United States; Chiang's has not.

His associates say that at the beginning of the undeclared 'war' he had repeatedly offered to place his military experience, as a private citizen, at the disposal of the country, but that the Cantonese rejected the offer and reminded him that he was merely one of the members of the Military Affairs Commission, and that the commission was subordinate to the government as a whole.

Hence it was merely in a political capacity that he returned to the government and went to Loyang. He had approved the removal of the government to the inland Honan city, and endorsed the explanation of T. V. Soong, who said, 'No government could function right under the guns of the Japanese warships at Nanking, which were already cleared for action.'

It was a gloomy group of government officials who assembled with Chiang at the Western Palace in Loyang March 1. The stubborn stand of the Nineteenth Route Army against vicious and repeated Japanese attacks had stirred the imagination of the world and had become a Chinese epic. But the stand had ended when the Japanese, after repeated reinforcements and changes of command, finally made the elementary military move that foreign military experts had expected for weeks. They landed a force on the Chinese flank, near Liuho on the Yangtse, and the Nineteenth Route Army retreated quietly and in excellent order. It was some time before the Japanese even knew of the withdrawal, but when they did learn of it, the Shanghai war was over.

Up at Loyang the Minister of War submitted a long military report. He told of the government's defense measures, explained the cause of the withdrawal at Shanghai, and told of the reinforcements which the government had sent. A heated debate took place on whether the government had or had not done enough to support the Nineteenth Route Army.

Finally Chiang barked out a few short phrases to end the argument. It was useless, he told his associates, to cry over what was past. The thing to do was to organize the country from a military standpoint, bring the war to the quickest possible conclusion without loss of national honor, and then to begin preparing for China's day of reckoning.

The C.E.C. decided to create the National Military Council, the highest military organ in the country. Consisting of a chairman and from seven to nine members appointed by the Central Political Council, it was given power to control all matters pertaining to national defense, military education, reorganization and disbandment of troops, suppression of 'bandits,' apportionment and distribution of military appropriations, and the appointment and dismissal of military commanders. The Central Political Council met immediately afterward and named Chiang chairman of the new body.

Most significant move in the establishment of the Military Council was the provision giving the chairman of the body power to issue all military orders. It was to prevent exactly such a state of affairs that the government had been reorganized after Chiang had resigned. The Cantonese wanted no military dictator. They insisted on a government in which the military arm was strictly under the control of the civil authorities, a government in which military authorities administered military affairs but were always accountable to a higher, many-membered, governing body.

The action at Loyang made Chiang's position exactly the same as that of commander-in-chief under the previous Nanking régime. It was a return to the emergency system under which Chiang had been given similar powers for the duration of the northern expedition from Canton.

CHAPTER XXV

RESISTANCE VS. NON-RESISTANCE

On March 18, 1932, with the Shanghai 'war' already history, Chiang assumed the chairmanship of the Military Council. Serving with him were the veterans Yen and Feng, Young Marshal Chang Hsueh-liang of the lost Manchurian provinces, Kwangsi war-lord Li Tsung-jen, and a quadrumvirate of Cantonese generals.

'China wishes a peaceful settlement of the dispute,' Chiang told an interviewer shortly before assuming his post, 'but if Japan increases her aggressive action, China is prepared to fight to the bitter end.' This was brave talk. Chiang realized that China was unprepared to fight, and that if she did it would necessarily be 'to the bitter end.'

The same tone was sounded by what was termed a National Emergency Conference at Loyang April 7. It was decided to offer 'prolonged resistance' to the Japanese aggression.

But it soon became apparent that any such program would be quixotic. The Japanese, having concluded the Shanghai adventure, were busy mopping up in Manchuria and driving every remnant of Chinese authority out of the northeastern provinces.

Meanwhile, seemingly taking advantage of the situation precipitated by the Japanese attack in Manchuria, the Communists in Central China resumed their activity. For a time Hankow itself was threatened.

The anti-Communist campaign was going on, as it had

for some time, desultorily. Chiang decided to make the campaign a live issue and to focus attention on the Red situation by assuming command himself. Some said Chiang was purposely dodging the real Japanese danger to cope with a more elusive menace. But Chiang was ready with his answer.

'It is useless for China to talk of resisting Japan,' he told his colleagues and the nation, 'when it has not yet stamped out the enemy in its midst. If China ventures to fight the Japanese, the Communists will attack from the rear and chaos will quickly overtake the whole country.'

There followed what was termed a 'rigorous military campaign' against the Reds. It was, indeed, the best display of Chinese military force since the night of the Mukden incident.

Reports told of the 'complete rout' of the Communists in three provinces and the capture of several Red strongholds. By the end of the year press reports were telling, as they had several times in the past, of the 'remnant' Communists.

The Communists, the nation was told, were retreating to the northwest. But it was easy to see that they were still a definite military force. They had not been stamped out; they were merely moving their location. There were more 'Communist-suppression' campaigns to come.

While Chiang was off to the Communist wars, sharp difference of opinion had developed between Wang Ching-wei and the Young Marshal. In June the two men met at Peiping and discussed measures for the defense of North China, which the Japanese army seemed bent on attacking forthwith.

Wang returned to Nanking, and in a strong speech to the Central Political Council indicated that his interview with the Young Marshal had not been satisfactory. Wang said that the son of Old Marshal Chang should either offer stubborn resistance to Japan or give way to someone who would. The Young Marshal, on the other hand, said his troops were poorly equipped and not regularly paid. If the government wanted him to fight, he indicated, it must give him enough funds to meet his military expenses.

The two leaders argued, and the argument concluded in the old familiar way. Wang resigned as President of the Executive Yuan, or Premier, and sent telegrams to everybody of importance to apprise them of the fact. Two days later, on August 8, the Young Marshal quit as commander of the North China area and member of the Military Council. Each, meanwhile, tossed another verbal brickbat at the other.

Wang then telegraphed Nanking urging the acceptance of the Young Marshal's resignation. Chiang Kai-shek and other leaders urged him to reconsider his own resignation, but he refused. Finally the whole government resigned on August 9.

There followed a series of new visits and conferences. Chiang was having difficulty holding his tempermental colleagues together. He first instructed the Young Marshal to stay at Peiping, under a new title which seemed to make no change in his actual status. Then, after some more discussion, Wang Ching-wei was granted three months 'sick leave.' He left Shanghai for Europe on October 21.

His departure gave rise to rumors about the organization of another government in North China, but Christian General Feng, who was generally believed to be mixed up in the suspected plot, denied the story and insisted on his utter loyalty to Chiang Kai-shek. As weeks passed and no sensational development occurred in the north, China settled down for a return to normality under Chiang Kai-shek and his government.

December 1 the government moved back to Nanking. Chiang took the occasion to emphasize again that the country would resist Japanese aggression, but there was still no evidence of action, and those to whom the statement was addressed concluded that it was just some more face business.

But two days after his return from Hankow to Nanking, where he had been directing the fight against the Communists, Chiang gave his own people and the Japanese something real to think about. He revealed that China was going to resume diplomatic relations with Soviet Russia.

He made no attempt to explain the desirability of a diplomatic rapprochement with the Russian Communists at the same time that he found it necessary to wage war against the Chinese Communists.

Meanwhile, something had to be done to reorganize the government at Nanking, and the C.E.C. convened December 15. Chiang, addressing the group, told about the anti-Communist campaign in Central China. He reported the Reds entirely routed and thousands killed. He explained how his expedition had not only staged a military drive against the Communists but had also rehabilitated the territory which it occupied, and how it had carried out a program of economic reforms and education to counteract the Red program. In so doing he paid unconscious tribute to the efficacy of the Red doctrine and its hold on the populace, a tribute which was at some variance with the government reports of Communist ravages and outrages in Central China.

The assemblage listened politely to Chiang's summary of operations against the Red enemy, but its thoughts were apparently full of another enemy whose depredations were more impressive.

T. V. Soong, Sun Fo, Mayor Wu Teh-chen of Shanghai

and C. C. Wu, former Minister to the United States, sprang a sensation. They proposed that China concentrate its troops and recover Manchuria as soon as the opportunity arose. They demanded a nation-wide boycott of Japanese goods, under government direction and sponsorship.

Despite the eminence of the men who made the proposal, Chiang was strong enough to defeat it. It would never do, of course, to bring the question to a ballot and to vote it down. The resolution was merely sidetracked, sent to a sub-committee, and finally 'not adopted.'

The government's attitude failed to command the support of the nation's intellectuals, and the students were openly hostile. When Nanking accepted the League of Nations resolution on Manchuria, despite the fact that the resolution condemned Japan and caused the Japanese to walk out of the meeting which approved it, thirty thousand Chinese middle-school pupils and twelve thousand university students struck in protest.

Again mass meetings of denunciation were held, parades moved through the streets, and student groups attempted to converge on Nanking. But this time Chiang Kai-shek was ready for them and determined to prevent the excesses of the year before. Repression, swift and ruthless, soon drove all student opposition underground.

Meanwhile, Chiang prepared to consolidate, to reorganize, to prepare. Eventually, he told his impatient countrymen, he hoped to strike.

CHAPTER XXVI

THE WAR ENDS

ENEMIES of Chiang Kai-shek are fond of saying that some time before or during the Manchurian adventure he and the Japanese reached an 'understanding.' Under the supposed agreement, Chiang would close his eyes to the Japanese incursions in the north, and they would respect his authority in the south.

The only thing wrong with the story is that the Japanese never acted as though they had heard of such an understanding. They bombed Shanghai, the seat of Chiang's power. They sent their gunboats scooting up to Nanking, and Chiang's government got out of the way, moving posthaste to Loyang. And they came swarming through the Great Wall, apparently more than willing to swallow up all of North China, which in name at least was Chiang's own territory.

Throughout the year 1933 Chiang was harassed by dissension and rebellion, but the Japanese gave no indication of either sorrow or support.

The Japanese presented Chiang with a New Year's greeting by suddenly bombing Shanhaikwan, the border town where the Great Wall meets the sea. The Japanese troops said the Chinese garrison fired first. The Chinese declared that the Japanese attacked without provocation. As in the case of countless previous incidents, the real story was of some interest but little consequence. What followed was of genuine interest. It was a new war.

The battle of Shanhaikwan raged for two days, with the Chinese troops offering considerable resistance. But the superior Japanese force captured the place on the third day, after completely wiping out one battalion and killing its commander.

A widespread conflict was soon in full swing, but it became apparent that the real Japanese objective was the remote province of Jehol, which, although never considered an actual part of Manchuria, would make a convenient extension of the territory which the Japanese were preparing to set up as a new state.

Bombing planes were sent over the Jehol cities. The helpless local civilian population bore the brunt of the attack. The war-lords charged with the governing and defense of the area moved out of the province with a speed approximating that of the better American track stars. But despite the rapidity of their exit they did not neglect to take with them all the cash, silver, and jewels they could lay their hands on, to provide the wherewithal for a comfortable old age. Nor did they leave their concubines behind.

When the Japanese started their final drive on February 27 they met practically no opposition. March 3 they marched into Chengteh, the Jehol capital, without firing a shot.

Jehol was always considered an appendage of Manchuria, but its ties to China for years had been tenuous. The Chinese government probably felt no great wrench at seeing the province go the way of Manchuria, but the loss did China's prestige no good. On the other hand, the warfare conducted against the civil population aroused the indignation of patriots at home and humanitarians abroad.

The first blast came from the south. The Canton leaders vigorously denounced Chiang Kai-shek's government for its 'weak-kneed' policy. On January 17 the southwestern governing bodies sent a joint telegram to Nanking demanding an explanation of its 'real attitude' toward Japan. The southerners minced no words. They bluntly accused Chiang Kai-shek of having reached a secret agreement with the Japanese.

The situation was exceedingly distasteful. Chiang couldn't spank the southerners. To do so might invite the extremist anti-Japanese elements to upset the entire government and reduce the nation to the feudal war-lordism which prevailed before the Kuomintang revolution.

On the other hand, the situation in the north was more than tense. The Japanese in the mood of imperial conquest might, if crossed, decide to snatch all China. They might have trouble doing so, but China would not profit by the experience.

Chiang finally went to North China March 6, three days after the end of the Japanese campaign in Jehol. He met the Young Marshal at Paotingfu. After several days of discussion, the Young Marshal realized that his own situation was hopeless. He could not hope to recover Manchuria alone. And Chiang was neither willing nor able to finance a Manchurian campaign. On the other hand, the former Manchurian troops were there in North China, drifting, helpless.

There was only one thing for the Young Marshal to do — hand the troops over to the Generalissimo to be made part of the national government forces. Then, off to Europe to give the nation a chance to forget his unfortunate connection with the Manchurian *débâcle*, and later, back to China to a fine new post with 'big brother' Chiang.

It was all decided within a few days. March 10 the Young Marshal was no longer a marshal. He turned his soldiers over to Chiang. March 11 the Minister of War was made commander-in-chief of all Chinese troops in North China. And two days later Chang Hsueh-liang left Peiping for Shanghai.

With the Young Marshal out of the way, Wang Ching-wei came back. He had been in Geneva for his health. On learning of the war in the East he decided to return to China to resume his duties in the government. He arrived in Shanghai March 17, and Chiang Kai-shek went to Nanking to meet him. The two leaders apparently found themselves in accord, and on March 30 Wang resumed his post as President of the Executive Yuan.

Canton, however, was still displeased. Its leaders accused Chiang Kai-shek of betraying a previous pledge to inaugurate constitutional government and avoid dictatorship.

The Canton leaders also derided Nanking for its previous decision 'not to yield another inch of ground to the Japanese.' Since then, they pointed out, Shanhaikwan and Jehol had been occupied by the Nipponese. Nanking was responsible, they said, because it had failed to map out a definite plan of resistance.

But if they expected an overwhelming national response to their denunciation of Nanking, they were disappointed. They thought that their telegram of April 4, in accordance with old Chinese custom, would be the signal for various regional war-lords and other anti-Nanking elements to rally to the cause of opposition. No such response came.

The Cantonese authorities decided to call their own 'national' congress at Canton at the same time that the Nanking meeting convened. The country was drifting back to the situation prevailing before the Manchurian incident, with one government at Nanking and another in the south. Only now there was a new disturbing régime north of the Great Wall, with the Japanese pulling the strings.

A Canton spokesman put the situation clearly to a Hong-kong newspaper interviewer. 'Before long we shall see another civil war taking the place of the war with Japan,' he said. 'As for the anti-Nanking elements, they have two alternatives. They either surrender or fight against General Chiang Kai-shek.'

But serious as was this threat of revolt in the south, the situation in the north presented an even more imminent danger. Fighting in North China was continuing, and the Japanese actually took several strategic Great Wall passes from the Chinese defenders.

The Japanese forces invaded North China proper and continued their advance until they arrived at Luanchow. From there they threatened to attack Tientsin and Peiping.

Chiang soon realized, however, that the Japanese had no real desire to grab the two North China cities. What they wanted to do was to bargain. They desired first of all a peace agreement recognizing their conquest north of the Great Wall. Their second consideration was a friendly Chinese administration in the area due south of their new Manchurian state. Those objectives gained, they were willing to leave Chiang nominal control of the Peiping–Tientsin territory.

It soon became evident that the Chinese authorities were planning to come to terms with the Japanese. The fact aroused widespread resentment, particularly among the patriotic North China students, who had behind them the glorious tradition of beating Japanese imperialism by force of public opinion. But the Japanese had a revolver at China's head. China had to answer, and there was only one answer.

Anyone acquainted with Chinese politics would have decided that this was the precise time for the Christian

General to raise his lusty voice. He would not have been disappointed.

On May 27, Feng suddenly issued a circular telegram announcing that he had assumed office as commander-in-chief of the 'People's Anti-Japanese Army,' which, it developed, was in Chahar Province. The telegram was a direct challenge to Chiang Kai-shek, although it did not mention the Generalissimo by name. Feng issued a general call to arms to all the people of China to rise up against the Nanking government's policy, which he, like Canton, called 'weak-kneed.'

His outbreak was the cue to Canton, which responded with another manifesto. Nanking in effect told Feng Yu-hsiang to shut up and get out. Canton objected to such lack of consideration for old Feng. But Canton's support was entirely verbal. Pai Chung-hsi, the brains of the southern military group, was still opposed to a military move against Nanking until the south was prepared for a real campaign. His views carried with the southern militarists, and the anti-Nanking movement virtually evaporated.

Feng, as a result, found himself without support and isolated. He removed himself from the neighborhood of Kalgan and betook himself to the sacred mountain of Taishan, in Shantung Province, where he arrived in August. The old Christian General went to the top of the mountain and closeted himself in a Buddhist monastery, under the protection of his one-time subordinate and betrayer, Han Fu-chu — now the Number One man of the neighborhood.

As soon as Feng made his exit an obscure general named Fang Cheng-wu reorganized the 'anti-Japanese army,' announced himself as commander-in-chief, and issued a circular telegram denouncing Chiang Kai-shek. He was a small potato. Chiang sent a subordinate to round up his troops and chase him off. The troops were incorporated into the Nanking army, and Fang Cheng-wu has been out of the limelight ever since.

But on May 31 the Tangku truce was signed, bringing the undeclared Sino-Japanese War to an end and adding another 'humiliation day' to the Chinese calendar. The truce, to save face all around, was signed, not by Chiang Kai-shek nor even by the Minister of War, but by a lieutenant-general who had not been heard of before and has not been noticed since. A vice-chief of staff signed for the Japanese army.

So tender were Chinese feelings at the time that the terms of the truce were not revealed. Even today there are many suspicious Chinese who insist that all the provisions have not been disclosed. But a series of Japanese protests when the terms were allegedly violated in later years soon indicated what the treaty did and did not provide.

In general, the Chinese authorities agreed to withdraw their troops to a line marking the boundary of a new 'demilitarized zone.' The Japanese 'after being satisfied that the Chinese troops have been withdrawn to the line stipulated' agreed to refrain from pursuing the Chinese beyond the line, and also to withdraw to the Great Wall.

The Chinese undertook to observe the boundaries of the demilitarized zone and to 'abstain from any provocative or disturbing acts.' The Japanese, however, in order to insure the carrying out of the Chinese withdrawal, reserved the right to make observations by airplane or otherwise, with the Chinese authorities giving the necessary protection and facilities.

Finally, the Chinese police were charged with the maintenance of peace and order in the areas south of the Great Wall and within the demilitarized zone.

In short, the Chinese were obligated to maintain peace and order in the northern demilitarized zone but were unable to dispatch special police to rid the area of bandits, as these would be considered armed forces and hence banned by the truce.

The Great Wall passes were slowly returned to Chinese authority, although one was held by the Japanese until December 1. The war was definitely over and, regardless of the humiliation involved, Chiang could, it seemed, start his program of preparation for '*der Tag*.'

CHAPTER XXVII

FLARE-UP IN FUKIEN

But Chiang realized that China's day of reckoning with Japan would have to be far in the future. Better than the prattling super-patriots he realized how ill prepared the nation was for real conflict. The lack of adequate arms and ammunition, the woeful state of communications, the absence of a large-scale supply system, and the chronically unbalanced budget were all good and sufficient reasons for biding his time.

Then there were the Communists. And soon there was the Fukien Rebellion.

Chiang had actually begun what he expected to be the final expedition against the Communists when he heard ominous rumblings in the south. He knew that the conservative southern militarists, like Kwangsi General Pai Chung-hsi, were opposed to an anti-Nanking military movement on the ground of unpreparedness. And he knew that there were others who were willing to fight him but who were afraid that, without allies, they would be crushed.

But his agents also reported that there were still other elements not only willing but ready to defy him. That they would have the temerity to revolt and set up an independent government seemed fantastic, but that was exactly what they proceeded to do.

As a rebellion it was considerably less serious than the Feng-Yen coalition movement three years before. As a war it was a joke. But its effects were tremendous.

For some time there was considerable uncertainty as to who was going to do the revolting. There were plenty of men, idealists and war-lords, intellectuals and politicians, who might have taken the leadership.

The early activity centered in Canton, cradle of revolution and hotbed of discontent. Almost everybody in the place was anti-Chiang in one degree or another. The conferences and plots began after Eugene Chen, balked in his effort to sever diplomatic relations with Japan, quit Nanking in disgust and retired to Canton when Chiang Kai-shek returned to power. Chen was the most voluble of the oppositionists, but others were the prime movers.

According to their plans, the anti-Nanking campaign was to start simultaneously from the north and the south. Feng Yu-hsiang would rise in Kalgan, and it was hoped that his old crony Yen Hsi-shan would join. In the south Chen Chi-tang, the Canton boss, was to assume full command of the anti-Nanking operations.

To win the support of the people, a new resounding political platform was to be drafted by Hu Han-min, to be announced when the campaign was under way. A vigorous and presumably anti-Japanese statement of foreign policy was to be drawn up by Eugene Chen and several fellow-rhetoricians. But Chen Chi-tang declined to assume the rôle prepared for him. He was against clashing with Nanking until he saw a good reason for clashing. As long as Chiang let him alone, he was willing to let Chiang alone.

Chiang did his best to remove all causes of grievance. A civil war was the last thing he wanted. But the Cantonese continued hostile. They trained their oratorical guns on the Tangku truce, the terms of which were just beginning to be suspected.

By this time Feng had proclaimed the organization of his anti-Japanese army, which turned out to be entirely an anti-

Nanking army. Other generals in his neighborhood pledged their support to him.

The southern malcontents decided it was a good time to strike. They began to organize an expeditionary force with troops from Kwangtung, Kwangsi, and Fukien Provinces. It went by the rather imposing name of the Anti-Japanese Relief Army for Marshal Feng Yu-hsiang. The army was supposed to fight the Japanese but the announced purpose, of course, fooled no one, least of all Chiang Kai-shek. General Tsai Ting-kai, commander of the Nineteenth Route Army and hero of the Shanghai war, was the commander of the expeditionary force.

This army was supposed to advance on Hankow, supposedly en route to North China to fight the Japanese; actually it planned to turn eastward and attack Nanking. If its leaders thought Chiang would wait for them at the capital they must have been naïve indeed.

Chiang held important and pointed conversations with the governor of intervening Hunan Province. The latter, having been assured a large supply of money and equipment, moved two divisions of troops to southern Hunan and blocked the advance of the southern forces. Tsai never hurled his forces against the Hunan troops. The major southern military leaders remained indifferent, and without their support no really strong expedition was possible. The northward march 'fizzled out.'

Meanwhile, Feng was making a brave show up in Kalgan, issuing fiery anti-Japanese manifestoes and refusing to compromise with Chiang. Feng, as a matter of fact, counted on support from the southerners. They let him down just as completely as he had let down the Kwangsi clique in 1929.

Patriotic groups in the south sent Feng $300,000 for military expenses, and attempted to rally all the anti-Nanking elements of the country. A call was issued to the Chinese people to 'rise up and do what you think is right to save the country,' but the Chinese people apparently had their own ideas of what was right, and didn't rise. Feng's movement collapsed, and the southern campaign remained unborn.

Throughout the summer and early fall Chiang had his hands full attending to Feng and another would-be anti-Japanese leader. One of Feng's subordinates, having been bought off previously, was sent to take over the Christian General's troops, and Feng went off to his sacred mountain in Shantung Province. Chiang urged him to come to Nanking, but old Feng declined the invitation, without thanks.

While Chiang was sending reinforcements to the north, the newest southern plot took shape. It was decided to establish an independent government in Fukien Province.

Chiang Kai-shek knew, all the time, what was happening. He sent the venerable figurehead President of China, Lin Sen, to Foochow, which had become separatist headquarters, in an attempt to reach an understanding. Lin, an amiable bewhiskered gentleman, much esteemed in China for his beautiful calligraphy but about as important as the King of Italy, made no headway.

The new government was launched at Foochow at a mass meeting, something in the manner of a new club. November 20 its personnel was announced. Tsai Ting-kai was chairman of the Military Affairs Commission, the Fukien counterpart of Chiang Kai-shek. Eugene Chen was Minister of Foreign Affairs.

The new government was rather grandiloquently named the Federal Revolutionary Government of China. Eugene Chen drafted a comprehensive statement of policy which included abolition of the unequal treaties, freedom to strike, religious freedom, state ownership of land, forests, and mines, prolonged resistance to the Japanese, and complete tariff autonomy for China.

Although Nanking denounced the new government as communistically inspired, there was little evidence of actual Red instigation. True, there was a fair-sized army of Communists in the immediate vicinity, with whom the chiefs of the new government were seemingly on cordial terms, but the Reds obviously had little faith in the new régime, and manifested only mild interest. The opportunistic nature of the elements comprising the so-called government was quite apparent to the Red leaders, who were wise enough to stake nothing on its survival.

The Federal Revolutionary Government of China abolished the Kuomintang flag and adopted a new ensign of red and blue. It was all ready to do business.

Its leaders thought that, with the new government actually in existence and functioning, the anti-Chiang elements would flock to its standard. They did not. On the contrary, anyone and everyone who might have been suspected of favoring or supporting the new régime rushed into print to repudiate the suggestion. The Southwest Political Council took pains to announce that it was out of sympathy. Cantonese leaders emphasized that they were loyal followers of the Kuomintang and would not join the new 'producers' party' which had been established as the ruling group in Fukien.

Chen Chi-tang issued a separate disclaimer, leaving no doubt that Kwangtung military aid to the new régime would be withheld. Even the old Christian General, usually willing enough to join any opposition movement, declined to become mixed up in this one.

Hu Han-min, who was believed sympathetic to the rebels, telegraphed them to 'reconsider' their anti-Nanking stand. Madame Sun Yat-sen, widow of the late great Leader and

uncompromising foe of Chiang Kai-shek, issued a statement denying any connection with the Fukien régime.

Chiang gave the rebels three days to reconsider, and then
acted. On November 23 the C.E.C. standing committee
expelled the Fukien leaders from the party. On the same
day, Chiang began to move his troops against Fukien. He
issued a final manifesto asking the Nineteenth Route Army
to come to its senses and pledge its loyalty to Nanking
before it was too late.

Canton, thinking that this was an ordinary political
crisis like those in the past, decided that it was a good time
to demand Chiang Kai-shek's resignation. On November 28
the Southwest Political Council called on him to quit.
Wang Ching-wei, again in opposition, said it was because
of Nanking maladministration that Fukien had come to
revolt.

Wang was specific enough in his denunciation of the man
with whom a short time before he had been associated.
'Since the signing of the truce at Tangku, the nation has
lost its power of control,' he announced. 'As the people of
the country are dissatisfied with the Nanking government,
the country wants to overthrow dictatorship. As the dangerous situation in China is caused by the Nanking government through the dictatorship of Chiang Kai-shek, it is
not right to blame the Kuomintang as a whole. We hope
you will accept our advice and leave the Nationalist government in order to free the party and the country again, and
let the people decide on national affairs.'

The declaration and the advice made no impression on
Chiang. He had left the government twice before in order
to give the various factions a chance to get together. Each
time they had found themselves stalemated and had bawled
for his return. This time he would settle things his own way.

Deciding that Canton despite its hostility would not fight,

he sent an envoy south to talk peace, and he himself proceeded to crush Fukien by force.

To the amazement of foreign observers as well as Chinese, Chiang brought out an aerial force that performed in the best manner of western sky armies.

Powerful bombing airplanes, mostly of American make, went winging their way over Foochow and vicinity, dropping missiles of death on the Nineteenth Route Army, which was caught completely by surprise. Young American-trained aviators, flying in perfect formation and releasing deadly cargoes with perfect aim, soon converted the Fukien front into a shambles.

The campaign started in earnest at the turn of the year. Government infantry advances followed the aerial bombardments. Within two weeks the Fukien government was wiped out and the heroes of Shanghai were completely routed. The nation was astonished. So was the rest of the world. The fighting ability of the Nineteenth Route Army had not been overestimated, as some said. It had demonstrated its effectiveness against the extremely powerful Japanese forces in a conflict which was decidedly no child's play. But against Chiang's formidable war machine it was helpless.

Tsai Ting-kai and his associate generals were forced into retirement. The remnants of their forces were reorganized into the Nanking army and transferred to Honan Province. A Chiang Kai-shek man was named governor of Fukien, and Chiang's own troops assigned to garrison duties throughout the province.

The revolt had lasted somewhat less than two months. It carried an object lesson to a number of parties. To the Japanese it indicated that Chiang Kai-shek, quietly but thoroughly, was preparing an army which might some day try conclusions with Nippon's best. But, even more, the handling of the rebellion showed unmistakably that here-after Chiang would not hesitate to use his strength to achieve a strong, unified country. No longer could Japan count on profiting by the existence of a weak, disorganized, chaotic China. Chiang would not hesitate to deal with the next revolt as he had dealt with Fukien. Outlying Chinese provinces would be subject to Nanking authority in fact as well as in name. If China needed a strong man, he would not hesitate to play the part.

The implication, similarly, was not lost on the Chinese leaders in or out of Nanking. The crushing of Fukien was notice to Christian General Feng Yu-hsiang, to Model Governor Yen Hsi-shan in Shansi, to the governor of Hunan, and above all to the southern generals, that it was no longer wise to risk rebellion. China was on its way to national strength.

There were those who cried Fascism. But there was a sur-prising number of others who hailed the new order with delight. What mattered labels and theories, they asked. What China needed was a leader to eliminate the vestiges of feudalism, and, by ending the weaknesses and abuses which the country itself had been unable to shake off, to make of China a really modern, potent state.

The lesson was most apparent in the south. The southern politicians who had been loudest in their condemnation of Chiang Kai-shek, and who had persisted in their efforts to promote an anti-Nanking military movement, discreetly ceased their agitation or left for non-Chinese territory.

Chiang pressed the opportunity to make a deal with Chen Chi-tang, the Canton dictator and 'King under Southern Skies.' He promised him a monthly subsidy of about $200,000 to defray 'military expenses' in return for Chen's aid in clearing the Reds from Central China.

At the same time he assured the southerners that if they

behaved themselves he would not interfere with their state of semi-autonomy. He let them know that he would not, for example, press for the abolition of the Southwest Political Council and the Southwest Military Council, which functioned for the provinces of Kwangtung and Kwangsi.

He went farther, and promised to include the two provinces in the national reconstruction program to be carried out and financed by Nanking. Thus, having made one show of strength at comparatively slight cost, he could be reasonably certain that his measures to keep the peace thereafter would be effective.

He was now free to deal with the remaining threat to his régime.

CHAPTER XXVIII

RED CHINA—AND NEW LIFE

CHIANG took a quick look at the country and decided that the next thing to be done was to eliminate the Communists. Seven years before, when his government was in its infancy, the Communists were a problem. Today they were a potent force, a government, an actual state within the state.

To Chiang's way of thinking a China harboring Communist territories could no more resist Japan than a man with a bellyache could battle a tiger. A separatist movement in Canton could be dissolved by negotiation. A rebel general could be outmaneuvered, beaten on the field in a few quick battles, or bribed to go abroad. But the Communist areas which coalesced in Central China and established their own capital at Juikin in Kiangsi Province, could be neither tolerated, defeated with ease, nor assimilated.

For the Reds had their own notions of government, of economics, of social welfare. They were not Nanking's ideas. The Communists favored the nationalization of natural resources, the taking of land from the wealthy absentee owners and its division among the peasants, the ignoring of the family as a social unit in favor of the individual. They interpreted Sun Yat-sen's principles in a manner that seemed almost blasphemous to Chiang. According to them the old man was a good socialist, a sort of first cousin to Marx. They were contemptuous of diplomacy, disdainful of religion, and hardly respectful to machine-gun fire.

Campaign after campaign to eliminate them had ended in abject failure. Chiang's forces had chased the Communists without overtaking them, had encountered them only to desert. The Reds, harried at one place, turned up at another, their organization seemingly intact and their morale unimpaired. Wherever they moved they brought dangerous ideas, made disconcertingly many converts. Residents of town and countryside welcomed their arrival, gave them covert aid after they departed, received Nanking troops and ideology with obvious distrust and displeasure.

Chiang took stock of the situation. He hated the Communists and what they stood for with a great and overpowering hate. But he was no fool; he saw the source of their strength, the nature of their appeal, and the reason for their sturdy resistance. He made his plans accordingly.

Their strength was in their Cause. The Red fighters received no pay but fought because they believed in the Cause. Many, being ignorant, knew nothing of Communist principles when they joined the armies, and marched with the Reds for the food which was assured them, but none could remain impervious to the systematic Red education in the ranks.

The appeal of the Communists to the peasantry was in their program: reduced taxes, lower rent, abolition of corruption, division of land in some areas, liquidation of the gentry — in general the subordination of the interests of the landlords and money-lenders to those of the soil-tillers.

The Reds' military power lay in their method of operation and in the weakness of their enemies. The Communist armies moved swiftly, attacked only when the enemy was unprepared or numerically inferior. They dissolved in the face of a determined attack by Chiang's forces in superior numbers. They were prepared to become, at a moment's notice, simple workers or farm hands, and Nanking forces which sallied forth to meet an enemy found themselves confronted by peaceful farmers who knew nothing of Communist-bandits or soldiers. This was possible, of course, only because of the friendliness of the real peasants and their willingness to harbor the Reds.

The Nanking forces, on the other hand, were handicapped principally by division of strength and lack of co-ordination. Chiang's own forces, comparatively well-organized and directed, were frequently surprised and beaten; the effectiveness of the provincial forces was immeasurably less. Theoretically all the anti-Communist forces were under Chiang's orders; actually the troops operating against the Reds in Hunan, Fukien, Szechuan, and parts of Kiangsi Provinces were those of the provincial war-lords, obeying only their orders. Each army conducted its own campaign, and the Reds had little difficulty out-witting all of them.

Chiang decided to revise the entire program of anti-Communist activity. He would fight the Reds with an intelligent, comprehensive plan which, while it might prove slow and unspectacular, would inevitably end successfully. He would meet the enemy's Cause with his own Cause. He would oppose their program with his own program. And he would offset their military tactics with his own entirely new and superior strategy.

The Cause was the New Life Movement. The program was the People's Economic Reconstruction plan. The strategy was economic blockade of the Red areas.

The program had to wait for victory and capture of Red areas. The Cause was prepared beforehand. On March 11, 1934, Chiang inaugurated the New Life Movement at a mass meeting in Nanchang, capital of Kiangsi. Its purpose was to give the essentially bourgeois Kuomintang nationalists something to live by and crusade for.

The movement, Chiang announced, was to encourage the industrious and Spartan life, as well as to cultivate good habits of personal appearance and the observance of the traditional Chinese virtues.

The reason for foreigners' contempt of Chinese, Chiang said, was that the Chinese were physically weaker and their mode of living not as regular and clean. The purpose of New Life, he informed the nation, was to make every Chinese citizen a 'civilized' person. 'Before a man can love his country,' he proclaimed, 'he must first love himself.'

Chiang outlined eight principles of the movement, some of which were somewhat vague but all of which were impressive.

1. 'Regard yesterday as a period of death, today a period of life. Let us rid ourselves of old abuses, and build up a new nation.

2. 'Let us accept the heavy responsibilities of serving the nation.

3. 'Let us observe rules, have faith, honesty, and humility.

4. 'Let us keep our clothing, eating, living, and traveling habits simple, orderly, plain, and clean.

5. 'Face hardships willingly, strive for frugality.

6. 'Acquire adequate knowledge and have moral integrity as citizens.

7. 'Let our actions be courageous and rapid.

8. 'Let us act on our promises, or, better, act without promising.'

The aims of the movement were epitomized by four Chinese characters, Li, I, Lien, and Chieh, each of which represented an ancient Chinese virtue.

The ethical import of New Life was obviously too lofty a concept for the masses to grasp. But the admonitions to he agreed in return to subsidize the commanders and help pay their armies.

The result — the commands of the anti-Communist forces in Kiangsi, Fukien, and Kwangsi Provinces were unified. The movements of the troops were correlated. The generals met in the latter part of June, 1934. By July the campaign was under way. Towns previously held by the Reds in Hunan, Fukien, and Hupeh Provinces were evacuated. The government pushed its circle of blockhouses into Kiangsi Province, heart of Red China.

The Communist area was made a closed country. Nobody from the outside was allowed to go inside. No one from the Red area came out. Food supplies were halted, transportation cut off, trade stifled. The irregular circle around Red China grew smaller and smaller.

July 18 another conference of commanders was held, this time in Kiangsi. Chiang gave them three months to clean up the Reds, and made it plain that this time he would brook no failure.

By the end of July the Communists were already reduced to dire straits. On the outer fringes of the Red territory they were on the run. They resorted to guerilla warfare, but Chiang's troops made no sallies, took no chances of being trapped. They advanced slowly, after the careful extension of roads and the establishment of adequate defense lines. No longer were huge supplies of guns and ammunition falling into the hands of the Communists.

The Reds finally broke through the blockade on the western side, and a large body fled into Fukien Province, occupying a number of large towns in the process. Chiang's forces, moving swiftly along the newly constructed highways, pursued the Communists, finally halted their advance at a place called Shuiching, in the beginning of August, 1934.

The Nanking troops then recaptured several important

districts. The Reds fled toward western Fukien. Here in the south was the weakest point of Chiang's cordon. By the end of the month the Communist movement in northern Fukien had collapsed, and in September Chiang Kai-shek's own troops were making rapid advances on the Red strongholds in southwestern Fukien.

Meanwhile the government forces operating in southern Kiangsi took the city of Hsinkuo, and in October, following a battle at Linfeng, two thousand Communists surrendered, a really rare occurrence in spite of the almost continuous press reports of huge government captures during the preceding five years. Foreign press correspondents used to keep tally on the number of Communists reported killed in Nanking press releases. The number soon exceeded China's total population.

November 9 the city of Changting fell into the hands of Chiang's advancing forces, and the defeated Reds started moving to the northwest. The Generalissimo's forces concentrated at Hsinkuo and prepared for a last round-up.

As the Nanking troops entered the territory once held by the Communists, they were under strict orders to behave themselves, to win the villagers and peasants with kindness. Chiang realized the hold of the Communists on the farmers among whom they had inaugurated semi-Soviet régimes. He knew that the farmers in many cases were loyal to the Reds, were sorry to see them go, and were distrustful of the approaching Nanking troops.

Chiang instructed his men above all to pay for everything they needed. This was a cardinal principle which his officers were under orders to enforce strictly. The effect was pleasing. The peasants, desiring above all to be let alone, were surprised to learn that the newcomers were not like the soldiers they remembered from former days. Chiang's soldiers did not loot or pillage; they paid.

AFTER THE FINAL ROUT OF THE COMMUNISTS

C. W. H. Young, the first outside observer to enter the area, accurately described the reactions of the people. One seventy-three-year-old woman summed it up.

'When the Generalissimo's troops arrived,' she said, 'we thought they would be no different from those who came before them, but we were wrong. We thought they would molest us as the soldiers molested us in the days gone by. But they did not. Instead they are a well-behaved lot, and we have much to thank them for. We are glad to sell them our tea and eggs.'

The peasants sold tea for a copper a cup, eggs at a copper each, and were happy. 'They pay for everything they take from us,' another peasant reported in astonishment. 'They do not seize our belongings. They even help us with our farming, and they teach our children.'

Chiang organized what he termed a 'Special Movement Force,' a political-military organization to maintain discipline. Actually it was a secret police group, obviously based on the Soviet model, but apparently devoid of terrorism. Its duties were to carry out secret-service work, capture army deserters, enforce the economic blockade, search travelers, arrest suspects, see that the troops behaved themselves and did not molest the people, and organize and train the masses.

All divisional commanders and high civil officials were amenable to its authority. The members of the force were comparatively well educated, generally young graduates of military academies, and consisted of about twenty thousand men scattered through Kiangsi, Fukien, Anhwei, and Hunan Provinces. Their identity in most cases, of course, was secret.

It was this corps which made the blockade effective, cutting off supplies of oil, salt, food, clothing, and cotton from the Reds and preventing the exportation of tea and tobacco from Communist China. They were charged with keeping communications between the Reds and the outside world disrupted.

They also saw action of the romantic and dangerous sort. They frequently plunged into Communist territory, wearing civilian clothes and carrying Red insignia. Once behind the lines, they fomented disturbances, diverted the attention of the Red leaders while the Nanking troops advanced.

Once an area was occupied by the government troops, however, their job turned to peaceful pursuits. They directed mass education for adults, acted on complaints against officials, punished corruption, and waged a vigorous moral campaign.

Young reported that the force drove out prostitutes, beat gamblers, burned cards and mah-jong sets, and confiscated opium. The Special Movement Force did a good job of carrying out Chiang's economic reconstruction program, and did it for a monthly wage of $12 Chinese currency per person — $3.60 American money. Some expenses were allowed the members for secret-service work, but the amount was sharply limited, and the effectiveness of their work depended on their moral fervor.

So the campaign progressed. Finally, Chiang was ready for the final drive. He closed in on Juikin, which the Reds had established as their capital and which had become the seat of the only Soviet government outside Russia. The Reds were cornered. They fled. Chiang's forces entered Juikin November 10, and plunged after the Reds, who were fast on their way toward the borders of neighboring provinces.

If the cordon had been equally strong at all its points, the Reds would have been hemmed in and a vast, bloody battle would have occurred. But the Reds broke through at a weak point and started a long trek which was eventually to take them to the far northwest provinces of China in one of the longest and most dramatic marches of all history.

Chiang's purpose, however, had been accomplished. He had removed Red China as a territorial entity, for the time being at least, and had dislodged the Reds from a position where they were a constant military menace to his régime. He appointed Ho Chien, old-time war-lord and governor of Hunan Province, to command the pursuing forces, while he devoted himself to rural rehabilitation work in the reclaimed areas.

Neither Ho Chien nor his successors scored any brilliant triumphs, but they harried the Reds and kept them on the march until they reached China's Wild West. That the Communists were to settle down eventually in far Shensi Province, as cohesive a unit as they were in Kiangsi, and indirectly cause the kidnapping of Chiang Kai-shek, neither he nor anyone else could foresee.

Congratulations poured in on Chiang. He had, it could not be gainsaid, freed all Central China from Red dominance. But he was under no illusions as to the nature of his success. In a statement to the nation he frankly said that the success of the campaign had been seventy per cent due to political measures and thirty per cent the result of military force. For 'political' substitute 'economic'; the ratio was correct.

Mass support, he proclaimed, had given real strength to his cause. This was palpably nonsense. The masses in the Red areas were in general friendly to the Reds; those outside were hardly interested in the campaign. Millions never knew that it was under way.

Chiang said that if the people supported the government in its dealings with other internal and foreign problems with the same spirit as they did the Red campaign, success was assured. To a majority of his countrymen the phrases meant nothing. Those who understood the implication and noted that Japan still held Manchuria and Jehol smiled bitterly and said nothing. Only in the Chinese communities abroad was it safe to comment; there the press printed unkind editorials and orators vilified Chiang for fighting fellow-Chinese while the flag of the rising sun flew over Chinese territory.

As the year ended Chiang admitted that the Communists were threatening to penetrate Szechuan and Kweichow Provinces, but he expressed confidence that they would give the government no trouble. Trouble they gave, and plenty of it, but it was nevertheless true that the Reds were definitely on the run.

CHAPTER XXIX

CONQUEST BY COUNSEL

THE months that followed the crushing of the Fukien rebellion witnessed the paradox of Chiang striding toward dictatorship and at the same time effecting a *rapprochement* with those who decried dictatorship.

The accelerated trend toward one-man government during the year 1934 was largely due to the need of so many drastic changes that only one strong man with a single purpose could effect.

It was apparent that regardless of the military advantages or disadvantages involved, governmental centralization would have to come to China. Nanking's word was law only in the Yangtse Valley. Beyond it, local chieftains held titles of governor under Nanking appointment, paid lip service to Chiang Kai-shek and the National government, and did as they pleased. If China was ever to become a strong, modern nation, this aspect of feudalism would have to go.

To dislodge the feudal war-lords was difficult. The wise course to follow was to extend the influence of the central government into the outlying areas. Through improvement of communications facilities, standardization of finances, and above all through the fostering of a truly national spirit among the masses, the provinces would have to be brought into the fold, so that eventually the regional chieftains would become in fact what they were in name —

subordinates to Chiang and creatures of the Nanking government.

Several events worked toward this end. At the end of 1933 Chiang and his brother-in-law, T. V. Soong, had come to the parting of the ways. Soong, the Number 1 financial man of China, the man responsible for the support of Chiang's régime by the Chinese bankers and bourgeoisie, the Harvard-trained budget-balancer, stepped out.

There were wild stories about the split. Some said Soong had been bitten by the bug of ambition, and fancied himself a rival to Chiang. There were reports of a stormy session in Chiang's house in which the Generalissimo threatened the financier with imprisonment, and the financier threatened the Generalissimo with ruin. Probably no one but the two men actually knows what happened. But the conflict between their policies was apparent to well-informed observers, and when the split came it was not surprising.

Soong stood for financial orthodoxy, a balanced budget, and the reduction of military expenditures to a reasonable percentage of the nation's income. The exact ratio of military expenditures to the total budget was always in some doubt. Long before Washington thought of the idea, Nanking had adopted the principle of the 'ordinary' and 'extraordinary' budget. The ordinary budget, which showed receipts from customs duties and the usual taxes, revealed a military expenditure ranging from thirty-five to forty-two per cent. The extraordinary revenues, such as receipts from the opium monopoly and a number of other imposts not legally existent, were paid out for extraordinary purposes, chiefly arms and munitions which never appeared in the public reports of the Finance Ministry. The ratio of military to total costs was therefore never known. Most observers placed the figure around sixty per cent.

Whatever the figure was, Soong said it was too high.

Chiang retorted that under the circumstances there was nothing to do about the matter. Soong questioned the need of such a huge military establishment for Nanking, opposed the large subsidies to the provincial militarists. Chiang pointed out that to reduce the Nanking military program was to hamper the nation's true interests, making possible civil war and postponing forever the day of successful Chinese resistance against Japanese aggression. As to the subsidies to the provinces, he insisted, to discontinue or reduce them would merely invite anarchy.

Furthermore, Chiang wanted to push forward with other projects, civil in nature, but military in purpose — new highway networks, long-distance telephone lines, subsidized land, water, and aerial transportation services, huge engineering projects. All of these took money, but the money was not in the treasury. They had to be 'financed,' which meant increasing the national indebtedness. Soong was working for a progressive reduction of the nation's loans and the improvement of the government's credit. Chiang maintained that the 'national emergency' transcended all other considerations, insisted that the money must be provided.

Chiang was not and is not an economist. He has made himself an expert in many fields where he has had no training, but finances have always been his weak point. Vaguely, he desired inflation, but was not precisely sure how to accomplish it, nor what the results would be. Soong put his foot down; Chiang was obdurate. The inevitable showdown between the brothers-in-law came, and Soong had to go.

There was no great conflict, not even a Kuomintang factional fight. Soong resigned his post as Minister of Finance and later went off to Europe and the United States. In America he arranged for the wheat and cotton loans as an official Nanking representative, but actually he was completely out of the government, and Chiang was left as the financial as well as the political and military chief of the nation.

Knowing nothing of routine finance, he named another brother-in-law, Doctor H. H. Kung, to the Ministry. Kung, although not a financier by training or profession — he had spent most of his adult years as an educator — had acquired some banking connections, and had previously held the portfolio of Commerce and Industry. His wife was the eldest of the Soong girls, Ai-ling, often regarded as the family boss following the death of Mrs. Soong. George Sokolsky says that when the final quarrel came between Chiang and T. V. Soong, she sided with brother-in-law Chiang against brother T. V.

With the presumably compliant Kung in the finance post, Chiang felt himself free to proceed with his reconstruction program without having to worry about monetary orthodoxy and heterodoxy.

Then Young Marshal Chang Hsueh-liang, who had gone to Italy, came back to China at the beginning of 1934. Once Chiang had been entirely dependent on the Young Marshal's benevolence. The movement of the Manchurian troops south of the Great Wall, if it led indirectly to the Japanese coup, had certainly saved Chiang Kai-shek from possible defeat at the hands of the Feng-Yen coalition.

Now the former Manchurian war-lord was on Chiang's bounty. Chiang realized that his 'younger brother' had to be taken care of, as a matter of gratitude and common decency. But he also saw that the Young Marshal, despite his Manchurian misfortune, was full of ambition and energy, and might make an admirable right-hand man. Chiang sent him up to Hankow with the imposing title of Vice Commander-in-Chief of Bandit Suppression for the

Provinces of Hupeh, Honan, and Anhwei. He was charged with fighting Communists, but incidentally was given the Hankow area as his territory in the capacity of Chiang's deputy.

With the Young Marshal to Italy and back had gone his extraordinary adviser, W. H. Donald. Australian by birth, formerly a newspaperman by profession, Donald years before had become associated with Sun Yat-sen, saw the monarchy out and the republic in, gravitated to Peiping, and finally joined the service of Old Marshal Chang Tso-lin. 'Uncle' to the original revolutionists and 'Grandpa' to their successors, he was, despite his complete ignorance of the Chinese language, one of the outstanding Chinese revolutionary veterans. Chiang Kai-shek acquired him. It was one of the most important decisions in his life, and one of the wisest.

Donald had ideas, in addition to principles. Refusing the title of adviser, and scorning all titles, he became, with Madame Chiang, a powerful influence on the Generalissimo's policies. In the capacity of a mere friend, and speaking to Chiang through Mei-ling as interpreter, he speedily convinced the Generalissimo that what China's administration needed was not a process of compromise and evolution but a drastic overhauling.

He did what no one else had had the courage to do. He stood up and told Chiang what was the matter with his government and his country. He minced no words. There was graft everywhere, and chicanery and inefficiency. The army had to be made a strictly military machine, with old-fossil politicians speedily ejected. The same for the navy, and the air force. Personnel of every government department had to be talked to, sat on, kicked in the pants when necessary, and bucked up.

Back-stabbers had to be removed and replaced with men

whose loyalty was unquestioned. Foreign advisers and technicians had to be hired in greater numbers; they would be needed for some time to assure efficiency in the government services and honesty in administration. A rigid system of control and audit would have to be instituted.

Finally, supporting the entire program, the Generalissimo himself would have to get out into the country, travel about, make himself known to officials and the public. The purpose was two-fold, to let the regional chiefs know that their work was being constantly checked, and to stimulate national patriotism among the masses.

Such a plan would necessarily center responsibility in one man. But what China needed, Donald insisted, was just such centralization of authority. Donald did not talk Chiang into dictatorship, nor did he plead for it. He merely concentrated attention on deficiencies and abuses, indicated how they had to be remedied.

Chiang Kai-shek had come to the same conclusion, was impressed by the foreigner's arguments. Madame Chiang was strongly in favor. The three of them settled down to the long, tedious task of carrying out the program.

There was considerable evidence that others in the country also felt that Chiang should play such a part. As early as February 23, twenty provincial and municipal Kuomintang headquarters telegraphed Nanking urging the appointment of Chiang as president of the party, a post which had been vacant since the death of Sun Yat-sen.

The party and the nation were stagnating, these petitions said. It was time for a new deal. They urged the complete overhauling of the party organization, the concentration of authority, and the selection of Chiang to succeed Sun Yat-sen.

Chiang gently reproved the petitioners. He denied, for the benefit of his enemies, that he was planning a dictator-

ship. He was opposed to dictatorship, he insisted. The
primary duty of Kuomintang patriots was to obey the
party constitution, and, he declared with emphasis, the
party constitution could not be changed at the will of a
minority.

'I have repeatedly pointed out,' he said, 'that the success of the Chinese revolution does not necessarily depend
on any one system or form of government. Italy and
Germany, it is true, accomplished their revolution by dictatorship, but if on the strength of this China were to
adopt a dictatorship, would the result be more successful
than our former adoption of the Russian committee form
of government? We adopted the Russian system, and
today our revolution is not yet realized. Why? Because
success is dependent on people and not on system or forms.
Revolution begins with the heart.'

But at the same time he called to account those who
would revert to decentralization. Upon the enthronement
of Mr. Henry Pu Yi as Emperor of Manchukuo in March,
1934, the Southwest Political Council in Canton planned
to issue a manifesto of denunciation; Chiang had Wang
Ching-wei, again back at Nanking as premier, warn the
southerners not to issue any manifesto to foreign powers.

Such action, he pointed out, would be a sign of Chinese
disunity. Nanking, too, was full of contempt for the new
puppet Emperor and his empire, but Nanking would do
the denouncing. The warning was heeded. Canton kept
quiet and Nanking issued its own pronouncement of disgust.

Chiang then set out to improve relations between
Nanking and the semi-independent régimes in Kwangtung
and Kwangsi Provinces. The word 'semi-independent'
understated the case. Both provinces were actually as
independent of Chiang as Manchukuo. They maintained
their own armies, navies, and air forces, assessed and col-

lected taxes, and carried out their own economic development projects without reference to or assistance from the national government. Customs collections to a certain extent were remitted to the national treasury, but only at the price of subsidies from Nanking to approximate the loss entailed by the remittances.

Chen Chi-tang, the King under Southern Skies, had made himself the dictator of Kwangtung Province by his willingness to let well-known political leaders occupy high positions and go through the motions of governing. His was the real power and his the financial benefit. He was intelligent enough to steer clear of political entanglements with discontented elements elsewhere in China. He was far more interested in Canton and Kwangtung than he was in China.

Li Tsung-jen and Pai Chung-hsi held forth in Kwangsi. Kwangsi was more remote, and its mountain fastnesses were more easily defended. As a result Li and Pai could afford to be more truculent than Chen Chi-tang in easily accessible Canton. On the other hand, the province was poor, and they had more to be truculent about. Bitterly anti-Chiang, they were for the moment pushing economic development of Kwangsi, inaugurating universal education, building highways, and enforcing universal conscription, so that in addition to their regular army they had a citizens' militia consisting of virtually the entire able-bodied male population of Kwangsi.

Chiang decided that Kwangtung presented the best prospects of *rapprochement*, and directed his efforts at Canton. To carry out the task he prevailed on the eminent Wang Chung-hui, China's justice on the World Court at the Hague, to act as go-between. Wang was a veteran revolutionary, a party elder, and a man unassociated with any faction.

Chiang sent him to Canton with a message of peace. 'Let us settle our differences by discussion' was its essence. The mission was received cordially. Even Hu Han-min, the old irreconcilable, said he was willing to co-operate with all parties for the sake of national unity.

October 21 the eminent envoy returned to Shanghai and reported that all the southern leaders were unanimously in favor of sinking their personal feelings in favor of national unity.

It was clear, however, that harmony was not to be so easily accomplished, that there would have to be much bargaining before the southern leaders were willing to come to a real understanding with Chiang Kai-shek.

Hu Han-min, for example, despite his declarations of friendliness, said he couldn't throw his policies to the winds 'for the sake of personal friendship.' He expressed the hope that Chiang would entirely change 'his present erroneous domestic and foreign policies.'

Getting down to cases, Hu said that 'those in control at Nanking have been selling the country through their policy of non-resistance.' He also had pointed remarks to make about the 'régime of terrorism through the organization known as the Blue Shirts,' and asserted bluntly that the unification of China by armed force and suppression was bound to fail.

It was Chiang's job to convince the southerners that he was not pledged to terror and force. Chiang's representatives argued the case eloquently. As a result, the southerners agreed to send delegates to the fifth plenary session of the C.E.C. which opened at Nanking December 10.

Hu Han-min's principal objections were directed against the proposal to give China's President, under the constitutional régime, vast emergency powers. Chiang's emissaries never succeeded in convincing Hu that Chiang had not set his heart on becoming Dictator-President, but the other Cantonese politicians drew closer to Nanking, and even the aloof Kwangsi clique sent a couple of delegates to the C.E.C. session.

At the meeting it was decided to hold a party congress November 12, 1935, and to have the congress fix the date of the National People's Congress. The latter was to approve the permanent constitution and inaugurate representative democracy for China, the final stage of government outlined by Sun Yat-sen.

The December, 1934, session of the C.E.C. adopted several important principles which enhanced the authority of the central government and to which the local representatives agreed. All economic matters, it was decided, would hereafter be controlled by the central government. Nanking would control the currency, and all local mints would have to close. Banks established by the regional governments were required to comply with Nanking regulations for issuance of banknotes.

Taxes of a national character, it was also decided, would be collected by Nanking, and budgets of the regional governments would have to be approved by the central government. On the other hand, taxes of a local character might be retained by the local units, and if deficits occurred the regional governments could look to Nanking for aid.

Nanking then allayed distrust of the provincial politicians by agreeing that officials would be nominated by provincial chairmen or municipal mayors.

The terms seemed to satisfy everyone, and the cause of national unity advanced noticeably. The Southwest Political Council, meeting at Canton, even passed a resolution to 'support and obey the central government'; it was proposed by Kwangtung's Chen Chi-tang and Kwangsi's Li Tsung-jen, and passed by unanimous vote! Just how much it meant was, of course, open to question, but the fact that it was considered at all was significant enough.

The latter part of the year also saw Chiang and Mei-ling following Donald's advice to tour the country, letting themselves be seen and known. Starting with the Young Marshal's headquarters at Hankow, they toured Hupeh and Honan Provinces, went up to Sian, where two years later Chiang was to be kidnapped, proceeded to Lanchow and the frontier province of Ninghsia, and returned to Peiping. From the old capital they went to Kalgan, where they were banqueted by Mongol Prince Teh, lineal descendant of Genghis Khan, cut across to Yen Hsi-shan's stronghold of Taiyuanfu, and conferred there with the Model Governor. Everywhere they were received with the greatest popular enthusiasm. The propaganda effect of the tour, as Donald had foreseen, was tremendous.

Chiang and Mei-ling returned to Nanchang after a forty-day tour. The Generalissimo issued a statement. He praised the highway and health work in the various provinces. He deplored the lack of educational reforms, and pointed out that afforestation and river conservation were being neglected, thus inviting a continuance of alternate flood and drought. There was no co-ordination of effort among the regional authorities.

His point was well taken, and it was listened to with respect by thousands who had heretofore regarded the question of regional and national administration as a purely political matter, of interest only to politicians.

The risk which the new policy involved, however, was indicated by an attempt to bomb the train in which the Chiang party was traveling. The circumstances were never confirmed by official sources, and the details are not known to this day. But it was learned that a bomb exploded in a coach occupied by bodyguards and troops accompanying Chiang between Tatung, Chahar Province, and Kwei-hua, capital of Suiyuan. A Japanese report said that two persons were actually killed and four wounded, but again confirmation was lacking.

At any rate, the bomb, hurled into the coach when the train reached a minor station, narrowly missed killing Chiang himself. With him at the time were Mei-ling, Donald, the Governor of Suiyuan Province, and a number of high North China officials.

Two suspects were arrested. Nothing was heard of them afterward, and they were presumably dispatched by the provincial authorities. The occurrence illustrated the perils of being a Strong Man, but it did not deter Chiang from his program, nor did it alter his practice of visiting the far-flung sections of his country.

CHAPTER XXX

NORTH CHINA CHESS GAME

THE Japanese apparently decided that if they were going to do any more pushing in China, it would be a good idea to get the pushing done before Chiang Kai-shek and his forces recovered from the effects of the anti-Communist campaign. It wasn't long before they were active in Chahar Province, next-door neighbor to Hopei.

Shortly after the year 1935 got under way, the Japanese army in Manchuria warned Chiang Kai-shek that unless Governor Sung Cheh-yuan withdrew his forces from two districts along the Chahar-Jehol border, the Japanese would drive them out.

The Japanese didn't like Sung Cheh-yuan anyway. His troops had fought hard and well against them in the battle of the Great Wall, and he had become somewhat of a Chinese patriot. High-school and university students all over China thrilled to the tale of Sung's resistance and sent his army 'comforts' of cigarettes, chocolate, mittens, and cash. Sung, the Japanese had decided, was too thoroughly anti-Japanese, a condition which they regarded as unnatural.

It pleased them not at all, then, to have his troops stationed along the Chahar border, adjoining the Jehol area which they had only recently added to the territory of Manchukuo.

In warning Chiang to pull Sung Cheh-yuan out of the border area, they said the Chinese troops had entered the

Tatan district near Kuyuan. Sung's forces had taken over the territory and, the Japanese said, 'had disrupted local administration.'

Chiang's foreign office in Nanking denied that there were any provincial troops in the disputed area; there were only a few militia. At any rate, Nanking replied, the territory in question was part of the Kuyuan district, and Kuyuan was in Chahar, and Chahar was Chinese territory, so what were the Japanese complaining about?

The Japanese retorted that Kuyuan was in Jehol. When they failed to get what they called satisfaction, they proceeded to prove that Kuyuan was Manchukuoan territory by taking it.

Five Japanese airplanes, equipped with bomb racks and full cargoes of bombs, went sailing over the Great Wall at Tushihkow. Twenty Japanese armored cars thundered along the plain, and the Japanese artillery laid down the most businesslike barrage. Three thousand Japanese and Manchukuoan troops poured across the country, with the armored cars in support, and began a general offensive against the Chinese troops.

Incidentally, the Japanese had a ready reason for the sudden onslaught. They said that the Chinese had started the trouble, by attacking the Japanese troops who had been dispatched to maintain their line at the Great Wall. No one except the Japanese ever heard of the attack.

The drive, which occupied the day of January 23, ended the same day. The following morning the Japanese announced that, since an aerial survey showed that the Chinese troops had retreated from the disputed area, 'no further clash will take place.'

The considerate Japanese not only did all the fighting. They did all the announcing as well. The Chinese were strangely silent. On February 3 the Japanese announced that a conference at Tatan had resulted in an agreement: the Japanese agreed to withdraw from the area in question, and Sung Cheh-yuan's army agreed not to trespass among the villages east of the Great Wall.

This was the first indication that there had been a conference at Tatan, and that an agreement had resulted from it. Chiang's foreign office at Nanking fumed, but was helpless. Sung Cheh-yuan, nominally subordinate to Nanking, had been forced into an accord with the Japanese under penalty of being driven entirely out of Chahar Province. He chose to comply rather than to depend on diplomatic protests from Nanking. Chiang Kai-shek certainly wasn't ready to go to war with Japan over the matter.

The terms of the agreement were never ratified by Nanking, and a few years later the Chinese government sought to repudiate it and all similar agreements made by foreigners with local military authorities.

In the meantime, the Japanese had exacted a pledge from Sung Cheh-yuan not to send his troops into the disputed Chahar area. Obviously, some time later the Japanese might find it necessary to invade the area again 'to preserve order' or for some other reason. But Sung's troops would still be effectively barred.

This procedure worked so well that the Japanese decided to try it out on a larger scale in a more important area. In Hopei Province there was a Chinese administration for which Japan had little taste. The military power was in the hands of the Northeastern Army, the Young Marshal's troops from Manchukuo. True, the Young Marshal was no longer in the neighborhood, but the commanding officers were his subordinates and the soldiers were the same Manchurians. Having been driven from their homeland by the Japanese coup which resulted in the establishment of Manchukuo, none of them bore any great love for Japan.

A series of clashes, most of them minor, occurred between the Japanese and Chinese troops. The Japanese proceeded to bring increasing pressure to bear upon the Chinese to put all of North China under Tokyo's influence, if not to convert it into another Manchukuo.

Chiang Kai-shek resisted the pressure with every possible resource. The Kwantung army had placed its trust in the Number 1 Japanese secret-service agent, Major-General Kenji Doihara, often called 'the Lawrence of Manchuria.' He it was who was credited with every intrigue in North China and Manchuria for the past twenty years. He was believed to be the man who brought Henry Pu Yi, the former boy emperor of China, from Tientsin to Mukden and put him on the throne of Manchukuo.

Doihara, an expert in blustering and bribing, told the Japanese army people that it was a 'set-up.' He would have the five North China provinces of Hopei, Chahar, Shantung, Shansi, and Suiyuan detached from Nanking in no time. They would declare 'autonomy' or independence, and proceed to join hands with Manchukuo.

Chiang Kai-shek realized what was in the wind. He knew the game Doihara was playing, knew that the wily Japanese secret-service man was poisoning the minds of the North China governors and generals against the Chiang régime. He was aware that Doihara was promising them the protection of Japanese guns and plenty of cash.

Chiang also knew that if the worst came to the worst and the Japanese army marched into North China and tore the five provinces from his grasp, he would probably be unable to do a thing about it. The Japanese army was in full fighting trim, ready for new conquests, and supported by the money and resources of a country which, indifferent at first, had been aroused to patriotic frenzy by the successful seizure of Manchuria and Jehol.

To hurl his own forces at the Japanese juggernaut, he realized, would not only be suicidal from his own standpoint but would result in the complete collapse of all authority in China. The Chinese people might rally to a campaign of resistance, but all the spirit in the world would not avail against trained regiments, barking guns, and bomb-dropping airplanes.

But he believed that the Japanese would not strike. He analyzed the situation and concluded that Japan preferred not to start a new military campaign but would try to detach North China by diplomatic means, with Doihara as the sole tool.

He did not discount Doihara's ability, and he realized that the man was able to exert tremendous pressure on the none too loyal North China militarists. But Chiang guessed that if Doihara was rebuffed he would stay rebuffed, and that no war would result.

Chiang further decided that some concessions would have to be made to the Japanese in North China. Two reasons prompted the decision. In the first place, 'incidents' were bound to result from the juxtaposition of a Chinese military force which was bitterly anti-Japanese and the Japanese garrisons of North China and near-by Manchukuo. Such incidents might conceivably result in a serious situation which would bring on actual war.

In the second place, the installation of a North China régime conciliatory to Japan would forestall Doihara's plans. If Chiang could satisfy the responsible Japanese officials that North China would make no trouble for them, he might be able to leave Doihara and his North China independence scheme high, dry, and helpless.

To carry out such a program, obviously, was dangerous from a domestic point of view. People were too ready to call him traitor. Students were likely to protest actively and start, in the name of patriotism, demonstrations which would bring the entire government tumbling and give the Japanese additional excuse for intervention in the rôle of 'protectors of East Asia.'

Chiang guessed right. Doihara had the confidence of the Kwantung army, but he was pulling a long bluff. The responsible Japanese officials, although eager for a friendly régime in North China, were not backing any move to snatch North China from Nanking.

Chiang Kai-shek played his hand carefully. He bolstered the North China governors and generals. He let them know that he was not letting any local officials handle the issue with Japan this time. If Japanese pressure became too great he was prepared to yield slightly, but only when he became convinced that resistance would bring conflict.

Meanwhile, he realized that the presence of the Young Marshal's former army in the Tientsin-Peiping area was a genuine thorn in the side of the Japanese. He forced the resignation of the Young Marshal's chief henchman as governor of Hopei Province, and sent the troops to far-off Kansu Province, in China's northwest. Sung Cheh-yuan was another gentleman who made the Japanese see red. Chiang removed him as governor of Chahar Province.

He then abolished the Peiping branch of the National Military Council, which had not functioned since the end of the Manchurian campaign and which was directed by the Minister of War himself. The Peiping Political Council was the next to go. Although presided over by men believed friendly to Japan, the Japanese disliked the Council's activities, and it was dissolved.

On the other hand, when so-called 'autonomists' staged demonstrations in Tientsin and other parts of Hopei Province, Chiang realized that the demonstrators were merely coolies paid by the Japanese to carry banners demanding independence from Nanking. He gave the word to the local Chinese authorities and the demonstrators were suppressed without difficulty. Police chased most of them into alleyways, tossed the rest in jail.

Doihara tried hard to confront Chiang with a *fait accompli*, and for weeks there were rumors of the imminent formation of an 'Autonomous North China Council' comprising the five provinces. Finally, when he thought that everything was going his way, and that the North China leaders were actually ready to declare independence of Nanking, Doihara let it be known that the establishment of the Council would soon be proclaimed.

The stipulated date came, a hitch developed, and a postponement was announced. Doihara again rushed around, saw all the military chieftains of the five provinces, shook his fist in their faces, pounded tables, and shouted that the Japanese army would blast them out of their jobs if they were not in Peiping on the appointed day.

Chiang decided that the zero hour was at hand. He summoned the Japanese Ambassador at Nanking, told him what was afoot in the north, and taxed him squarely with responsibility for what would be an undoubted act of hostility toward China. What, Chiang inquired, did the Ambassador have to say?

Ambassador Ariyoshi replied that Japan was sponsoring no autonomy movement in the north, that if what Chiang said was true, Doihara was acting entirely without authority.

That was all Chiang wanted to know. He telegraphed the northern commanders to stand pat, and assured them that there would be no consequences such as Doihara had promised.

They stood pat. One governor suddenly entered a hospital, where it was announced that he was suffering from 'stove-fume poisoning.' Another went off to the country to 'visit his sick mother,' and under no circumstances could he leave her to attend the meeting in Peiping. Old Yen Hsi-shan in Shansi was detained by urgent business. The Number 1 man of Shantung took a train trip into the interior. All of the others developed similar errands which prevented their attendance. Doihara sat in Peiping and bellowed with rage.

Not long afterward Chiang demanded that Doihara be withdrawn from China. He insisted that the man was a public nuisance. If Japan wanted China to be conciliatory, he said, Japan must play the game. The Japanese Ambassador, genuinely friendly to China, agreed, and Doihara was pulled out of North China, assigned to routine work at Mukden, and eventually brought back to an obscure position in Japan. As an intriguer his great days were seemingly over.

The Japanese, on the other hand, proceeded to run roughshod over North China to an extent which Chiang had not counted upon. They objected to the man he had installed as Governor of Hopei, announced that they now had no objection to the very man they had ousted from the governorship of Chahar, Sung Cheh-yuan.

Apparently Sung had come to an understanding with the Japanese. There was nothing to do but name him governor. The Japanese quickly increased their garrison in North China to nearly eight thousand men, constructed military airdromes at Tientsin and near-by points, built barracks for their troops at many stations along the railway to Manchuria, and prepared to stay there, regardless of China's protests.

Sung became not only governor but chairman of the Hopei-Chahar Political Council, which was set up to satisfy the Japanese demand for a liaison body in the two provinces.

Chiang was forced to look the other way while the local authorities dissolved the local Kuomintang branches in Hopei and Chahar Provinces. These Kuomintang locals had been bitterly anti-Japanese, and were accused by the Japanese of fomenting disorders.

The Japanese aim was to conduct negotiations with the Hopei-Chahar Council — negotiations in which Nanking might be unwilling for reasons of face to participate. The Japanese sought, for example, recognition of Manchukuo, which Nanking could not grant without signing its own death warrant. Another objective was Sino-Japanese economic co-operation.

Economic co-operation they got, recognition they did not. In general, the Council failed to prove the tractable organization that Japan expected, but at the same time it bowed to Japan far more than the patriots could tolerate. Student demonstrations against the Council broke out again and again; the Japanese accused the body of being too pro-Nanking, Nanking believed it too pro-Japanese, and altogether nobody had the slightest use for it.

CHAPTER XXXI

THE FASCIST BOGEY

CHIANG, meanwhile, was strengthening his régime elsewhere as best he could. For some time his government had been trying to get the major powers to raise their legations to the rank of embassies. It was a matter of prestige, giving China the status of a major power. Only Soviet Russia had complied, and the Soviet wasn't quite respectable, diplomatically speaking.

Italy had been taking special pains to gain China's favor. Plenty of Chinese leaders looked kindly at Fascism, and Italy wanted to sell China airplanes. The major powers had an agreement that none would establish an embassy without the consent of the others. Chiang played Italy as the best bet to break the powers' united front.

It worked. Italy had little love for the other powers, and agreed to raise her legation to the rank of an embassy without consulting the others. March 11 the deed was done. The united front not only cracked, it crumbled. Eager to convince China of their everlasting good will, the remaining powers engaged in a most undignified scramble to be the first to follow Italy.

Japan, strangely enough, beat the rest. Then within a few hours of each other came Great Britain, the United States, and Germany. Chiang let it be known that he had enough embassies — China couldn't afford to maintain too many reciprocal embassies in foreign countries.

He then settled down in Kweichow Province for a short time, and drove off the Communists who had attempted to enter there after fleeing from Kiangsi. It was a short campaign. The Reds weren't disposed to battle, they were looking for a haven, and they kept on marching.

Kweichow was another one of the provinces which had nominally paid allegiance to Nanking but was actually more than semi-independent. The Communist invasion which the local militarists were unable to handle gave Chiang a good excuse to extend the influence of the Nanking government into that area.

When Chiang himself came into the province, the provincial leaders and local bigwigs staged a tremendous welcome for him. Chiang replied by denouncing the whole lot of them for corruption and misgovernment. It was true. The province had been bled badly by rascally officials and the local gentry. He immediately began reorganizing the provincial administration. He visited all the outlying districts by airplane, appraised their situation, and extended his reforms. By the time he left, Kweichow was very much part of the national government, and Chiang's own appointees were in charge of the administration.

Chiang went on to Szechuan. There also the Communists were penetrating. The campaign was longer drawn-out than it had been in Kweichow, and the fighting more severe. But Chiang's troops probably never came in direct contact with the main body of Communist troops. His forces fought only stray units, which they harassed from the air as well as on the ground.

The governor of Szechuan was seemingly amenable to the Chiang reform program. He had just driven his uncle out of the province and was glad to have some backing from Chiang to avert an unwelcome return of the old man.

Szechuan was probably the worst-governed province in

China. Taxes had been collected from the suffering peasants as much as twenty years in advance. Years of oppression and misgovernment and the ravages of civil war had made the people almost desperate. Their condition accounted in part for the progress made by the Communists through the province, and also explained the presence of numerous bands of actual bandits.

Chiang announced that official corruption must end, that interference of military men in political affairs must halt. No military man, he announced, might serve as a local magistrate, nor might he interfere in the administration of law cases. He prohibited business enterprises operated by military officials in competition with private enterprise, and called a halt to extortion of taxes.

He was able to make his drastic reform program effective, despite the magnitude of the task. The opium evil was the most serious problem. The poppy had supported armies for ages. Chiang realized that the evil could not be eradicated in a few days. He knew that thousands of addicts could not be cured immediately, saw that the mere banning of opium would not solve the problem. He inaugurated a control scheme under provincial administration with Nanking supervision, and gave strict orders for the execution of a program of gradual suppression.

A foreign resident of the area noted the change that had occurred in Chiang in recent years, as evidenced by his activity in Szechuan.

'At one time he seemed not far different from any other militarist, seeking his own ascendancy by fair means or foul, enriching his relatives and friends, merging himself with the corrupt surroundings in which he found himself. But owing to the critical times and partly no doubt to his own innate greatness of character, Chiang Kai-shek has come out of his long ordeal a different man. He has been

made modest and humble by the task ahead of him.'
It was a fair appraisal.

Unfortunately, the reforms didn't stick. When Chiang
finished his Communist campaign and withdrew his troops,
much of his program went with them. Enough of it remained, however, to afford some evidence of his visit.
And the influence of the Nanking government over the
Szechuan provincial chiefs had, without a doubt, been
strengthened.

Friction with the Japanese, meanwhile, broke out in an
unexpected quarter. On May 4, 1935, at Shanghai, a
magazine called the *New Life Weekly* published an article
dealing with the emperors of the world. Remarks about
the Japanese Emperor drew a prompt protest from the
Japanese. The periodical was banned by the Chinese
authorities. The editor and author of the article were
ordered arrested. The publisher was tried and sentenced to
fourteen months in prison. After much agitation by the
Japanese at Shanghai, the incident was settled the following July with profuse apologies and the punishment of all
those deemed responsible.

The incident gave the Chinese authorities a bad case of
nerves, and thereafter they leaned over backward to avoid
giving offense to the Japanese. Chiang Kai-shek issued a
manifesto against anti-foreignism in speech and writing.
Censorship became even more severe than before, punishment of radical agitators even more harsh.

But resentment also broke out more fiercely. At a plenary session of the C.E.C. in November at Nanking, an
obscure reporter shot and wounded Wang Ching-wei.
Rightly or wrongly, Wang had been regarded as conciliatory to the Japanese.

Wang straightway resigned as President of the Executive
Yuan. Chiang Kai-shek was named to replace him. As a

result, Chiang's power expanded to a greater extent than ever before in his career. The C.E.C. named Wang Ching-wei chairman of the Central Political Council and Chiang Kai-shek vice-chairman — but Wang was wounded, out of action, and Chiang accordingly wielded the real power. Hu Han-min was named chairman of the C.E.C. standing committee, in a gesture of friendliness to the veteran dissenter, and Chiang was chosen vice-chairman — but Hu remained sulking in Europe, and here also Chiang wielded genuine power.

He held, in short, the three most powerful executive positions in the government. And he still headed the Military Affairs Commission, the Number 1 military post. Lin Sen was reappointed to the figurehead presidency of the government.

Chiang made a ringing speech to the nation. Despite pressure from extremist elements, he announced, he would continue to follow a moderate foreign policy until he felt the nation could afford to take a stronger stand. It was the only thing, he emphasized, that the nation could do.

'So far as I am concerned, I shall not evade my responsibility,' he informed the nation. 'We shall not forsake peace until there is no hope of peace. We shall not talk lightly of sacrifice until we are driven to the last extremity which makes sacrifice inevitable. The sacrifice of an individual is insignificant, but the sacrifice of a nation is a mighty thing. For the life of an individual is finite, while the life of a nation is eternal.'

The pronouncement, in general, struck the Chinese as good common sense. The Japanese termed it 'most statesmanlike.'

He still had to deal with Canton's suspicion that he was planning a military conquest of the two southern provinces, as well as a personal dictatorship. He invited his old enemies Feng and Yen to come to Nanking, presumably to convince themselves that there was no dictatorship. To the surprise of everyone, both came. Whether or not they were convinced they did not say, but both were apparently more kindly disposed toward Chiang and his régime than at any time in the past.

Further to still the fear of dictatorship, Chiang again affirmed his recognition of the southern branches of the C.E.C. and the political council.

But his increase of power in the party and government was extremely real, and if it did not represent dictatorship, the Cantonese could not see much difference.

But some showed no fear of the word and said that what China required was, precisely, a dictator. A veteran Kuomintang member and close associate of Sun Yat-sen for years openly declared that China needed a strong man like Mussolini or — this was in 1935 — the Emperor of Ethiopia. What the speaker had to say later about the example of the Lion of Judah has not been revealed.

But Chiang himself decried dictatorship, and the Kuomintang Congress at the end of the year rejected a resolution to reform the party along Fascist lines, by making the C.E.C. merely an advisory council and elevating the president of the party to full control.

But the party had had no president since the death of Sun Yat-sen, and it was agreed to let the organization remain unchanged. Chiang himself sought no presidency. He held all the power he wanted or was likely to require.

CHAPTER XXXII

THE SOUTH REVOLTS

CHIANG hoped for quiet, to consolidate his internal position and press forward his program of strengthening the nation's military forces. By February, 1936, a foreign military expert who was in a position to know said that China's air force was already equal to that of Japan. Millions of dollars had been spent in the previous few years on the latest and most powerful fighting planes, most of them purchased in the United States. Japan probably was quantitatively superior in the air, but in armament and performance, the expert said, her force was likely to prove no match for China's.

But the army itself still needed years of training and millions of dollars' worth of equipment and supplies before it could hope to compete with Japan's highly mechanized legions. The number of Chiang's German military advisers increased to more than one hundred, stationed at Nanking, Loyang, and Nanchang, the military centers of the nation.

The anti-Communist campaign had not, as some foreign observers seemed to think, served as a practice war for Chiang's troops. As he himself said, the campaign against the Reds was more political and economic than military, and the military phases presented conditions far different from what the Chinese troops were likely to meet in fighting the hypothetical enemy, Japan.

The Japanese, meanwhile, had continued their push into Chinese territory. Toward the end of 1935 they had done what might have been expected. They sent Mongol cavalrymen into the six North Chahar districts adjoining Jehol, the scene of the previous dispute and the one-day war.

The cavalrymen, directed and financed by the Japanese, occupied and assumed control of the entire area. The Chinese provincial troops, bound by the Tatan agreement wrung from Sung Cheh-yuan when he was governor of Chahar Province, were barred from the area, and had to stand by helplessly while the Japanese-instigated Mongols virtually annexed the territory for Manchukuo.

Then in January, 1936, the Japanese-sponsored Mongol raiders seized Kalgan itself, capital of Chahar and the central section of the Peiping–Suiyuan railway. Thus the passage between Kalgan in China and Ulan Bator in Soviet-controlled Outer Mongolia swung to Japanese control. The leader of the Mongols, an opportunist tribesman named Jodpajak, was made hereditary ruler of the Chahar 'league of Mongols,' and his forces were encouraged to strike at five districts in eastern Suiyuan.

Chiang could do nothing in the Chahar situation except protest. The area which the Japanese claimed for Manchukuo was in dispute. It had originally been part of independent Mongolia, anyway, and the Chinese claim had merely been one of possession by virtue of encroachment. Furthermore, the Japanese had Sung Cheh-yuan's assent to the Tatan agreement, and Chiang could not repudiate the agreement without admitting that Sung, then and now, was independent of Nanking's authority.

The Mongol investiture of Kalgan was eventually lifted, but the Japanese continued to keep a 'military mission' at the city, and the area which it commanded was no longer to be considered purely Chinese territory.

Chiang during this time was trying to strike a bargain with Hu Han-min. With all of Hu's obstinate opposition to

Chiang's plans, Chiang still wanted him in his government. Hu carried an enormous amount of prestige, and despite his constant quarrels with one and another of the Kuomintang leaders was held in considerable awe by reason of his early close association with Sun Yat-sen.

Chiang wanted to compose every section of the nation, and was ready to make large concessions to bring Hu back into the Nanking camp. Some believed Chiang was ready to give up the presidency of the Executive Yuan, equivalent to the post of Premier, in favor of Hu. But Hu knew that Chiang held real power, and would continue to hold it even if he surrendered the premiership. Hu would be nobody's puppet. He demanded the right to reform government policies drastically. Besides, remembering his detention at Nanking five years before, he placed no confidence in Chiang's guarantee of safety. He demanded that two divisions of Canton troops be brought to Nanking to protect him.

Hu also had some pointed remarks on dictatorship. There was much to substantiate his contentions. Despite Chiang's deprecations of efforts to elect him supreme Kuomintang leader, and despite the rejection of the proposal to make the C.E.C. a purely advisory body, the Kuomintang was fast moving toward more rigid control.

In March, 1936, occurred a change of the greatest importance to the nation which went almost unnoticed by the Chinese people and was entirely overlooked by foreign observers. The Kuomintang was re-formed on the Italian Fascist pattern. The committee system which had prevailed since Canton days in the organization of municipal, district, and provincial Kuomintang offices was discarded, and a system of special commissionerships was inaugurated March 2. On that date all executive committees and supervisory committees in the local Kuomintang branches, which had insured a degree of democracy in party affairs, came to an end. Simultaneously special commissioners for each branch assumed office. The commissioners were appointed by Nanking.

For political reasons, the committee system was maintained at the central party headquarters in Nanking. To have replaced a committee by one man there would have aroused too much attention and would undoubtedly have stirred opposition. Newspapers were instructed not to 'play up' the change in the local branches, and the reorganization went almost unnoticed.

Party members explained, to those who had doubts, that the committee system had served to encourage internal strife. Chiang described the Kuomintang as 'a spiritless skeleton,' and many agreed with him that the condition was due to the spreading of responsibility through the committee system.

There were any number of leaders who were ready even then to elect Chiang as President of the Kuomintang, making him the successor to Sun Yat-sen, but more moderate elements counseled delay. The reason was that the elevation of Chiang at that time would undoubtedly have resulted in hot opposition from Wang Ching-wei and Hu Han-min. Either of them would have regarded himself as having a far better claim than Chiang to be Sun's successor, and Chiang at the time was trying to keep both gentlemen pacified.

The negotiations with Hu, however, were interrupted by the outbreak of the southwestern revolt. Early in June, 1936, to the amazement of everyone, the military leaders of the southern provinces, Chen Chi-tang of Kwangtung and Li Tsung-jen and Pai Chung-hsi of Kwangsi, called upon Chiang Kai-shek to mobilize the military forces of the nation against Japan.

Not getting what they thought was a satisfactory reply, the Kwangsi leaders sent the vanguard of their troops into Hunan Province, and the Kwangtung troops prepared to march into the Nanking-controlled provinces of Kiangsi and Fukien. It was easy to see that the enemy as usual was not Japan but Nanking.

The southern proclamation and even the initial movement of the troops came with such suddenness that many believed it a hoax. The Japanese, well informed as usual, had reported the movement, but a check of official sources brought only expressions of ignorance or outright denials. The foreign newspaper correspondents cabled denials.

But they soon learned that the Japanese were right. The Kwangsi troops were on the move, crossing the Hunan border into the 'Balkans of China.' The highest Nanking committees were immediately summoned to discuss the situation. But without waiting for discussion, Chiang rushed his own troops into Hunan and Kiangsi provinces to meet the threat of the advancing southerners.

As with the last revolt of the Kwangsi clique six years before, the situation largely hinged on the attitude of the Hunan governor, crafty Ho Chien. Kwangsi undoubtedly counted on his joining the revolt and letting the southern forces sweep through Hunan to the head of the Yangtse Valley, threatening the heart of Chiang Kai-shek's domain.

Chiang forestalled them. Possibly he outbid them. At any rate, before the government organs had time to assemble at Nanking, he had reached an understanding with Ho Chien. The Hunan war-lord disposed his own troops through the southern part of his province, blocking the advance of the Kwangsi divisions. Seeing Ho Chien against them, and realizing that their cause was already lost, the troops of Li and Pai did not advance beyond Hengchow, about fifty miles inside the Hunan border. The

Kwangtung forces of Chen Chi-tang never even marched out of their own province, but marked time along the Kiangsi and Fukien borders, where they remained, potentially but not immediately menacing.

The southern military chieftains were apparently not worried by the erection of the Hunan barrier. They settled down and proceeded to wait for negotiation, in the time-honored Chinese fashion. They anticipated making some demands of Chiang, and receiving some from him, and then, after both sides had made compromises and concessions, reaching a new understanding which would certainly better their own position even if they hadn't actually gone to war and overthrown Chiang.

They failed to count on two developments which presently ruined their composure and made them wonder if they had not maneuvered themselves out of power and into oblivion. The first was the overwhelming popular opposition to the southern revolt. The second was Chiang Kai-shek's decision to bargain no more, but to treat rebels as traitors.

The brave announcement of an anti-Japanese army marching to fight the invader in North China and Manchuria, the resounding call to the nation to rally and fight the foreigner, deceived no one. Hundreds of telegrams descended on the southern leaders, imploring them not to betray the nation. Ardent patriots who had denounced Chiang Kai-shek as strongly as anyone were among those who condemned the rebels, urging them not to split the country but to abide by Nanking's decisions.

The highest and the lowest in the nation joined in the denunciation. Other telegrams poured in from Chinese in America, England, and the South Seas. The messages were invariably of the same tenor: Chinese must not fight Chinese, and the time had not come to fight the Japanese.

It was an impressive vindication of Chiang Kai-shek's own policies. As a demonstration of loyalty, it could not have been improved upon if it had been staged at Chiang's own orders.

The action of the southern military leaders proved unpopular even in their own ranks. Kwangtung had its own air force of more than forty airplanes with efficient American-trained pilots. On July 1 the airmen left Canton, flying all forty of Chen Chi-tang's planes to Chiang Kai-shek's base at Nanchang. Nine of them went directly to Nanking, and the pilots pledged their loyalty to the Generalissimo. Whether genuine patriotism motivated the aviators, or whether, as many hinted, Chiang had offered large financial rewards to pilots bringing planes into his territory, remained a matter of speculation. Perhaps both factors entered into the situation. Rewards may have induced the fliers to take off in their dramatic gesture, but it was known that many leaders in the southern armies sincerely opposed the anti-Nanking adventure.

Eight days later, as the C.E.C. was about to convene at Nanking to decide how to treat the rebellion, General Yu Han-mou, most trusted associate of Chen Chi-tang, flew to Nanking. He was deserting the King under Southern Skies. In his case there was little doubt that he had received substantial inducements. He had been too close to Chen Chi-tang for years to decide so suddenly that Chen was a rascal.

Chiang received Yu with rejoicing, told him Chen Chi-tang's days of power were numbered. He offered Yu the position of Number 1 man in Canton, conditional on his leading military as well as moral opposition to the Kwangtung war-lord. Yu agreed.

Other commanders deserted Chen Chi-tang in rapid succession and pledged their loyalty to Chiang Kai-shek.

Some denounced the Canton chief for despotism. Others decried his 'passion for money-grabbing.' Still others urged him to resign and 'do penance for plunging the country into imminent hostilities.'

With all these defections, Chen's position became extremely precarious. The Kwangsi chieftains, on the other hand, held the loyalty of their subordinates, and in the mountain fastnesses of their home province they knew they had a comparatively safe refuge. Even against modern bombing airplanes and Chiang Kai-shek's German-trained army, Kwangsi was likely to be impregnable.

The C.E.C. and the Central Supervisory Committee met in Nanking July 10. It wasted little time in circumlocution. It decreed the abolition of the Southwest Executive Committee and the Southwest Political Council. The legalized autonomy of the southern provinces was ended. Yu Han-mou was named commander-in-chief of the Kwangtung provincial troops and given all the posts held by his old boss, Chen Chi-tang. The proposal for an anti-Japanese expedition was flatly rejected.

Nanking moved cautiously, however, against the Kwangsi clique. It was not on as solid ground as in dealing with Chen Chi-tang, who was on the run. The C.E.C. renewed the appointment of Li Tsung-jen as commander-in-chief of the Kwangsi forces, and of Pai Chung-hsi as vice-commander.

Speaking to the C.E.C., Chiang Kai-shek defined his foreign policy. He gave his answer to the demand for an anti-Japanese expedition. He announced that China would not bow down to any nation seeking to destroy her territorial integrity, and would not sign any treaty detrimental to her sovereignty.

'If and when any nation should force China to sign any paper for the recognition of Manchukuo,' he said, 'that will be the time for China to make the supreme sacrifice!'

To those who were eager for sudden and spectacular resistance, he called attention to the case of Ethiopia. World opinion had been sympathetic to the Ethiopians, but where was their country today? Under the heel of a conquering Italy.

'The defeat of Ethiopia, however, does not mean that we should not follow the path of Ethiopia,' he announced. 'China will not be afraid to be another Ethiopia if that is the only way to save the nation and the race. But if the entire nation and all the Kuomintang members stand together solidly under the central government, China can never be a second Ethiopia.'

The session was closed by Feng Yu-hsiang, of all persons. The chronic rebel had seemingly made a lasting peace with Chiang Kai-shek, and was remaining in Nanking as a high official of the national government, nothing less than vice-chairman of the Military Affairs Commission under Chiang.

The southwestern revolt was all over. Yu Han-mou led a southward march of troops loyal to him. They were Kwangtung soldiers, and hence did not impress the residents of the province as northern invaders, but they were termed national troops and actually represented Nanking. This was an ideal arrangement for which Chiang was responsible. It was his idea to deputize a Kwangtung military force to take over Kwangtung. This would have the double purpose of salving local feelings and saving his own troops for more important work.

But Yu's troops encountered no resistance. It was a march and not a campaign. The King under Southern Skies himself fled to Hongkong from Canton, taking with him plenty of cash and valuable possessions. Yu took over Canton at leisure. The world press headlined the capture of Canton by Nanking forces as though it were the culmination of a bitter war. Actually the issue had been decided weeks before, and Yu arrived in Canton with no more excitement than if he had been on a few weeks' vacation in the north.

Chiang Kai-shek, after vainly appealing to the Kwangsi clique to conform to Nanking orders and reaffirm allegiance to the central government, flew to Canton August 11 to supervise negotiations and military preparations to deal with Kwangsi's resistance.

The Kwangsi leaders by this time had withdrawn all their troops to their own province, but showed no signs of incorporating their troops into the Nanking armies, as had been done in Kwangtung. Nor were they willing to hand the provincial civil administration over to Chiang's appointee.

Chiang Kai-shek established his headquarters at Whampoa, seat of the academy whose foundation had meant so much to his career. Everybody expected the same thing to happen that had happened in Kwangtung. Chiang would negotiate with the Kwangsi chiefs; if unsuccessful, he would wage war.

He failed in all his efforts, and he did not go to war. The Kwangsi leaders were obdurate. They had their own ideas about national policy, but, of more importance, they were determined to run Kwangsi themselves. They rejected every offer Chiang made. They refused to give up their control of Kwangsi to the slightest degree. And their subordinates stood pat.

For a while it looked as though hostilities were inevitable. Both sides seemed to be preparing for conflict. But at the last moment, Chiang retired. He was beaten and he knew it. He didn't want to go to war against Kwangsi. The result might be eventual victory, but the cost would be too great. Kwangsi could not be subjugated overnight.

It would take months, probably many months, and Chiang could not persuade himself to waste man-power and resources on what might, after all, prove an empty victory. He did not need Kwangsi as a territory. So long as he could be assured of the Kwangsi leaders' good behavior, he could afford to back down.

There had to be some face-saving formula, naturally, and Kwangsi was not unwilling to co-operate, if assured of being left unmolested. The appointment of Li Tsung-jen as Pacification Commissioner of the province was affirmed by Nanking. Pai was named to the Military Affairs Commission and urged to come to Nanking to assume his duties. The Kwangsi armies were designated 'national armies.'

Li and Pai played ball with Chiang. With a solemn oath they assumed the 'new' jobs to which they had been named, and informed their troops that henceforth they were the Fifth National Army instead of the Eighty-ninth Kwangsi Army. It was harmless play-acting which fooled no one. Chiang could go back to Nanking and say that the Kwangsi situation was settled, and no one could dispute him.

Kwangsi, as everyone knew, had given Chiang his first domestic setback in years. But there was no indication that the defeat had damaged anything except possibly his pride.

The question arises, why did the southern leaders who had consistently opposed an anti-Nanking expedition in the past suddenly embark on a venture which they must have known was doomed to failure? Chen was an extraordinarily cautious man, Li was shrewd, and Pai was brilliant. Surely their common sense must have argued against the campaign.

The answer is that they were misled. They had been

assured that if they started the revolt, support would be forthcoming. Certain northern military leaders would join the movement as soon as the southern troops were on the march, the southerners were told. Outstanding political leaders would issue manifestoes denouncing Chiang Kai-shek and Nanking, and calling for a policy of strong resistance against Japan. Even some of the Nanking officials would support them. Chiang Kai-shek would have to resign and the government would be reorganized.

The armies moved, but the support never came. The northerners were either not ready or had been cowed at the last moment by Nanking pressure. Maybe the northern leaders changed their minds and decided that the moment to strike had not come. The political leaders kept silent. And of course the oppositionists in Nanking, with no cue from the rest of the country, had to remain under cover.

The surprising aspect of the entire episode was the strength of genuine popular feeling against the revolt. Times had definitely changed in China. There was a strong man at Nanking and, for better or worse, the people were going to support him. Political opposition might be tolerated to some extent, but military revolt was now treason to China. Chiang Kai-shek had a program. The Chinese people, despite occasional extremist outbursts, were determined to let him carry it out.

CHAPTER XXXIII

CHINA STRIKES BACK

BUT even before the Southwestern revolt episode had been concluded, Chiang found himself facing renewed Japanese pressure, this time on the diplomatic front. A series of 'incidents' involving attacks on Japanese subjects had brought strong demands from Japan, seeking more than mere satisfaction for anti-Japanese activities.

They had begun the previous November with the murder by unknown persons of a Japanese marine in Shanghai. Only a few months later a Japanese civilian met death in a similar attack. At Chengtu, in far-off Szechuan Province, a bitter argument between the Chinese and Japanese governments over the reopening of a Japanese consulate in the port had so aroused anti-Japanese feeling that a mob attacked four Japanese visiting Chengtu, killed two, and seriously wounded the others.

Down in Pakhoi, in Kwangtung Province, an aged Japanese druggist, resident of the town for years and married to a Chinese woman, had been dragged out of his shop by a mob and killed. There followed the mysterious murder of a Japanese policeman in the Japanese Concession at Hankow. Finally, another Japanese marine was shot down and killed in a Shanghai street by an unknown assailant.

The Japanese made a serious issue of the killings, and demanded that Nanking assume full responsibility in each case. But they went farther. Japanese diplomats insisted that Nanking take steps to prevent similar occurrences in the future. This, they said, called for the dissolution of many Kuomintang branches, including the Shanghai headquarters, which they accused of dangerous anti-Japanese activity. The Japanese also demanded the revision of Chinese schoolbooks, which they said were teaching Chinese children to hate the Japanese.

As the negotiations on the various incidents slowly proceeded, punctuated by threats of direct action by Japanese naval units and marines, the Japanese extended their demands. They pressed for economic co-operation between China, Japan, and Manchukuo, and also for a three-cornered alliance against communism.

What angered the Japanese was Chiang's insistence on remaining behind the scenes in all the negotiations. They knew that he was really in control of the government, that all policies were outlined by him, and that every aspect of Sino-Japanese relations was subject to his review and approval. Yet he remained outwardly aloof. Much of the time he was away from Nanking.

The Japanese Ambassador would call at the foreign office and be interviewed by a vice-minister of foreign affairs. Once in a while, he would have audience with the Foreign Minister. But the Japanese regarded the Foreign Minister as merely a 'front' man for Chiang Kai-shek. They knew he had no power and little authority.

Finally, Chiang having returned to Nanking in mid-October, 1936, he agreed to receive the Japanese Ambassador. He greeted the envoy with perfect courtesy, even with cordiality. But he resolutely refused to talk business with him. It was a courtesy visit, he insisted. With all politeness, he informed the Japanese that China's foreign relations were being handled by the Foreign Minister, and that the Foreign Minister was the only proper person to see.

Baffled and enraged, the Ambassador resumed his discussions with the Minister, fully aware that the latter did not dare to enunciate a single principle without consulting Chiang Kai-shek.

Came a day when the Ambassador, tired of negotiating, made a blunt demand for what he had previously been making more or less polite requests — economic co-operation and an anti-Communist alliance between China and Japan, and Manchukuo. To the speechless amazement of the Japanese Ambassador, and later to the surprise of the whole world, the Chinese Foreign Minister just as bluntly rejected, completely and finally, each of the Japanese demands. And to give point to the rejection he actually presented counter-demands — demanded the abrogation of the Tangku truce which had ended the Manchurian and North China hostilities, and of the Shanghai truce which had brought to a close the war on the Whangpoo in 1932.

A new era had arrived. China, tired of face slaps, was slapping back. The world sat up and took notice. Japan was too confused to act.

Meanwhile, the Japanese-instigated Mongols had enlarged the scope of their campaign and had attempted to invade Suiyuan Province. China resisted, with real guns and bullets. The nation cheered. The Mongols were hurled back from the Suiyuan border and then, to the astonishment of Chinese and foreigners alike, the Chinese crossed into territory which the Mongols had taken a year before, and captured Pailingmiao, seat of the principal Mongol government.

The truth was that the capture of Pailingmiao had been achieved by purchasing the defection of a large number of Mongols in the region who were dissatisfied with their government. But the fact was not generally known, and the seizure of the town stirred China to wild enthusiasm. Money poured in for the 'gallant Suiyuan fighters' from every section of the country and from abroad. China, at long last, was striking back.

Chiang sounded the keynote. The capture of Pailing-miao, he told the nation, proved that 'with determination and unity China need not lose a single inch of territory through foreign invasion.'

CHAPTER XXXIV

JUBILEE

CHIANG's fiftieth birthday was approaching. He was only 49 years old by foreign reckoning. By Chinese calculation he became one year old on the lunar new year which followed his birth by only a few months, and in Chinese eyes he was therefore nearing the half-century mark.

The lunar calendar, however, had been abolished, and ever since the establishment of the Kuomintang republic the solar dates had been observed by government fiat. It was ascertained that his birth date had actually been October 31, and his family and the government decided to observe it on that date henceforth.

As the day drew near it was obvious that it would not bring unmixed joy. Ominous rumors were coming from Sian in the northwest, where Young Marshal Chang Hsueh-liang and his troops were now stationed. Although the Young Marshal's forces were supposed to be battling the Communists, who, after their long trek from Kiangsi, had settled down in Shensi and Kansu Provinces, the campaign was at a standstill. The northeastern armies objected to fighting the Chinese Reds. They wanted to turn around, battle the Japanese, and recover their old homeland. The Communists had made an open offer for a common front against the Japanese. The ex-Manchurians could see no reason for not accepting it.

The Young Marshal had telegraphed Chiang Kai-shek

that the situation was serious. On October 22, 1936, Chiang went to Sian by airplane. He stayed at the near-by hot springs resort of Lintung, which less than two months later was to be the scene of his kidnapping.

It was apparent that the Red situation in the northwest was stalemated. The Communists held southern Shensi and large parts of Kansu, but there was no fighting.

Chiang had scant patience with the lassitude of the campaign, angrily rejected all talk of accepting the Reds' proposals for a united front. He conferred with the Young Marshal and with Yang Hu-cheng, the native Shensi military chieftain. The latter two were at loggerheads. Chiang ordered them to get along, to prosecute the anti-Red campaign, and then returned to Nanking.

But he celebrated his fiftieth birthday not at the capital city but at Loyang. Ostensibly he went to the Honan city out of modesty — he wanted to be away from the capital when his birthday was celebrated with such enthusiasm. Actually he went to attend a military conference which he himself had summoned. To it came Young Marshal Chang, Model Governor Yen, two Honan military chieftains, and Suiyuan Governor Fu Tso-yi, currently a national hero for his defense of Chinese territory and capture of Mongolian Pailingmiao. Madame Chiang flew from Nanking to Loyang. Hundreds of telegrams of congratulations poured into the Nanking telegraph office. Others went directly to Loyang, still others to Sian. The nation's birthday gift to Chiang was a huge collection of modern fighting airplanes. Funds had been raised for the purpose for months previous, and remitted to the United States to purchase the latest models.

As the *North China Daily News* put it, 'At first it seemed that the movement for the presentation of planes was strictly official in inspiration. As time passed, it was apparent that it was taking the form of self-dedication to the national cause.'

At Loyang a deafening discharge of thousands of giant firecrackers, mingled with the salute of countless guns, ushered in the day. Chiang and Mei-ling had a simple breakfast party, where the candles of two large cakes lit the faces of the military leaders gathered there on the most serious of business — the threatening northwest situation and the Communist impasse.

Madame Chiang cut the two cakes, handed out slices to the assembled generals, whose thoughts were on graver things than birthday celebrations.

While Chiang pondered the problem of which the nation was entirely ignorant, Nanking went wild. More than two hundred thousand persons thronged the Ming Palace airdrome. Fifty-five airplanes were presented to the government in honor of Chiang's birthday, but it was believed that more than one hundred and fifty planes had been bought. For obvious reasons, it was best not to emphasize the number of craft thus added to the Chinese air force.

Large photographs of the Generalissimo were displayed everywhere in the capital and all over the nation. More often than not his portrait appeared side by side with that of Sun Yat-sen.

Over the Ming Palace airdrome flew first sixteen and then nineteen planes in perfect formation, outlining the Chinese characters 'Chung Cheng,' the Generalissimo's courtesy name. Fifty-five planes then flew by in single file, each dipping in salute to Chiang Kai-shek. Foreign aeronautical observers acknowledged that the show was a good one, comparable to the best in Europe and America. The thousands gathered at the airdrome bowed three times to the portrait of Chiang Kai-shek, shrilly shouted the slogans, 'Long live the Republic! Long live Chiang Kai-shek!'

He was achieving a status comparable to that of Sun Yat-sen himself.

In Shanghai the enthusiasm was quite as evident. Flags were broken out by foreign and Chinese stores, shops, offices, and public buildings. From countless structures were flung banners wishing Chiang 'a thousand autumns.' Protestants and Catholics, Buddhists and Mohammedans, officials and clerks, millionaires and laborers, joined in the observance. Hundreds of Protestants, Chinese and foreign, gathered at the Moore Memorial Church and prayed for long life for Chiang. Buddhists mixed worship with merrymaking. Mohammedans went to their mosques. The Catholics sent three delegates to Nanking bearing good wishes, and, more to the point, checks for $520,000 to buy three Red Cross planes, which were presented to the government in Chiang's honor.

Gaiety prevailed all over the nation. In far-flung towns of remote provinces, the Chinese people celebrated the birthday of their leader, and foreigners wished them well. Music and dancing were a prominent part of the observance. Cabaret dance bands played the Kuomintang anthem, and taxi-dancers stood at attention while their escorts shouted, 'Long live Chiang!'

One of the gayest affairs, however, in the Metropolitan Hotel at Nanking, was abruptly terminated when Tai Chi-tao, President of the Examination Yuan and long-time friend of Chiang, strode into the ballroom, rebuked the merrymakers, and told them such expensive pleasures were unseemly 'in this time of national emergency.' The dance broke up and the crowd dispersed.

Motion-picture screens flashed the portraits of Chiang and Sun Yat-sen, and whole audiences, Chinese and foreign, arose and cheered. Trains were decked with flags, sirens shrieked.

Chiang rejected all gifts with thanks. In a message from Loyang, he noted that many had economized on food and clothing in order to contribute to the airplane fund. He pledged himself to redoubled efforts on behalf of the nation.

In a statement entitled 'Some Reflections on My Fiftieth Birthday,' he was careful to emphasize that the airplanes were not for himself but for the Chinese government. He told of his debt to the state, stressed his failure to accomplish his objectives, and in characteristic Chinese fashion castigated himself for general unworthiness. He charged the people 'not to imitate the superficialities of the West, nor to plagiarize the doctrine of might of the imperialistic nations.'

After enumerating the struggles of his early life and paying tribute to the fortitude of his mother, he concluded: 'For my own part, I have been painfully conscious of my inability to discharge my responsibility in such a way as to fulfill the expectations of my countrymen and the fervent wish of my late mother.

'I am always mindful of two things — that, so long as the people are in distress, I have not fulfilled my mother's long-cherished wish, and that, so long as the task of national salvation is not yet accomplished, I shall be responsible for the distress and sufferings of the people.

'Therefore I sincerely appeal to my countrymen to help me fulfill my mother's ardent wish — to fulfill the great task of national salvation.'

CHAPTER XXXV

SNATCH AT SIAN

EXACTLY one month and twelve days after the nation had exultantly celebrated his fiftieth birthday, Chiang suffered the greatest possible anticlimax. He was kidnapped. For thirteen days he languished at Sian, the captive of his military subordinates, until with a suddenness that startled the world he came back to Nanking, a Christmas present to the nation.

Newspapers in America and Europe blazoned the story with large-sized headlines, but neither the readers nor the editors ever made much sense of the strange episode. As long as it appeared that Young Marshal Chang Hsueh-liang had seized the Generalissimo for a huge ransom, the story appeared plausible. Even when it developed that what the Young Marshal wanted was not money but a stronger foreign policy, preferably war on Japan, the story did not tax the credulity of the western world.

But when it was learned, indisputably, that Chiang had been released without any conditions or stipulations, and that the Young Marshal had followed him to Nanking, demanding punishment, the outside world gave it up as one of those mysteries for which the East is famous, and editorial writers dragged out the old word 'inscrutable.'

Actually what happened was simple enough to those who knew the situation. The difficulty was that so few people really knew, and that those who knew were in no position to tell. The publication six months later of extracts from

Chiang's own diary of the fortnight at Sian, and Madame Chiang's exposition of the coup, provided many interesting sidelights to the story, but neither account touched the underlying events which gave the story meaning.

The truth was that Chiang's kidnapping was caused by his own personality and temperament. The fact that the force of his character also led to his release did not alter the reason for the staging of the coup in the first place.

As mentioned previously, the Northeastern Army of the Young Marshal, charged with harrying the Communists in the far northwest province of Shensi, had become tired of the job. The anti-Communist campaign had been at a standstill for months. But the army was more than indifferent. It was hostile to the idea of even making a pretense of fighting the Reds, and it was thoroughly in accord with the Reds' proposal for a united front against Japan.

It must be remembered that the army's home was in Manchuria, from which it had been roughly separated. In China it was always a stranger. For a time it had been quartered in the neighborhood of Hankow. Now it was in the barren province of Shensi. The soldiers were bitterly anti-Japanese and resented Nanking's order to keep fighting the Communists.

The northeasterners believed that Chiang Kai-shek was using none of his own troops in the anti-Red campaign, that they themselves were given the assignment to keep them out of mischief. The Communists were Chinese like themselves, the Young Marshal's men pointed out. They urged resistance against Japan. If Chiang himself didn't want to send his own troops against Japan, at least let the Communists and the northeasterners march against Manchuria and fight the invaders.

But from Nanking came the insistent order to keep fighting the Communists, a repeated refusal to begin a campaign against Japan until the time was ready. The northeasterners simply stopped listening to Chiang. They reached a complete understanding with the Communists. They insisted that Young Marshal Chang Hsueh-liang tell Chiang Kai-shek they were determined to turn about-face and fight the Japanese.

The Young Marshal was entirely loyal to Chiang Kai-shek. But he knew how his men felt, and to a certain extent he sympathized with them. When the news of the Japanese-German alliance reached Northwest China it stirred new resentment. The Young Marshal argued with his officers and men, explained Chiang Kai-shek's views and his long-range program. But they refused to be convinced. They insisted that Chiang preferred civil war to war on Japan.

It was in October that the Young Marshal sent urgent telegrams to Chiang Kai-shek urging a policy of resistance, and a common front with the Communists, who were now calling themselves the Anti-Japanese Red Army. Chiang's answer was a flat refusal.

But he realized that all was not well in the northwest, and he went to Sian a few weeks before his birthday. The Young Marshal thought he would be able to convince the Generalissimo of the urgent necessity of a new policy if the Northeastern Army was to be held in check.

But Chiang was sure of the wisdom of his own policy, and had no hesitation in reiterating it. Speaking to the Sian Military School, he announced with finality that the Communists were the real enemy of China, and that Japan, although undoubtedly a menace, was remote.

The student-soldiers did not take kindly to Chiang's statement. They were free with their criticism of Chiang. A few rose up in the school assembly and bitterly attacked the Generalissimo. The Young Marshal, still loyal to Chiang, dismissed three of the critics from the school.

But Chiang repeated his remarks in another address to the Loyang Military Academy, and indicated clearly that his mind was unchanged.

Meanwhile a number of secret groups loyal to Chiang Kai-shek began to function at Sian. They worked with and through the local Kuomintang branch. The Generalissimo knew there was hostility at Sian, and this intelligence service was to keep him informed.

After Chiang left the northwest these groups swung into action. A number of students and workers' leaders who had been active preachers of union with the Reds disappeared, supposedly kidnapped. This activity aroused the North-eastern Army and its sympathizers almost to the point of frenzy.

The Young Marshal wrote Chiang Kai-shek asking the 'right and the opportunity to drive out the Japanese and return to our homeland.' He concluded on an ominous note. 'In any case, I must tell you that I cannot control my army much longer.'

But no answer came from Chiang. The secret groups not only failed to subside, but increased their activity. Three students who had come as 'delegates' from North China to the anti-Japanese center at Sian were seized. The Young Marshal telephoned the Kuomintang office to inquire, and was told that nothing was known of the missing students.

That night Chang Hsueh-liang closed the city gates, raided the Kuomintang headquarters, located the missing students, banished the secret agents, and wired a protest to Chiang Kai-shek.

In the meantime one of Chiang Kai-shek's own divisions, one of the best of his crack units, had been left at Sian to show the Young Marshal's troops how to fight the Communists. This division renewed the anti-Red campaign. It ventured twenty-seven miles into Red territory, and struck disaster. The Reds suddenly appeared from all sides, fell on the would-be attackers and forced the majority to retreat. Two brigades of the crack division were captured.

This convinced Chiang that the situation was really serious. He flew to Sian December 7 to consult the northeastern leaders. He also learned that the Shensi native troops under Yang Hu-cheng had also just voted to fight the Japanese. The situation was even more grave than he imagined.

Chiang established headquarters at Lintung, a hotsprings resort about twelve miles northwest of Sian. With him was his nephew, the leader of the secret groups whose activities had aroused the ire of the students and soldiers at Sian. A number of Nanking generals put up at the guest house of the China Travel Service at Sian.

The northeastern leaders expected a general conference for the discussion of the situation. At first Chiang antagonized them by insisting on seeing them one at a time. Finally he agreed to a meeting with the principal generals.

They all told him, with the greatest politeness, that they were entirely loyal to him and to Nanking, but that they refused to fight fellow-Chinese any longer. They again requested permission to return to Manchuria and fight the Japanese.

Chiang was obdurate. 'You have only one duty before you, to destroy the Communists,' he told them. The conference was deadlocked.

Two days after Chiang arrived, a student demonstration was held in Sian. Thousands marched through the streets, carrying banners with patriotic slogans, demanding that regular Chinese army troops be sent to Suiyuan to fight the Japanese-sponsored Mongol irregulars who were attacking.

Chiang ordered the Governor of Shensi Province, his

own appointee, to break up the demonstration, above all to prevent it from marching out to Lintung. That was exactly what the students were determined to do. They wanted to demonstrate not to the sympathetic Sian audience but to the unsympathetic Chiang.

The students moved out of the city gates, intent on marching the twelve miles to Lintung. The police ordered them back. They defied the police and streamed out of the city. The police fired, seriously wounding two youthful demonstrators, twelve and thirteen years of age. The demonstration broke up, with the students and soldiers at white heat. The Young Marshal himself lodged a vigorous objection to the shooting down of helpless students.

On December 11 a report went around that the secret groups had armed and were preparing a coup. Chiang Kaishek himself, the rumor went, had approved a list of anti-Japanese agitators to be arrested in Sian.

The night of December 11 a conference was held by the northeastern generals and the leaders of Yang Hu-cheng's Shensi troops. The Shensi group in particular was insistent that the suspected raids be nipped. They denounced the secret groups which they said were sponsored directly by Chiang himself, and demanded that Chiang be taken into custody for the double purpose of frustrating the coup and making him change his policy to accord with theirs.

At six o'clock on the morning of the twelfth, Chiang's headquarters were surrounded. The troops who staged the attack were those of Young Marshal Chang Hsueh-liang. Among the first to be captured was Chiang's nephew. As soon as the soldiers satisfied themselves that this was the leader of the secret groups, they shot him forthwith.

Chiang heard the commotion, dashed out a rear door, clad only in his nightshirt. He was barefoot. It was bitterly cold. One bodyguard went with him. Some distance at the rear of the resort hotel was a high wall. Its gate was locked, and Chiang had to scale it. He scrambled up the wall with considerable nimbleness, and let himself drop from the other side. He did not know that a deep moat ran the length of the wall on the other side. His fall was far deeper than he expected. The moat had only a few inches of water in it, and Chiang fell into it heavily. He arose, and found that his back was badly wrenched. It was painful to walk, but he had to run.

He dashed to the protection of a near-by foothill, where after some walking about he took refuge in a cave. His legs were badly scratched by the brambles and weeds, and his back was excruciatingly painful. Bullets began to whizz all around the small mountain.

Finally Chang Hsueh-liang's troops located him. One story said that the guard who accompanied him to the mountain turned back and disclosed the Generalissimo's hiding-place, but there is little to substantiate the tale. From all accounts Chiang's bodyguards were loyal, and practically all of them died defending him.

The soldiers who captured Chiang were extremely polite. Although engaged in the extreme act of mutiny, they still followed military discipline by saluting him scrupulously. Chiang for his part scolded every one of them roundly and loudly. He invited them to kill him, but they insisted on merely saluting him.

Yang Hu-cheng's Shensi troops, meanwhile, had captured the guest house in Sian, and all the Nanking generals were seized. Other military detachments rapidly raided the headquarters of the Chiang-appointed civil government and the police bureaus. The headquarters of the secret groups were among the first places invested, and their staffs captured. A number of the suspect secret agents were immediately killed.

Chiang was taken to a waiting automobile, under the direction of one of the Young Marshal's chief officers, who reportedly kneeled down on the ground before him and greeted him with tears in his eyes.

Chiang was taken to Sian, where he was placed in Yang Hu-cheng's headquarters. This was somewhat of a surprise to Chiang. Until then he thought that Yang Hu-cheng was entirely loyal. Later he was to learn that the Shensi leader was the guiding spirit of the coup.

Chiang went to bed. His legs were bleeding, his back was aching fiercely, and he was in a frenzy of rage. He denounced everybody about him. When the Young Marshal came to see him, he heaped abuse on him, refused to listen to a word from his 'Younger Brother.' Chang Hsueh-liang was surprised and puzzled. He expected to find a meek prisoner; the Generalissimo stormed about, and it was the Young Marshal who was meek.

Meanwhile a new Sian administration was set up. It announced an eight-point program which, among other things, called for the reorganization of the Nanking government to include all factions, a halt to civil war, and the immediate convocation of a 'National Salvation Congress' to plan measures against Japan.

The northeastern army freely fraternized with the Communists, who began to stream into the city. A provisional government was formed which included several Communist members.

The Young Marshal made daily broadcasts from the Sian radio station, telling of the efforts made to induce Chiang to fight the Japanese. Agnes Smedley, American left-wing writer, read news bulletins in English. But nobody heard the station. Its power was weak, it was unknown to most Chinese radio-listeners, and the Nanking authorities did what they could to interfere with reception of its signals.

OLD AND NEW CHINA REVIEW THE MODERN NATIONALIST ARMY

BEFORE THE KIDNAPPING
On the left, the 'Young Marshal' Chang Hsueh-liang
On the right, the 'Model Governor' Yen Shi-shan

CHAPTER XXXVI

RELEASE

Two days after the capture, Chiang was still refusing to have anything to do with Chang Hsueh-liang. The Young Marshal was beginning to wonder what to do with the Generalissimo. Chiang might refuse forever to discuss the important matters of national policy which he was trying to broach. The Generalissimo even refused to listen to the Young Marshal's suggestions of personal comfort. Chang wanted him to move to another house; Chiang absolutely refused.

Then Donald arrived. He flew by plane from Nanking by way of Loyang. He had for years been adviser to the Young Marshal, who welcomed him to Sian as an intermediary.

Chiang was also glad to see Donald. It touched him that a foreigner, with no official position in the government, was willing to brave the danger of an armed uprising to come to Sian to be with him.

Donald found the two men as far apart as on the day of the coup, with Chiang upbraiding the Young Marshal every time the latter opened his mouth. Donald first of all persuaded Chiang to move to another house, and moved in with him. Then he started to talk.

But Donald wasn't able to speak a word of Chinese. And Chiang understood no English. There was no interpreter. They had to call in the Young Marshal.

Donald started out by praising the Young Marshal, whom

he described as absolutely honest and reliable and a sincere patriot. The Young Marshal had to interpret, and being a modest fellow, objected to speaking his own praises. He left out whole sentences. Chiang Kai-shek scolded him for not translating fully; Donald scolded him for the same thing, although not quite as vigorously. It took them some time to get straightened out and down to business. While the three argued about interpretation a nation of more than four hundred and fifty million people was going frantic in the excitement of its greatest modern crisis.

Donald finally put the most pressing point. Nanking was determined to launch a punitive expedition against Sian. That very day thirty-five central government airplanes had appeared over the city and dropped pamphlets warning the rebels that unless Chiang were released, the city would be bombarded from the air and reduced to ruins.

In Nanking two factions were in open conflict. Chiang's family, including his wife, Doctor H. H. Kung, and T. V. Soong, were insisting on moderation, negotiation. They were naturally concerned with his safety, but Madame Chiang was also arguing for a sane solution of the case and the avoidance of bloodshed. Others, however, said that a mutiny was a mutiny, that it must be crushed, that the life of one individual, however respected and important, must not stand in the way of national discipline. They hinted that the Chiang family was putting personal considerations above patriotism.

It was a clever argument. The truth was that too many of the seeming patriots really wanted Chiang killed in the course of a government bombardment. They were more than ready to seize control of the government machinery. Donald saw the situation, realized the difficulty of combatting it. So did Madame Chiang.

Donald impressed Chiang with the necessity of ordering

Nanking, peremptorily, to call off all plans for hostilities for the time being. Chiang was induced to send an emissary with a letter to the Minister of War. The letter said that Chiang expected to be released the following Saturday, December 19, and urged that no hostilities be undertaken before then.

Even this letter failed immediately to still the cry at Nanking for prompt drastic action against Sian. Some argued that Chiang had been forced to write the letter. But the emissary assured them otherwise. He gave a faithful account of affairs at Sian, and the bombardment was called off until Saturday.

The deadline approached. Chiang remained captive. Nanking announced that hostilities would begin Sunday morning.

T. V. Soong left Nanking by airplane Saturday afternoon. A number of leaders tried to dissuade him, said he also would be held prisoner. But he had learned of the real situation at Sian in indirect messages from Donald, and insisted on going. The Nanking government felt itself embarrassed by his trip, announced that he was going to Sian only as a private citizen and not as a government emissary. It was emphasized that the government did not intend to make terms with the rebels.

The rebels by this time had found their captive a tiger whom they held by the tail. They couldn't hold him, and to let him go was dangerous. They had been genuinely impressed by the nation-wide denunciation which had greeted the seizure of Chiang. They had never imagined the extent to which the removal of the Generalissimo would stir national feeling.

Men who had been Chiang's enemies for years decried the kidnapping, denounced the Sian leaders, demanded his release. And if the Sian leaders expected any of the restive military leaders to join them in establishing a new régime, they were disappointed. All Chiang's old military opponents pledged him their support, called on the rebels to free him.

Christian General Feng Yu-hsiang at Nanking actually became the Nanking spokesman, was named acting chairman of the Military Affairs Commission in Chiang's absence, called loudly for Chiang's release, and hinted that if the kidnappers freed the Generalissimo, he, Feng, would do all in his power to make the Nanking government take a more forceful anti-Japanese stand.

The Kwangsi clique pledged loyalty to Nanking; so did Yen Hsi-shan, Sung Cheh-yuan of Hopei, the governors of semi-independent Shantung, Szechuan and Yunnan Provinces. Disciples of Hu Han-min, who had died the year before, declared that the kidnapping was a blow to China. Leading intellectuals like Hu Shih and spokesmen for the democratic opposition all joined the chorus of regret and denunciation.

The rebels decided that the best thing they could do was to sit tight and bargain. Particularly was Yang Hu-cheng nervous. He felt that the Young Marshal might get out of the scrape without harm, but he wanted a deal for himself. The rebels waited for overtures from Nanking, but no overtures came — only the threat of bombardment.

As Madame Chiang clearly saw, the opportunity to arrange for the Generalissimo's release was waiting. It was ignored because of Nanking's insistence on hostilities, on the one hand, and Chiang's own refusal to negotiate, on the other.

The Young Marshal and Yang Hu-cheng had read Chiang's diary, which he had kept for years. They were impressed. They became convinced that, despite his faults and the difficulty of dealing with him, he was sincerely working for the welfare of the country. They even came to believe that he would, in time, adopt an anti-Japanese policy every bit as strong as their own. But he would, it was clear, stand for no dictation. He wanted to do things his own way, and he took few men into his confidence.

Chiang told the Young Marshal more than once, with asperity, 'Since you call me President, then you are my subordinate. You can treat me only in two ways. If you recognize me as your superior official, you should immediately escort me back to Loyang. Otherwise you are a rebel, and you should immediately kill me. There is nothing more to be said.'

The Young Marshal tried to get Chiang to accept his eight-point program. Chiang said he was in sympathy with some of the points of the program but would promise nothing under duress, and would not even pledge himself to recommend the program to the other Nanking government officials.

T. V. Soong went back to Nanking and then came back to Sian with Madame Chiang. She was able to plead with the Generalissimo to adopt a more reasonable attitude, and she served as his spokesman in the endless conversations with the rebel leaders. Yang Hu-cheng, it soon developed, was the stumbling-block to an agreement. He foresaw ruin if the Generalissimo left Sian without making any definite pledges.

But Chiang repeated again and again that he would make no pledges. As a matter of fact, he had decided he would never escape from Sian alive, and had resigned himself to death. He read the Bible regularly, and repeatedly urged the rebels to shoot him if they would not release him unconditionally.

'If I make any pledges to gain my own release,' he told them, 'I should be a contemptible coward and should deserve to be killed.'

Finally the Young Marshal himself decided to go to Nanking with the Chiangs. The purpose was two-fold, to convince the nation and the world that he had not seized the Generalissimo for money or other private gain, and to persuade Yang Hu-cheng to let the Generalissimo and his party go. On the one hand, he would submit himself to Nanking's punishment for the treasonable act of seizing Chiang's person. On the other, he would accept sole responsibility and thus save his own army and Yang Hu-cheng's troops from punitive action by Nanking.

On December 25, after more conversations in which the prospects of release appeared to grow dimmer, Chiang and his party, Madame, T. V. Soong, the Young Marshal, and Donald finally left Sian by plane. At the last moment, Chiang himself complicated matters again. Yang's attitude seemed likely to change, and the attitude of his associate generals was extremely doubtful; there was the prospect that they might try to "highjack" the release and keep the Generalissimo captive. It was suggested that Chiang go to the airport in disguise. He flatly refused. He would go openly or not at all. He was commander-in-chief; to steal out of the city was beneath his dignity. And there the matter stood.

It was finally arranged. The plane at the airport was warmed up. The guards had their orders. Chiang and his party drove up in the Young Marshal's car. They boarded the Young Marshal's plane, and were off to Loyang. There they changed planes, Chiang, Madame Chiang and Donald travelling in one and T. V. Soong and the Young Marshal following in another.

The news had preceded them. China went wild. Guns boomed. Firecrackers roared. Flags broke out like a rash on every building. Sirens screamed. Chinese New Year was nothing like it. Far into the night and well into the next morning the people, from millionaires to ricksha coolies, joined in one vast spontaneous celebration. Christian General Feng Yu-hsiang broke a long-standing rule of temperance and drank a glass of wine to Chiang's health. Only the celebration of the first armistice report after the World War could compare with the spectacle that staid old China staged to mark the return of its Strong Man.

That Chiang did not, as the experts predicted, suffer an irreparable loss of face and straightway pass into obscurity as a result of the kidnapping, was due less to any iron grip which he held on the Chinese government than to the fact that he had become indispensable to the Chinese people.

He resigned, of course. That was to be expected. He blamed himself for the mutiny, asked the government to punish him. His resignation was rejected. He resigned once again, lashed himself verbally for personal faults, official laxity. Once again his offer was dismissed, his strictures ignored. It was more than face business. The government, including those who had slyly sought to profit by his elimination, realized fully how much it needed Chiang if it was to remain a government.

A Chiang dead, a martyr to the revolutionary cause, might have proved as great an influence upon the Chinese nation as the spirit of Sun Yat-sen. But a Chiang alive and not in control of China's destinies would have been as inconceivable as a Lenin in Mexican exile, a Mussolini in a monastery after the March on Rome.

CHAPTER XXXVII

SEQUEL

CHIANG's release from Sian did not, of course, solve the problem of the disaffected Northeastern Army, nor did it dispose of the Communist appeal for a united front against the Japanese. Nobody realized the pressure of those problems better than Chiang after his fortnight in the Shensi capital.

The army problem, it was apparent, could be solved. The former Manchurians could be transferred, they could be promised a chance to fight the Japanese, they could be given additional funds for 'expenses.' Chiang was used to dealing with matters like this. But he could not postpone a reckoning with the Communists, nor could he continue to wage what more and more Chinese were beginning to call a 'civil war' without precipitating serious domestic trouble.

Much as he must have hated to make a deal with the Reds, he realized that he had no choice. The Communists had not only proposed a united front with Chiang and the Kuomintang. They offered to abandon all attempts to form a Soviet government in China, to 'give up the class struggle,' as they put it. They were ready to pledge not to engage in Communist propaganda in Kuomintang China henceforth. They agreed to incorporate their forces into Chiang's national army, and to submit completely to Chiang's military command.

The Communists, in short, were ready to cease being Communists and to make themselves primarily Chinese

nationalists. All they asked in return was a pledge that China would fight Japan.

Even on this point they were conciliatory. They realized the difficulty of declaring war on Japan immediately; they were aware of the obstacles to the successful prosecution of such a conflict. But they wanted an anti-Japanese program, a promise that China would start preparing for the inevitable struggle.

Chiang might retort that he was already engaged in such a program. The Communists merely wanted definite word to that effect, and an end to speeches in which Chiang insisted that the Reds were the real enemy and Japan only a remote menace.

Chiang finally came to the realization that it was useless to fight the Reds further, and that it would be better to use them, if they could be depended upon to keep their promises. On this point he was none too sanguine. He always felt that the Communists in 1927 had betrayed the Kuomintang revolution. But he believed that the betrayal had been made possible by unwise encouragement of the Communists by a number of the Kuomintang leaders.

Now he was in sole control. He should be able to avoid the pitfalls of 1927. If the Communists were sincere in their professions, he was ready for a rapprochement.

Also, Chiang owed the Reds a certain amount of gratitude. The Red Army did not directly participate in the plot which led to the Sian coup. The leaders were aware of it, although their representatives did not enter Sian until the fourth day after the kidnapping. But to the surprise of everyone, they actually exercised a moderating effect upon the masses and the younger staff officers who were full of rebellion.

Undoubtedly astute, the Red leaders sensed that the Sian mutiny, being a military conspiracy, could not form

the basis of any revolutionary program. Such a plan would lead only to incessant civil war, thus weakening the country and defeating the Reds' real objective, resistance to Japanese imperialism.

The Reds, erstwhile bitter enemies of Chiang, argued most eloquently for his release. And they carried great influence with the Sian military leaders.

After the departure of Chiang Kai-shek and the Young Marshal, extreme excitement prevailed at Sian. Reports circulated that the Young Marshal was being detained at Nanking. Some of the radical younger officers attempted to assassinate sixteen of their superiors, whom they accused of selling out to Nanking, and actually killed several leading Manchurian officers on February 2. Here again the Reds acted as mediators, and prevented the situation from flaring into an open anti-Nanking rebellion.

When the first definite overtures were made remains in doubt. The Communists had made their original proposals not long after the Manchurian seizure, but their manifesto had gone unnoticed by official China. Subsequently they renewed their offers and their assurances, but the nature of the first definite Nanking-Communist conversations is still vague.

It was a popular story in China that Chiang Kai-shek met the chief Communist diplomatic liaison man, Chow En-lai, during the captivity at Sian, and that during their conversations they reached the basis of the Kuomintang-Communist rapprochement. This account circulated in some left-wing circles in China and was given considerable credence by the Japanese, who were growing extremely nervous at the prospect of a Nanking-Red alliance.

Chiang himself makes no mention of any such conversations in his diary of the Sian days, nor does Madame Chiang refer to Communist negotiations. The omission

proves nothing, of course; neither Chiang nor his wife would be likely to comment on the matter.

But there is considerable evidence that the first actual conversations did not occur until Chiang returned to Nanking. Chow En-lai, it is now known, did come to Nanking after the conclusion of the Sian episode. Whether it was his first contact with high Nanking officials or not is a matter of debate. To judge by general Chinese practice, however, it seems most likely that the Communist envoy did not interview Chiang Kai-shek at Sian but that he did communicate with him through the military leaders in the northwest, who were favorable to a rapprochement.

Chiang, as has been seen, resolutely refused to discuss any conditions, make any pledges, while he was held captive. He probably indicated his willingness to consider the Red proposals, but insisted on being returned to Nanking first and receiving the Communist spokesman there without any semblance of duress.

The date and nature of the original conversations are, after all, of minor importance. Significant is the fact that the overtures resulted in conversations and that the conversations soon became negotiations. Chow En-lai visited Nanking on two occasions. If Chiang himself preferred not to be seen in conference with the Red spokesman, he at least had responsible Nanking officials conduct the discussions. A member of the C.E.C., but not one in the public eye, later flew to Sian, where he met Chow and other Communist representatives, and the details of the cooperative understanding were slowly worked out.

The C.E.C. member was sent to Sian ostensibly to arrange for the taking of Nanking propaganda motion pictures, but as a matter of fact his mission was referred to almost openly in the Chinese newspapers. Despite the ordinarily strict censorship affecting Chinese news organs,

the most respectable of them commented several times on the C.E.C. member's mission to settle the 'North Shensi' problem, which everyone understood to mean the Communist question. The envoy's comparative obscurity prevented too great attention being paid to his movements.

Slowly, with much maneuvering and the laying of verbal smoke screens, the two erstwhile hostile forces came together. At Nanking on February 19, 1937, after submitting his resignation twice and seeing it rejected, Chiang resigned once again.

Before doing so, he delivered a verbal report to the C.E.C. on the Sian mutiny, and presented the members with extracts from his diary in Chinese, detailing the events of his captivity. After blaming himself for dereliction of duty he outlined the eight-point program which the Young Marshal had submitted to him. He pointed out, with great care, that he could neither accept nor reject the proposals; China had a central government, and it was up to the central authorities to pass on the program.

Then, with emphatic independence, he submitted the program to the C.E.C., but recommended rejection.

The C.E.C., after noting its 'especial gratification at Comrade Chiang's attitude' in not trying to decide the matter himself, followed his advice and rejected the Young Marshal's program. It also rejected Chiang's third resignation.

Having thus put itself on record as absolutely repudiating the radical program, the C.E.C. two days later outlined 'conditions for reconciliation with the Communists.' The conditions made delightful reading.

They were: (1), Abolish the Red army and incorporate it into the nation's armed forces under a unified command. (2) Unify the government power in the hands of the central government and dissolve the so-called Chinese

Soviet Republic and other organizations detrimental to
governmental unity. (3) Cease Communist propaganda.
(4) Stop the class struggle.

Lest they be accused of softening their policy, the
C.E.C. went on to enunciate the history of the Communists
in China, denouncing them for bad faith and betrayal of
the revolution and heaping maledictions on the Reds for
their past behavior.

Nanking in 'outlining conditions' was obviously accepting the Reds' own offer. It was confusing to the outsider;
it was intended to be. Nanking was making peace with its
sworn enemies, but was trying to divert attention from the
fact.

The Japanese, obviously the people most interested in
the change of policy, were certainly too clever to be taken
in by such bandying of words. Yet the Japanese press,
naïvely enough, hailed the C.E.C. manifesto and praised
Nanking's 'ringing denunciation of the Communists.'

The C.E.C., significantly, also issued a statement on
foreign policy which despite its circumlocutions immediately
impressed alert observers by its change of tone from pro-
nouncements of the past several years.

Starting out with the flat declaration that the government 'sees no need of revising our foreign policy,' it wound
up with the declaration that 'even when we are driven to
armed resistance, in the event that our rights are violated
beyond our tolerance, we shall only be fighting in defense,
and not because of anti-foreignism.' It was a direct warning to Japan not to encroach farther on Chinese territory
or to press China with new demands. Its meaning was not
lost on either the sapient Japanese or on alert Chinese
observers.

The Chinese Communists quickly replied to the C.E.C.
action, announced that they were altering their policies

immediately. They would stop working for the overthrow of the Nanking government. They would change the 'Chinese Soviet Government' into the 'Government of the Special Region of the Republic of China.' The Red Army was the Red Army no more. Henceforth it was to be the 'National Revolutionary Army' under the direct leadership of the central government and the Military Affairs Commission.

Finally, the Reds reported, they were halting their policy of expropriating the land of rich owners, and were concentrating hereafter on the common program of the anti-Japanese united front.

The C.E.C. of course elaborately ignored the Communist manifesto, but it was obvious that an understanding had been reached and that it was being ratified by both sides.

The Communists recommended a program calling for a number of reforms, including freedom of speech and press, the release of political prisoners, and 'preparatory work for the war of resistance against the Japanese.'

The C.E.C., still carrying on the game, rejected the program. But, without any fanfare and with no publicity, it proceeded to accept a proposal submitted by some of its own delegates which appeared to coincide in many respects with the Young Marshal's program and the Communist proposals. The plan called for a united front of all parties against 'foreign aggression,' abolition of newspaper censorship, the release of all political prisoners, and the calling of a conference of all elements to consider steps for the recovery of lost territories.

Chiang Kai-shek himself removed all doubt as to what was happening. In an interview with a semi-official Chinese news agency he announced, startlingly, that the National government was modifying and relaxing its restrictions on the freedom of speech and press. Not only would the national regulations be lightened, but Nanking would actively oppose the curbing of press freedom by provincial governments.

He went farther and announced that the release of political prisoners would depend on their 'repentance.'

And Wang Ching-wei, obviously speaking for Chiang, announced that China's program henceforth would be the 'recovery of lost territories.'

Chiang moved with characteristic swiftness once his mind had been made up. All press matters were quickly transferred to the Central Publicity Council. The chairman of the council was the ex-governor of Shensi, and he immediately announced a program of enlightened non-interference with media of news and publicity so long as they steered clear of treason and gave away no military secrets.

Political prisoners by the hundreds were released from prisons. The press made no mention of the exodus, but countless families were presently surprised and delighted at the unconditional release of their left-wing friends and relatives. Some of the outstanding Communist leaders of the country, including the celebrated woman writer, Ting Ling, were turned loose and given *carte blanche* to roam the country, an unprecedented state of affairs. Many of them immediately dashed off to the Communist centers of northern Shensi, and no obstacles were placed in their way.

Chiang Kai-shek announced frankly that the government had adopted a policy of magnanimity in the hope of achieving internal peace and stability.

But it took some pressure to get the C.E.C. to exercise its magnanimity toward the Young Marshal, Chang Hsueh-liang. After Chiang Kai-shek's release he had been sentenced to ten years' imprisonment and deprived of his civil rights for five years. The prison sentence was suspended on a special pardon granted at the insistence of Chiang Kai-shek. For some weeks, however, he was plain 'Mr. Chang,' without any civil rights. Only after some sharp orders from Chiang Kai-shek did the C.E.C. issue a mandate restoring his rights, thereby avoiding the danger of renewed revolt by the Northeastern Army. The action, as the editor of the *Shanghai Evening Post* remarked, 'cleared up a position which required sense, not vengeance.'

Having achieved his objectives and seen the government do an almost complete about-face on policy, Chiang asked for and received a two months' leave of absence to recover his health.

CHAPTER XXXVIII

AFTERMATH

FOR some time the physical result of Chiang's ordeal at Sian remained unknown to anyone outside his family circle and his physicians. Gradually the truth leaked out. His back injury was by no means slight, and it gave him considerable pain. Although he had been granted leave of absence immediately after returning to Nanking, and although the leave had been extended, Chiang refused to take the rest which his physicians had prescribed.

Too many important matters cried for attention despite his ostensible retirement. For one thing, he had a pressing problem in the question of government personnel. He now realized fully that some of the men who had been his most ardent supporters were only too eager to see him out of the way in order to seize power themselves.

These included some of the officials on whom he had leaned most heavily for counsel. Several among them were outspoken advocates of dictatorship. They had constantly preached China's need for a strong man, urged Chiang to assume more and more and more power for the good of the nation. He now faced the ugly fact that they wanted all power concentrated in him, only to exercise control more easily when he should have disappeared from the scene.

It was a sobering thought, and Chiang took himself off to quiet places to consider it, and to confer with those whose loyalty he need not question — his wife and Donald.

But no matter where he went there were conferences and

interviews. He made no effort to rest nor to avoid strain to his injured back.

Just before the February C.E.C. meeting at Nanking, Chiang had been in Hangchow. He suddenly flew to Shanghai and consulted a bone specialist. Only then did the seriousness of his injury become generally known. The specialist had a brace made to support the injured portion of the spine. He told Chiang the injury would have healed already had he not insisted on overworking.

Previously, X-rays showed that he was also suffering from a severe rib bruise which had not completely healed. This injury was comparatively slight, but the strained back continued to worry his medical advisers.

Finally, at the insistence of Madame Chiang and Donald, Chiang agreed to rest for a while, and received no callers at his Shanghai residence. But in a few days he was off to Nanking for the C.E.C. meeting, which he insisted on addressing personally.

Another result of the Sian detention appeared to be an intensification of his religious faith. On March 28 without prior announcement he sent a Good Friday message to the Eastern Asia Conference of the Methodist Episcopal Church, in session at Nanking. It was his first public religious pronouncement.

When captured at Sian, he recalled to the church workers, he had asked only for the Bible, which he had read earnestly. 'The greatness and love of Christ burst upon me with a new inspiration, increasing my strength to struggle against evil, to overcome temptation, and to uphold righteousness,' he testified.

On going to Sian, he said, he had been aware of danger, but he remembered that Christ on entering Jerusalem for the last time, although knowing of the danger ahead, rode into the city without fear.

'What greatness! What courage!' commented China's Buddhist-born Generalissimo. 'In comparison, how unimportant my life must be. So why should I hesitate?'

He recounted how during his captivity he had recalled Christ's forty days and nights in the wilderness, and also Doctor Sun Yat-sen's prayers during his imprisonment at the Chinese legation in London in 1895.

'With the spirit of Christ on the Cross, I was preparing to make the final sacrifice at the trial of the so-called "people's front." Having determined upon this course of action I was comforted and at rest.'

But he hastened to deprecate any suspicion that he was comparing himself with the great ones of the past. 'I offer this account of my experiences as testimony,' he emphasized, 'and not in any sense to exalt my own worthiness or achievements.'

He still remained away from official activity, but he continued to work as hard as at any time in the past. Finally Donald and Madame Chiang informed him what the physicians were afraid to tell him — that if he rested his body he would eventually recover completely, but that if he continued to exert himself he would be an invalid for life.

The news sobered Chiang. He had to function perfectly for the sake of the state, they told him, and he agreed. Again he went to Shanghai from Hangchow by airplane, and entered a hospital.

When he descended from the plane at the Shanghai airdrome his pain was apparent to the few spectators. Madame Chiang, after settling him in a waiting automobile, returned to the plane and obtained a large soft cushion, which she placed behind his back. The car moved off slowly, to avoid jolting the Generalissimo, and traveled to the hospital at a snail's pace.

While at the hospital, Chiang had several teeth removed, leaving only a few original teeth in his mouth. During the confusion of his escape from the Lintung hotel, it was recalled, he had lost his dental plate and Madame Chiang had taken him a 'spare' when she flew to Sian.

He left the hospital a short time later, and for a while took somewhat better care of himself. But his physical recovery was accompanied by some vexation in connection with the return of his long-absent elder son from Moscow.

Chiang Ching-kuo was the son of Chiang by his first marriage. He had gone to Moscow in 1926, during the era of the original Kuomintang-Communist co-operation. Chiang Kai-shek, who had then just returned from a tour of inspection to the Soviet Union, sent his son to study in the institution for Oriental students which later became Sun Yat-sen University.

When Chiang rose to power and purged the Kuomintang of Communists, his son was already an ardent Communist. But his activities and even his fate became something of a mystery. In 1934 Moscow dispatches reported him making a scathing attack on his father, in a letter to his mother at Chikow. But his mother never received the letter, and the suspicion arose that the report was merely Moscow propaganda.

Many Chinese believed that he had died in Russia. Rumors said he had been killed by the Communists in retaliation for Chiang's split with the Hankow government in 1927. Prominent Chinese visiting Moscow were said to have tried in vain to see young Chiang.

Then suddenly in the spring of 1937 Chiang's first wife, still living at Chikow, received a letter from Ching-kuo. He was well and returning to China with his Russian wife and young son. His mother, overjoyed, prayed that he might become reconciled with his father. The Chikow villagers prepared a grand celebration to mark his return.

Ching-kuo finally arrived in Shanghai the latter part of April aboard a Soviet steamer from Vladivostok. Deepest secrecy attended his short stay in Shanghai. Nanking officials took charge of him, kept him away from curious newspapermen. Ching-kuo, his wife, and their eight-year-old son were taken to Chiang's house in the French Concession of Shanghai. Chiang and Mei-ling flew to Shanghai, and father met son for the first time in eleven years.

Soon afterward Ching-kuo went to Chikow to meet his mother. His mother's relatives and friends said that the son had already quarreled with his father. When Chiang introduced his son to Mei-ling and said, 'This is your new mother,' Ching-kuo retorted hotly, 'My only mother is in Chikow.' An argument ensued, and Ching-kuo departed. The story lacked all confirmation, but the Chikow people attributed the account to Ching-kuo himself.

Chiang's first wife, at any rate, greeted her son with tears of joy. She immediately ordered a three-day theatrical performance to thank the gods for the fulfillment of her long-cherished wish to look on her son once again.

Ching-kuo as far as is known is still at Chikow with his mother.

Another son of Chiang gave him even greater vexation. Wei-kuo by name, he is not Chiang's own son. When Chiang was a student in Japan, a close friend, now a high official in the Nanking government, had an affair with a Japanese waitress. A son was born. The friend, disliking the idea of bringing home to China a half-Japanese son, declined to take care of the child. Chiang obliged and, following Chinese custom, adopted him as his son.

Wei-kuo's Japanese features have led to the baseless theory that Chiang Kai-shek's own ancestry is Japanese. Wei-kuo for years was a trial to Chiang. He was shiftless and extravagant. Madame Chiang tried to be kind, but the youth refused to be friendly. Chiang made his wife responsible for Wei-kuo's allowance, hoping to force the youth to cultivate her good-will. Wei-kuo remained surly, called Mei-ling 'Mother' with obvious reluctance.

Late in 1936 Wei-kuo, who spent most of his time at Soochow, came to Shanghai, engaged a hotel room, and began spending money like the traditional drunken sailor, mostly on sing-song girls. When he ran out of money, which was frequently, he obtained 'loans' from the Mayor of Shanghai, the Garrison Commander, and other officials.

Chiang heard of his son's goings-on, and telegraphed him to leave immediately for Germany to study military science, or to sever relations forever. Wei-kuo sailed.

While Chiang was recovering from the effects of the Sian episode, Wei-kuo suddenly appeared in London for the coronation of King George VI. He turned up without invitation and attached himself to the official Chinese delegation. The Chinese envoys were unable to disown him without causing comment. He was without a doubt Chiang Kai-shek's son, and they were forced to accept him.

Young Wei-kuo had a grand time in London. At Nanking, Chiang Kai-shek sputtered helplessly.

CHAPTER XXXIX

THE MAN

THE world learns about Chiang Kai-shek principally from foreign, that is non-Chinese, sources. As a result, all information about him is curiously filtered.

Most of the newspaper and news agency correspondents stationed in China speak no Chinese. Chiang speaks no English. Hence the chronicle of his movements, the reports of his speeches and manifestoes, depend on translation by third parties.

Hitler addresses large crowds in huge stadia; his appearances are carefully stage-managed; the Germans see and hear and feel him, and his words spoken into microphones are broadcast to all Europe. Mussolini thunders at throngs from palace balconies, and interested observers watch him as he flings his arms about and rouses audiences to frenzy. Englishmen troop to the House of Commons to listen to the debate of government and opposition leaders. President Roosevelt confronts a huge press delegation as a regular part of his office routine, and his 'fireside talks' bring his personality into the houses of the great and the humble throughout the land.

But Chiang Kai-shek appears at no vast concourses of people; his radio broadcasts are rare, and are never connected with the weighty announcements of domestic or foreign policy which one associates with the rulers of the western nations. His work goes on behind the scenes; his decisions are transmitted to a few individuals; his declamations are restricted to small groups. The C.E.C., of less than two hundred members, is generally his largest audience.

True, he frequently addresses commencement exercises of military and aeronautic schools and less frequently makes appearances at official functions, but on these occasions he confines himself to expounding lofty patriotic principles and charging his hearers to devote themselves to the welfare of the country. His talks are often long-winded and usually full of platitudes.

A few years ago he used to deliver diatribes to selected groups, and now and then rose to shrill denunciations of the Japanese. But the word got about, there were explanations to be made to 'certain quarters,' and he finally gave up the practice.

The Chinese learn about him from official bulletins released by government departments and the semi-official Chinese news agencies. They report his comings and goings, but carry hardly an interview with him from one year to the next.

Chinese actually interested in the man's policies resort to the editorials of the English-language press, which is free from much of the censorship applying to the Chinese organs, but even there, their gleanings are few. More information about Chiang appears in American and British newspapers and magazines than in the combined native and foreign press of China.

That the information appearing abroad is frequently erroneous is not surprising in view of the difficulty of 'covering' him. Until recently staff writers and free-lance commentators from foreign countries used to drop into China and interview Chiang with regularity, while the permanent correspondents residing in the country found it almost impossible to see him except on matters of the most urgent importance.

ONE OF CHIANG KAI-SHEK'S RARE BROADCASTS

Donald changed all that. Himself a former newspaperman and correspondent, he recognized the unfairness to the regular correspondents of barring them from Chiang's presence while every Tom, Dick, and Harriet with a card from some foreign paper or magazine walked in for a chat with the great man.

But, aside from the equity of the situation, Donald realized that Chiang's public relations were suffering. Persons with no knowledge of China or things Chinese were passing through the country, interviewing Chiang, and then frequently writing nonsense about him. He saw that in the long run foreign opinion of Chiang would benefit if the Generalissimo were seen and interviewed by observers with some knowledge of China and an appreciation of its problems.

Donald spoke to Madame Chiang, who agreed with his view. Today Chiang, and more especially Madame, is fairly accessible to resident correspondents. Obscure freelancers are barred, and visiting journalists have to be of real importance before they see Chiang.

Recently the 'March of Time' sent an expert camera crew to China, and some intimate shots of Chiang and Madame were obtained; the reel was subsequently shown in most parts of the world. Audiences never realized the tremendous feat those seemingly casual shots represented. For Chiang and his wife to take the time to pose for the scenes was a concession of the greatest magnitude; as though they were bidding the affairs of state to stand still while they idled. Only Madame's realization of the importance of public opinion abroad accounted for the fact that the photographing was done at all. And the scene in which Chiang addressed a C.E.C. meeting at Nanking and was photographed by a foreigner while doing so represented an absolute shattering of precedent.

Photographs of Chiang which are printed in China and abroad are mostly all of the conventionally posed type. He is almost always standing in uniform, gazing into the distance, his countenance grave with the cares of state. Or he stands with one or more associates and looks stiffly at the camera while the shutter clicks. Only in recent months has permission been given to an official photographer of the Officers' Moral Endeavor Association to accompany him on excursions, snap him and Madame in human off-the-record actions.

Americans are familiar with the figure of President Roosevelt on a fishing trip, his shirt open at the throat and a slouch hat jammed on his head. He has even been 'shot' sucking his thumb after biting into a sandwich on a picnic. It will probably be a long time before Chinese see 'candid' photos of Chiang Kai-shek engaged in Chinese shadow-boxing or lifting noodles into his mouth with expertly poised chopsticks.

His physiognomy is fairly well known to the public abroad. But his physical characteristics are vague.

He is, for example, of only medium stature to western eyes, although his thinness gives the impression of greater height. He stands about five feet eight inches, comparatively tall for a Chinese.

Before 1930 he was clean-shaven, and appeared extremely youthful. Chinese are likely to look younger than their age; Chiang appeared a mere stripling. In 1930 he blossomed out with a small mustache, which he has worn to this day; it has made him look a bit older, but he still gives little indication of his fifty years. The mustache is not of the Hitler variety, nor is it of military proportions. Chiang keeps it clipped short, and he avoids the appearance of the much caricatured mandarin with scraggly droopy hairs.

His eyes, like those of most Chinese, are black and penetrating. But small wrinkles at each side indicate the jovial side of his nature. As a matter of fact he laughs frequently when among his intimates; the grim side of his nature is reserved for his infrequent public appearances. His nose is straight, strong, regular, not prominent. All his features are generally undistinguished. He looks like neither a peasant nor an aristocrat. His face is that of an honest bourgeois. His skin is brown rather than yellow, and he is often deeply sun-tanned.

Chiang's general build is slight. His figure is thin and trim, prompting an American news magazine's adjective 'wasp-waisted.'

Although his once-black hair has turned gray, his head is closely cropped, and he has the brisk appearance of a still youthful business executive. Edgar Snow interviewed him during the course of the anti-Communist campaign and found him gray and aged, but he has seemingly recovered his spirit and agility in the past few years.

The injury to his back has of course curbed his customary activity, but he still carries himself with military jauntiness and is characterized by quick, decisive movements which have impressed most observers as extremely un-Chinese. He shakes hands firmly, easily.

His hands are small and delicate. With them he gestures frequently, reveals anger, impatience, nervousness. But with foreign visitors he is almost invariably calm, careful. The nature of his foreign interviews easily accounts for his somewhat changed attitude.

The visitor speaks. The interpreter, generally Madame Chiang, must translate. Chiang listens, considers, ponders his answer. The interviewer, usually a journalist, watches him carefully for manner, characteristics, 'color.' It is all highly unnatural. Chiang replies to the question, precisely; he must above all avoid misquotation. The interpreter looks from the translator to Chiang, perhaps jots down a note or two. The entire atmosphere is strained. It is difficult to get a clear idea of the man's nature from these brief glimpses of infrequent visitors.

With his associates, it is different. To his wife and intimate friends he is kindly, jovial. He shows teeth, even, white and artificial. In conference, with military commanders or civil officials, he is attentive, earnest. He fires questions, demands clear, clipped answers.

He often shows temper. Chiang has many vast projects to deal with, progress is slow, obstacles are frequent. He yearns for sweeping, drastic reforms, learns that changes are difficult, often requiring months or years to accomplish. He verbally lashes his subordinates, drives them to action, tries to fill them with the incessant urge to achieve which characterizes his own life and activity. On such occasions he barks out orders, shouts, gesticulates.

He is respected by his subordinates; he is not loved. Chiang has little patience for the traditional Chinese politeness of phrase to hide a criticism or rebuke. Many have resented what they call his bad manners. Some term him vindictive. Certainly in dealing with business or affairs of state he shows little warmth of personality. His is the brusqueness of the military man in action. He knows how to negotiate, to compromise, but he wastes little time in circumlocutions. He speaks clearly, briefly, and to the point. Often he punctuates his remarks with grunts. He also grunts when foreign observers say something that strikes him as good sense.

He never wears foreign-style clothes nowadays, although on his wedding day he wore a morning coat and gray trousers. Most of the time he is garbed in what is known as the Chungshan uniform, popularized by Sun Yat-sen, and called by Sun's courtesy name. This is a semi-military uniform, not particularly trim. It consists of a fairly long coat buttoned down the front, with a high turn-down collar and no necktie or belt, completed by long trousers of comparative narrow cut.

Chiang's Chungshan uniforms are either gray or olive-drab, and worn with a simple cap, bearing the white sun of the Kuomintang on its peak.

On ceremonial occasions he wears a standard foreign-style military uniform, with a general's insignia and appurtenances, a gold-braided cap, and a modest amount of medals. He rarely strides about in this garb, but most of his formal photographs show him in it.

Most of the time he wears ordinary Chinese dress, a long, loose gown with short jacket. For ordinary wear the gown is gray in winter and white in summer. For more or less formal appearances the gown is dark blue and the jacket black silk; this is popularly known as the 'Chinese tuxedo.'

When traveling, particularly in cool weather, he wears an over-garment with a cape effect which gives him a rather patriarchal air, and a plain foreign-style soft felt hat which always strikes foreign observers as comical, something like the cartoon character of the cannibal chieftain with grass skirt and top-hat.

CHAPTER XL

LUCRE

THE years have treated Chiang well from a material standpoint. It is a far cry from the days when he had to shuffle out on the street and buy his copper's worth of hot water. But if he is no longer poor, neither is he the millionaire that some allege.

Although he had few resources when he went south to Canton from Shanghai, he has been well paid since then, and he has saved money. His enemies mutter that he has made millions in speculation, that he owns vast amounts of real estate and controls many industrial companies. There are reasons to doubt it.

For one thing, no information leaks out about his specific holdings. Concerning several other high officials in the Nanking government, people have come to know, through underground channels of information, that this one owns that company, that the other one is interested in such-and-such an enterprise. But through the years that he has been at Nanking, no one has said that Chiang is the landlord of this building, or that he holds the controlling interest in that firm.

Allegations are freely made that a portion of the revenue from the opium traffic goes to swell the government coffers. One is never told that Chiang himself banks the profits from the trade. Where there is smoke there is sometimes fire; where there is no smoke the existence of the fire seems doubtful.

His manner of living belies any piling up of a great fortune. Nobody outside the Chiang family knows how much he draws as salary for his government and party positions. The figures appear in no budget reports. But if he receives really vast sums, he gives no evidence of spending them.

He lives in comfort, travels freely, buys an airplane now and then. But he makes no consistently large purchases, cultivates no extravagant hobbies. On the contrary, his mode of life is decidedly simple, and he gives every evidence of practicing the frugality he preaches in the New Life Movement.

But he is extremely generous to those close to him and to those who have served him well.

While his mother lived, he provided for her to the limit of his ability. There were times when he was poor and could give her no help. But when he had money he remitted generously, and her last days were free from want. When she died in 1921, Chiang was not too well off, but his mother was given every care and convenience he could provide. He spent heavily on her funeral, and later erected a monastery at Chikow in her memory.

In the village where he was born is the Wulin School, which he established in 1927. It is a model institution. Chiang has enlarged its campus until it now covers three hundred and fifty acres. There is the school itself, a library, an agricultural station, and a hospital. The most modern equipment has been installed throughout. One thousand students receive their education there. Chiang regularly sets aside forty thousand dollars in Chinese currency each month for the expenses of the school and its allied institutions.

He has also donated generous sums for the construction of highways in the vicinity of Chikow and Fenghua, has erected a number of public buildings, and has financed a village hospital.

His first wife, now referred to as Miss Mao, is well supported by him. Reliable reports say that he sends her three thousand dollars in Chinese currency each month. She lives in the Tze An Temple, where the spirit of Chiang's mother is honored.

A few years ago Miss Mao, a devout Buddhist, decided to make a pilgrimage to Kiuhwashan, a sacred mountain in Anhwei Province. Chiang ordered his subordinates to charter a special ship for her, and furnished her with a bodyguard. He also urged her to invite a number of her friends to join her, and a sizeable party made the trip, all expenses paid.

Chiang's living quarters are modest. At Nanking the government erected an imposing mansion for him while he was President of the National government. Chiang never lived in it. He and Mei-ling stay in an extremely modest bungalow.

In Shanghai they live in a French Concession house which, although comfortable, is far from elaborate. It is exactly like five or six other houses in the same block, and considerably less impressive than the homes of many of the managers of foreign firms.

At Kuling for several years they rented a bungalow from the missionary association which administered the resort. Today they own a bungalow, but it is no better than dozens of other simple dwellings in the vicinity.

In Chikow they own the Chiang family home, and at Hangchow they have a small villa; neither is in the mansion class. While on the Kiangsi front during the anti-Communist campaign, Chiang and his wife stayed in a rented cottage which Mei-ling described as 'bitterly cold.'

On the other hand, Chiang makes lavish monetary awards

to military men who have performed well in the field or who have remained loyal when they might have rebelled.

He supports his adopted son Wei-kuo, who until he was packed off to Germany to study military science was a free and easy spender.

And a comparatively small if constant expense is his support of relatives at Chikow besides Miss Mao. Family relationships in China are observed far more extensively than in the west; fifth and sixth cousins are still considered part of the family.

A number of Chiang's distant relatives are still poor. Many are sedan-chair coolies by trade. Whenever Chiang visits his old home, his coolie cousins crowd around him. Partly as a matter of face and partly from real generosity, Chiang gives them sizeable sums of money, tells them to stop carrying sedan chairs. They take the money, quit carrying chairs, and enjoy life. But when Chiang next appears in Chikow, they trot out the chairs once more, inform him loudly that they have run out of money, have had to go back to coolie work. He pays off again.

CHAPTER XLI

REGIMEN

LIKE most of the world's rulers, Chiang has a tremendous amount of energy, works extremely hard, and follows a routine day after day which can only be described as grueling.

From his boyhood days he has retained the habit of arising at dawn, and he never varies from the routine. He takes a light breakfast, the Chinese equivalent of coffee and rolls, and immediately goes to work. He is at his office desk, whether at Nanking or in the field, until noon. After lunch he rests for an hour, and then is back at work. All day long he interviews commanders, officials, an occasional diplomat or journalist; he reads reports and sends telegrams.

The matters which he is called upon to deal with each day are impressive in number and scope. Military plans, once against the Communists, now against Japan, naturally form an important part of his activity. But until the un-declared war with Japan he was also constantly concerned with rural rehabilitation programs, the extension of the nation's highways, educational reforms, foreign policy, the ever-present danger of some war-lord's disaffection, financial matters of every description. Of necessity he has be-come an expert in a number of fields which were alien to him less than a decade ago.

He has even devoted considerable time to such a highly specialized matter as architecture. Interested in making Nanking a model capital, he enlisted the aid of Henry

Killam Murphy, noted American architect, who devised a modified Chinese architectural style retaining the character of the native structures but incorporating advantages of modern-style construction. Chiang had long talks with Murphy on construction and city planning. Becoming intensely interested in the subject, he asked Murphy to recommend a good book or two on the subject.

Murphy instructed a Shanghai book store to send a few books on architecture to the Generalissimo for selection. The shop, eager to please, sent a whole case of books. Chiang kept them all. For a while afterward he could be seen taking a walk along Nanking streets late in the afternoon, accompanied only by one or two aides. He carried a book on architecture, which he read as he walked, and surveyed the streets and squares of the city with a critical eye, planning needed changes and developments. Other affairs intervened, however, and he had to leave architectural worries to Murphy and Chinese experts.

He and Madame, with Donald and possibly another one or two members of his entourage, dine quietly at home. The Chiangs attend no official dinners; they leave that duty to the foreign office and the comparatively minor officials of other departments. Nor do they entertain. Once in a while Chiang will have a few important officials or military commanders to a simple meal, but the occasions are rare and are usually prompted by important business.

After dinner he and Madame go to work again, devoting themselves to important but non-routine affairs. Madame Chiang is with him most of the time. She deals with his foreign correspondence, reads foreign newspapers from which she digests world news for him. She does her best to keep him in touch with European and American thought, and his general knowledge of events outside of China frequently surprises foreign visitors.

The Chiangs used to find time for an automobile drive or a walk during the day. Pressure of work in the past few years has eliminated even this slight relaxation. People acquainted with the routine followed by Chiang and his wife often wonder how they continue the pace. The answer lies in their frequent excursions to Chiang's old home at Chikow and to Hangchow, where he has a villa. In each place the work goes on, and official visitors continue to come, but the Chiangs are able to snatch a slight amount of leisure and to reduce the pressure to which they are subject at Nanking and Shanghai.

Madame Chiang, as a matter of fact, regularly overworks herself, and frequently is ordered to bed by her physicians. So far she has managed to stave off the breakdown which they tell her is sure to come unless she expends less energy. In the summertime the Chiangs go to Kuling, a mountain resort in Kiangsi Province. This used to afford them some relaxation, but for the past few years the Executive Yuan and the entire government have moved to Kuling, the resort has become China's summer capital, and the routine is as burdensome there as it is at Nanking. Only the heat of Nanking in the summer is missing.

Religion plays an important part in the Chiangs' daily lives, particularly since Chiang's baptism. He reads some part of the Bible daily, no matter how busy he is, and says his prayers regularly. Grace is said before each meal. A minister, friend of the family, is generally with them Sundays at Nanking. When they are in Shanghai, Madame Chiang and her sister, Madame H. H. Kung, hold a Sunday-School class at the old Soong home, which some of Shanghai's most eminent gangster overlords attend regularly and faithfully.

Chiang's personal habits tend toward the austere. He neither smokes nor drinks. An American observer several years ago noted that at a luncheon party he had wine served to his guests, but took grape juice himself. Today even the guests go without wine, which is frowned upon by the New Life Movement.

During a recent luncheon for high officials, Chiang set a new record for simplicity, even for himself. Following the precepts of the New Life Movement, he restricted the meal to four principal dishes — even modest meals served by Chinese hosts to strangers often run to fifteen or twenty courses. And each guest was expected to fill his own rice bowl, which in the old days would have involved terrific loss of face. Chiang has made it fashionable to be simple and frugal.

Chiang likes to listen to western classical music, enjoys hearing good phonograph records. He often has the phonograph played while he naps.

Considering the fullness of his days, he does a surprising amount of reading. But much of it is re-reading, and his favorite volumes are few — the Bible, the lectures of Sun Yat-sen, the works of the Ming Dynasty theorist Wang Yang-ming and the modern Chinese statesman Tseng Kuo-fan. He also absorbs chapters from standard books on military strategy. His interests are kept catholic by Madame Chiang, who transmits to him the gist of her own voluminous reading.

He reads with thoroughness, frequently taking notes, making comments, marking important passages.

Since his youth he has kept a diary, and for the past twenty years he has never failed to make a daily entry. He started it, he says, to develop the trait of persistence. Besides narrating events of each day, and commenting on his reading and conversations, he invariably records observations on himself. In his entries he has never hesitated to criticize himself — this is not merely the usual humility of a Chinese in conversation with others; the diary has been kept for himself alone, and only the account of the fortnight at Sian has ever been made public.

The note of self-criticism is revealing. He points out to himself his harshness of temperament, tells himself he is too severe in dealing with subordinates. It is understandable that Chang Hsueh-liang and Yang Hu-cheng were impressed by what they read when they seized his diary at Sian; with its constant self-assessment, its general effect must have brought the two rebels conviction of the writer's sincerity.

It is characteristic of Chiang that he travels as he acts — quickly. The airplane is his usual means of transport. He owns a large Douglas transport plane, a Ford tri-motored plane now used mostly by his entourage, and a Sikorsky flying boat similar in design to the Clipper planes used for passenger transport service in various parts of the world.

He sometimes travels on gunboats, rarely on trains in the past few years. For one thing, train travel is potentially dangerous. He remembers how Old Marshal Chang Tso-lin met his death, has the vivid recollection of the attempt to bomb his own train during the Mongolian trip of 1934.

Whatever may be the hazards of planes in the air, he is comparatively free from assassination attempts between take-off and landing. Also, movements by private plane can be satisfactorily variable; train times are easily ascertained by would-be assassins.

When Chiang arrives at an airport, the local military authorities close the area to traffic, carry out the most minute precautions to avoid mishap or danger. But Chiang is nevertheless not heavily guarded as he goes about the country. He has a detachment of bodyguards, but in size and strength it does not compare with the units surrounding western rulers. Often, particularly in the outlying districts, he walks about the countryside with practically no protection.

The fact that on one occasion a member of his own bodyguard attempted to assassinate him, and was only prevented by a sudden alarm which frightened him away from Chiang's bedroom, has apparently not resulted in any great nervousness on the part of Chiang or those near him. His conception of himself as a man whose life is already dedicated to his country has seemingly made him indifferent to assassination attempts. The precautions attending his movements are the concern of his associates, not of himself.

But the events at Sian apparently convinced him that as the head of the state he would do well not to wander too far afield. He has noted his own recklessness in exposing himself to the danger of kidnapping. Whether in the future he will curtail his practice of keeping in personal touch with the outlying administrative areas remains to be seen.

CHAPTER XLII

POWER

A FEW years ago Chiang was generally classified as a military opportunist. The circumstances of his break with Hankow were well remembered. The frequent denunciations of his régime by Madame Sun Yat-sen were effectively publicized. And the terror that was periodically instituted in his name filled liberals with distaste, if not disgust.

In more recent times there has been a tendency to exalt him as a great statesman. Foreign criticism has virtually disappeared; foreign critics in China have been labeled 'die-hards'; those in other countries, Communists. Blind reverence has replaced the former attitude of blind enmity.

Yet neither point of view does him justice. On the one hand, Chiang was as much the instrument of the anti-Hankow movement as he was its agent. The break with the left-wing element and with the Communists was bound to come, sooner or later. The nation as a whole was not ready for a proletarian revolution. The Kuomintang leaders who roused the peasants and workers in the cause of nationalism were not willing to see the peasants and workers carry the anti-imperialist program to its logical conclusion.

The Chinese bourgeoisie were ready to fight any genuine economic revolution. Whether they would have succeeded in quelling it or not can only be guessed at. But there would have been a sanguinary struggle, and certainly there were enough powerful independent war-lords to promise continued civil war for many a year.

Whether Sun Yat-sen would have gone Communist, or whether he would have rebelled and done as Chiang has done, is also open to argument. There is evidence to support either view. He was obviously grateful for Russian support, esteemed the U.S.S.R. as a nation willing to treat China on terms of equality. But he also indicated on more than one occasion his growing distrust of the Communist allies in the Chinese revolution, and the visit to the north which ended in his death is seen by some as an indication of that distrust.

Terror can never be condoned. Nor are the attempts to clear Chiang of responsibility very convincing. That he approved, encouraged, and directed the Communist purge of 1927 is not even denied by his apologists. That he was just as aware of the less publicized but equally drastic drive of the succeeding eight years is patent to any impartial observer. Chiang was too firmly in control of the government, too obviously the source of all policies, to escape responsibility. The writings and utterances of those who have been alternately his associates and his opponents tell the story of the terror all too conclusively.

But political realists know that in any government ruled by minorities the ruling group has had to stamp out opposition by ruthless means. It has been true in Russia and Germany, as the world well knows; it has been demonstrated from India to Yugoslavia. China's example was neither better nor worse than those of other countries. And Chiang was no more to be exonerated or excoriated than the chiefs of a dozen other régimes, in or out of China.

The truth was that he saw his chance and he took it. The praise or blame must lie in the eventual success or failure of his effort. If China becomes a powerful unified nation, blessed by peace and prosperity because of its strength and unity, Chiang will be hailed by his people as greater than Sun Yat-sen, and in the years to come his faults and weaknesses will be forgotten until resurrected by some 'debunking' historian. If the structure which he has erected collapses and China emerges from the Chiang era to a period of chaos and conflict, he will be charged with the fault, and the people will look upon him as they now regard ambitious, unfortunate Yuan Shih-kai.

On the other hand, the present tendency to exalt Chiang can do neither him nor the nation any good. The fact is, as Edgar Snow has pointed out, that his strength in the past has really rested in the weakness of his enemies. They have in the past distrusted each other, failed to make common cause against him when such action might have unseated him. Realists would say that it is just as well that his enemies have neglected their opportunities. China has thereby been spared much needless bloodshed, regardless of the counter-revolutionary bloodshed which it has entailed.

But to overestimate strength is dangerous, as the Sian situation clearly showed. Most observers, prior to the coup, would have ridiculed as fantastic the prediction that in the year 1936 the nation's Strong Man could be kidnapped and held captive for two weeks. It was accomplished with surprising ease. But the fact that emerged from the occurrence was that facilities for criticism and a willingness to act on it would have made the kidnapping unnecessary and certainly averted the crisis that followed.

But in this respect also, the eventual result may be pure good fortune. Chiang's disappearance and his danger united the nation as nothing else could have done. The understanding with the Communists which followed his release undoubtedly eased the tension which had previously prevailed. China suddenly became far stronger than it had been for the previous five years.

The task is far from finished. As this is written, Chiang's

troops are locked in combat with the Japanese, and the outcome cannot be foretold with certainty. But, regardless of the result, national reconstruction remains a gigantic task. The conversion of the nation from Kuomintang party rule to democracy, as Sun Yat-sen envisaged, is even greater. Chiang, if he survives the conflict with Japan, probably faces his sternest task in the years to come.

He is a more likable personality today than when he was rising to power. Power has brought self-confidence and a certain amount of tolerance. The Sian coup must have increased his realization of responsibility. That it induced him to relinquish some of his prejudices is already evident.

The question is regularly asked: Is Chiang a dictator?

'I am not a dictator and refuse to be one,' he told Paula Lecler in 1936. 'I am against so-called dictatorships for China. I am for constitutional government, and when the People's Congress meets at Nanking, it will inaugurate popular government, the period of tutelage provided under our organic law having expired.'

But the fact remains that the People's Congress has been postponed once, and may be postponed again. This gathering, charged with promulgating China's permanent constitution and inaugurating a representative democracy, seems an anachronism in a world which sees the number of totalitarian régimes ever increasing. It may be that, under the stress of the continued 'national crisis' in China, the nation's political leaders will be persuaded to defer the Congress and constitutionalism in favor of continued military control under an essentially dictatorial régime.

For it must be remembered that the masses of China are still illiterate, inarticulate. The people who decide problems of government are the politicians and the intellectuals. They in turn abide by the policies of a small group which does the actual governing, and that group looks to Chiang.

He cannot, however, make a decision on a vital question affecting Sun Yat-sen's Three Principles, like this one of constitutionalism, without consulting other leaders, and in fact he does not attempt to do so. To that extent, then, Chiang's régime differs from that of, say, Mussolini or Kamal Ataturk. And to that extent he is not a dictator as the world has come to understand the term.

Before Chiang rose to power at Canton, an official of the Soviet Embassy at Peking who was active in furthering the Kuomintang-Communist entente surveyed the Chinese leaders in the south and reported to his superiors. Of Chiang he wrote: 'He is a man who possesses the quality of being able to unravel problems affecting both China and the world. He is well aware which path has to be taken in order to obtain and retain power, and he realizes that the support of the masses is an uncertain quantity.'

It was a shrewd assessment. Today Chiang has the power. He guides the destinies of a nation with a greater population than all of Europe. He controls, for every practical purpose, more people than any other individual on earth. His territory is inextricably bound up with pressing problems which affect not only Asia but the whole world. What he thinks and what he does may well change the lives of countless people, in far-off countries, who have never even heard his name.

It becomes increasingly likely that in the days to come, the western world will have to reckon, for better or for worse, with this Strong Man of the East.

THE END

The following publications have also been consulted by the author:

China Weekly Review, Shanghai.
People's Tribune, Shanghai.
North-China Daily News, Shanghai.
Shanghai Evening Post and Mercury, Shanghai.
China Press, Shanghai.
Bulletins of the Council of International Affairs, Nanking.
International Press Correspondence, London.
Asia Magazine, Concord, N.H.

BIBLIOGRAPHY

The Chinese National Revolution — Wang Ching-wei and others, Tientsin, 1931.

New Life for Kiangsi — C. W. H. Young, Shanghai, 1935.

Two Years of Nationalist China — M. T. Z. Tyau, Shanghai, 1930.

China In Revolt — T'ang Leang-li, London, 1927.

Far Eastern Front — Edgar Snow, London, 1934.

Political Parties in China — Jermyn Chi-hung Lynn, Tientsin, 1930.

China, The Pity of It — J. O. P. Bland, London, 1932.

Is China Mad? — D'Auxion de Ruffe, Shanghai, 1928.

The Far East — Payson J. Treat, New York, 1928.

The Capital Question of China — Lionel Curtis, London, 1932.

The Chinese Revolution — Arthur N. Holcombe, Cambridge, Mass., 1930.

New Lamps for Old — Anatol M. Kotenev, Shanghai, 1931.

Far East in Ferment — Guenther Stein, London, 1936.

China Today — Stanley K. Hornbeck, Boston, 1927.

Five Years of Kuomintang Reaction — Harold R. Isaacs, Shanghai, 1932.

Sian, A Coup d'Etat — Madame Chiang Kai-shek. A Fortnight at Sian — Chiang Kai-shek. One volume, Shanghai, 1937.

Covering the Far East — Miles W. Vaughn, New York, 1936.

Far Eastern Crisis — Henry L. Stimson, New York, 1936.

China's Millions — Anna Louise Strong, New York, 1928.

Eminent Asians — Upton Close, New York, 1929.

China's Red Army Marches — Agnes Smedley, New York, 1934.

General Chiang Kai-shek, Builder of New China — Chen Tsung-hsi, Wang An-tsiang, and Wang I-ting, Shanghai, 1929.

The Biography of Chiang Kai-shek — in Chinese — Wang Chieh, Shanghai, 1937.

Weak China's Strong Man — Edgar Snow, in Current History, March, 1934.

The China Year Book — edited by H. G. W. Woodhead, Tientsin and Shanghai, 1927–1936.

BIBLIOGRAPHY